pets

pets

every owner's encyclopedia
The Diagram Group

**PADDINGTON
PRESS LTD**

NEW YORK & LONDON

OPTIMUM PUBLISHING COMPANY, LTD. CANADA

Library of Congress Cataloging in Publication Data

Diagram Group
  Pets: every owner's encyclopedia.

  Bibliography: p.
  Includes index.
  1. Pets. 1. Title.
SF413.D53   636.08'87   78-9311
ISBN 0 7092 0146 X
ISBN 0 448 22208 6 (United States only)

Published simultaneously in Canada by
Optimum Publishing Company Ltd.
ISBN 0 88890 094 5

Copyright©Diagram Visual Information Ltd.
All rights reserved.

Printed and bound in Hong Kong

In The United States
Paddington Press
Distributed by
Grosset & Dunlap

In The United Kingdom
Paddington Press

In Southern Africa
Distributed by
Ernest Stanton (Publishers) (Pty.) Ltd.

Foreword

The relationship between animals and humans has always been potentially rewarding for both sides. Over the centuries, animals have provided us with food, clothing, protection, transport, muscle, and companionship. In the process many creatures have become totally dependent upon people for their well-being.

In an age of growing awareness of the risk of exploitation of animals by humans, many people are concerned for wild animals that have been hunted and collected to near extinction. Equally important is the potential exploitation of the tame animals that join our households as pets. A pet-owner's lack of basic knowledge can result in unintentional cruelty.

Owning and caring for a pet is a serious responsibility which must be approached with a full knowledge of each animal's particular requirements. **PETS: Every Owner's Encyclopedia** provides all the facts and practical advice necessary for the humane fulfilment of this responsibility. It is the first book to combine clear wording, simple diagrams, and attractive illustrations to give a full and comprehensive guide to everything you need to know, from choosing the right animal to breeding and showing a prize winner. Above all **PETS** will ensure that your animal, whether a mongrel dog or an Arab stallion, is always in peak condition, free of disease, and happy in the environment you provide.

Over 500 species and varieties are described and illustrated, from familiar household pets to exotic animals of every kind, grouped in chapters which reflect their zoological classification. There is also a section on conservation and its relevance to pet keeping, and information on observing and helping animals in the wild. The editors and publishers would like to thank the many individuals and organizations, including veterinarians, zoological societies, and conservation bodies, which were consulted during the compilation of the material and who gave professional help and advice.

The Diagram Group

Managing editor	Ruth Midgley
Research editor	Elizabeth Wilhide
Contributors	David Black, David Lambert, Anna Sproule, Maureen Cartwright
Picture research	Linda Proud
Index	Mary Ling
Editorial assistant	Susan Leith
Art director	Roger Kohn
Art editor	Richard Hummerstone
Artists	Steven Clark, Sarah Fox-Davies, Sheila Galbraith, Robert Galvin, Susan Kinsey, Pavel Kostal, David Lightfoot, János Márffy, Kathleen McDougall, Graham Rosewarne, John Woodcock
Art assistants	Nigel Bailey, Brian Hewson, Rosemary Vane Wright

Contents

Mammals

Artiodactyls

Wild mammals

Fish

**3**

Invertebrates

**4**

Amphibians

Explanation of symbols
For easy reference, each
chapter has a general symbol (**a**)
which is repeated at the top of
each right hand page in the
chapter. This symbol stands for
the animal group discussed, or
the main chapter topic. Another
symbol (**b**) below the main
symbol indicates a major group
within the chapter, such as an
animal family, or may stand for a
particular species discussed on
the page.

a

b

Reptiles 5

Birds 6

Cage and aviary birds

Fowl

Conservation

Explanation of circles
To indicate the comparative
sizes of the animals illustrated,
each drawing is accompanied by
a circle. A circle 1in (2.5cm) in
diameter (**a**) has been chosen as
a basic measure. The circle will
appear small next to a large
animal such as the tabby cat (**b**),
and big next to a small animal. If
the animal is very small, only
part of the circle appears; as
with the glowlight tetra (**c**).

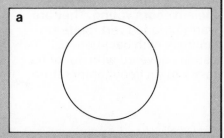

1

Mammals

Many species of mammal were domesticated early in man's history, and for centuries have been providing milk, meat, clothing, protection, transport, and companionship.

Most mammal pets come from these domesticated species, and have already become adapted to living with humans. Mammals are generally more responsive, more intelligent, and easier to train than other types of pet. In many cases, their care must include a type of relationship to substitute for the natural animal society that has been forfeited in the course of their domestication.

Mammals are distinguished from other animals by the fact that they produce milk to suckle their liveborn young. They are warm-blooded vertebrates (animals with backbones), usually covered with fur or hair to maintain body temperature.

Right Classical scene with domesticated mammals (Codex Romanus, Ms. lat 3867 f.44v, Biblioteca Apostolica, Vatican).

Keeping mammal pets

Most people's idea of a pet animal is usually some kind of mammal, often a cat or a dog. In the United States alone, there were over one hundred million cats and dogs known to be kept as pets in 1975 — and probably many more were unaccounted for. Many other types of mammal are commonly or sometimes kept as pets, varying in cost, ease of care, and general suitability.

Dogs are traditionally man's favorite animal companion. There are many breeds but generally all require exercise, training, veterinary care, and human companionship. The large number of strays and abandoned puppies shows that many people find it difficult to meet these basic needs. Owning a dog is a responsibility that lasts the animal's lifetime — sometimes over 15 years.

Cats are fairly easy to care for, but it is a mistake to assume that they can fend for themselves. All cats require regular, balanced meals, even if they hunt. Other aspects of care include handling and training. Unless kittens are definitely wanted, all female cats should be spayed.

Mustelids / weasel family The most commonly kept members of this family are the ferret and, in North America, the skunk. They are not recommended to inexperienced petkeepers, and odor can be a serious problem.

Rabbits are good children's pets. They are hardy, and can remain outside in most weathers, given a warm, secure shelter or hutch. Feeding is simple and cheap. Many breeds are available, varying in color and size. Rabbits are timid animals and must be handled gently.

Rodents are among the easiest mammal pets to obtain and care for. They make good pets for children. Avoid keeping breeding pairs, unless a large number of animals can be catered for. Many commercially available cages are too small. Several species are suitable.

Horses and ponies are the most expensive to buy of all the mammals commonly kept as pets. Feeding and care are also costly, and a lot of space is needed for exercise. Riding can be an extremely enjoyable activity, but many people considering buying their own horse or pony would be better advised to follow their sport at a riding school.

Donkeys are generally hardy and rather easier to keep than horses and ponies, given adequate space. Most are gentle and affectionate, and their reputation for stubbornness is largely undeserved.

Farm animals are commonly kept in large numbers for their products, but families living in the country may consider keeping one or two as useful, if unusual, pets. Goats are probably the most interesting, but as with the other animals in this group, no-one should embark on keeping them without obtaining expert advice.

Wild mammals In general, very few wild mammals make suitable pets. Laws prohibit their keeping in many areas. Expert care will be needed to raise a young animal, and many wild mammals are aggressive when adult. Some wild species can be tamed as free "pets."

Dogs

History and uses

The dog is one of the few domestic animals that has become man's companion primarily because of the high value placed on its friendship and loyalty. A breed of domestic dog is believed to have existed in Europe as far back as the Stone Age. The Egyptians, Assyrians, Greeks, and Romans all kept dogs as pets and working animals. Today there are over 500 distinct breeds of domestic dog, probably all descended from one or two species of ancestor. The extraordinary variety in structure and appearance of the different breeds is unique among domesticated animals. Man has benefited from his long association with the canine species, gaining a willing and intelligent partner in hunting, herding, tracking, and defense. Dogs are naturally social animals, and adapt well to man's community. Keeping one as a pet is a responsibility that involves effort and commitment, but the rewards are well known, and make the dog one of the best loved of all pet animals.

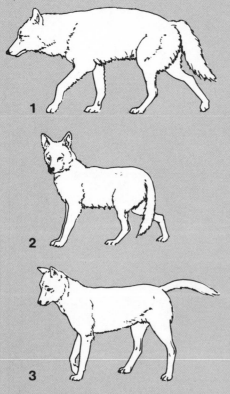

Ancestry Dogs are carnivores and members of the family Canidae, which contains 37 species including wolves, foxes, and jackals. The domestic dog *(Canis familiaris)* probably originated 10,000-12,000 years ago somewhere in the Middle East. The ancestors of the dog are unknown, but evidence suggests the wolf was one of them, and the jackal, with its similar hunting behavior, may be another. It is possible that different wild species of dog were domesticated at different times and places for specific reasons. Domestication probably occurred when early man reared puppies from a wild pack for use as hunting dogs.
1 European wolf *(Canis lupus).*
2 Black-backed jackal *(Canis mesomelas).*
3 Dingo *(Canis dingo).*

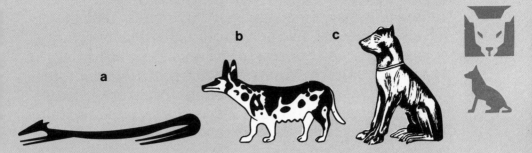

a

b

c

Early representations Dogs were one of the first animals to be domesticated. This long association between man and dog is reflected in early objects of art.
a A galloping dog from a Persian cup c.3000 BC.
b An Egyptian painting of a bitch from the tomb of Khumhotep c.1900 BC.
c A basalt dog from the Ptolemaic period in Egypt (323-30 BC).

Working dogs Many of the dog breeds now popular as pets were bred originally for specific abilities. Dogs can be trained for highly skilled work.
1 St Bernard Rescue work.
2 Golden retriever One of the breeds used as a guide dog.
3 Husky Originally bred by Eskimos to pull sleighs.
4 Border collie Herding sheep.
5 German shepherd Used as a guard and tracker by police.
6 Foxhound Hunting.

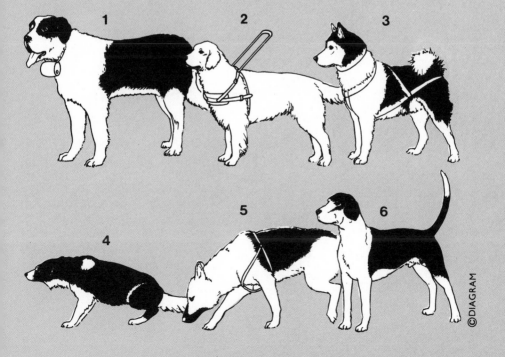

©DIAGRAM

19

Anatomy of the dog

Modern domestic breeds are not only smaller than their wild ancestors, but also quite different in proportion, temperament, and general appearance. Through selective breeding directed by man's requirements, the structure of dog breeds has changed considerably over centuries of domestication. Certain qualities can be emphasized by breeding, and some recessive tendencies encouraged.

Points of a dog The external features — or "points" — of a dog are listed here and located on the numbered diagram given below.

1 Stop.
2 Muzzle.
3 Jaws.
4 Shoulder.
5 Prosternum.
6 Forechest.
7 Elbow.
8 Pastern.
9 Dewclaw.
10 Ribs.
11 Flank.
12 Feet.
13 Metatarsus.
14 Pastern.
15 Hock.
16 Lower thigh.
17 Stifle.
18 Upper thigh.
19 Tail.
20 Croup.
21 Loin.
22 Withers.
23 Occiput.

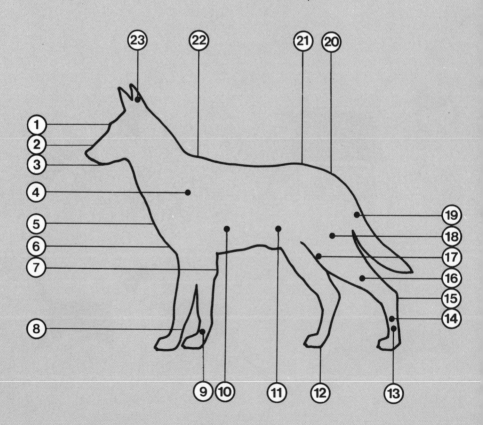

This type of selection is often useful when developing a specialized working animal, where shape and physique must be matched to a willing disposition. Unfortunately not all breeding has improved the general stock. Some animals bred solely for their show appearance have weak conformation and exhibit recessive qualities that would have been selected against if man had not interfered.

Skeletal structure The skeleton of a small dog, a Scottish terrier (**a**), shows the result of miniaturizing certain features, particularly the legs. In contrast with the skeleton of a large dog, a German shepherd (**b**), the head is proportionately larger and the legs have to support a greater weight. The effect of this miniaturization on the dog is to preserve the proportions normally associated with puppies or young dogs.

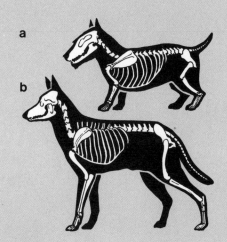

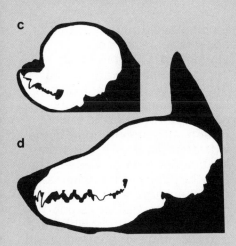

Types of skull There is no other species of animal that shows such variation in the proportions of its skull as the dog. The skulls of short-faced breeds differ chiefly from those of long-faced breeds in the length of their nasal bones. This largely accounts for the difference in facial type between, for example, a pug (**c**) and a German shepherd (**d**). Short-faced breeds are mutations of the original long-faced wild dog breeds.

Teeth The dog is born without teeth. By 5-6 weeks there are 28 temporary teeth. By 4 months these have been replaced by 42 permanent teeth (see diagram).
a Incisors (12).
b Canines (4).
c Premolars (16).
d Molars (10).

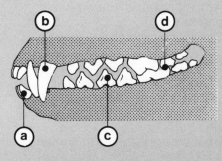

©DIAGRAM

Choosing a dog

Every year thousands of dogs are abandoned by their owners. These people were often unprepared for the amount of care and expense involved in keeping a dog. Unhappy mistakes can be avoided if time is taken to consider the implications of owning a dog, and to decide which breed would be the most suitable. All dogs require exercise, may be expensive to feed, and should be trained

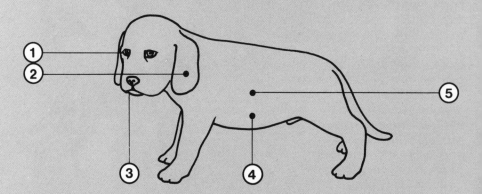

Choosing a puppy Points to consider when choosing a puppy include the following.

Age Avoid taking puppies from the litter before they are 10 weeks old. Contact with their mother, littermates, and humans is essential for young puppies. Puppies kept too long in pet store cages have often been starved of vital contact.

Size Remember that puppies grow: try to choose one that will not grow too big for your home or your pocket (obviously a problem with mongrels of uncertain parentage).

Sex Decide which sex is preferred. Males may wander and fight; females need care to prevent unwanted litters (p.56).

Temperament To select a puppy of good temperament it is wise to visit the litter at 8-10 weeks. Observe the puppies at play and feeding: avoid any puppy that appears aggressive or submissive. Observe which puppies come forward without fear when you call them. Clap loudly: a puppy that recovers quickly will be easier to train.

Health All puppies should come with a certificate of health from the breeder. Even so, it is wise to take the puppy to a veterinarian for a check-up and to arrange to return it if there are any signs of illness (except worms, which are quite common in young dogs and can easily be treated). A quick health checking guide follows.
1 Eyes should be clear and shiny.
2 Ears should not smell.
3 Make sure there is no cough.
4 Puppies should be plump but not fat.
5 The fur should be thick and not dull-looking.

at least to a minimum standard. They all need some
veterinary care, such as inoculations.
Luckily breeds vary considerably in size (and hence
appetite), temperament, and type of fur. Choose your dog
carefully to get the healthiest and liveliest individual, and
buy only from reputable sources. Dog breeders can often
give good advice on the requirements of particular breeds.

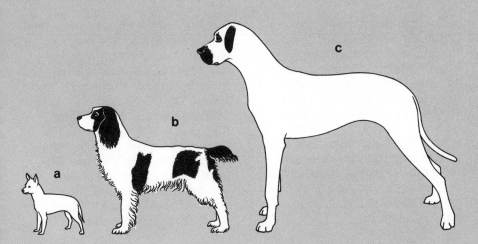

Size This is perhaps the most important single consideration when choosing a pet dog. It affects not only the amount of space needed but various other requirements and features too.

Small breeds such as the chihuahua (**a**) need less exercise and less food than larger breeds. They can be kept easily in an apartment. Shrill barking may be a problem. Some small dogs are extremely nervous.

Medium-sized breeds such as the springer spaniel (**b**) need regular exercise and are best not kept in town apartments. Food requirements are moderate. Dogs of this size make good pets for children.

Large breeds such as the great Dane (**c**) require a lot of food and are expensive to keep. They need a lot of exercise and are best kept in the country or where there is plenty of space for supervised daily runs. Temperament is usually good, but careful training is essential. Some large breeds have a slightly shorter lifespan than average.

Different-sized breeds Some dogs, notably the poodle, have been bred in a variety of sizes. The toy (**d**) must be under 11in (28cm) high at the shoulders; the miniature (**e**) measures 11-15in (28-38cm); and the standard (**f**) is over 15in (38cm).

Classification of dogs

The time, place, and origin of many breeds of dog are unknown. In the past 500 years, exchanges of breeds from one country to the next have further confused relationships between the various types. Most Kennel Clubs and professional breeders' associations divide the breeds of dog into five groups, first devised over a century ago. These are hounds, gundogs, terriers, non-sporting

1 Greyhounds Dogs of this group were developed for hunting and racing. Their streamlined build enables them to run extremely fast in pursuit of prey. Great reliance is placed on their excellent eyesight. (See p.26.)

2 Mastiffs Originally developed as war dogs, mastiffs are now used mainly as guard dogs or for rescue work. They are heavy in weight and build, with large heads. (See p.28.)

3 Spitz These dogs originated in Arctic regions, where they are used for hauling, hunting, and herding. Typical appearance includes a thick, rough coat, and a curled tail. (See p.30.)

4 Sheepdogs Developed for their shepherding prowess, these dogs show considerable variations in physical type. All have keen senses and show considerable adaptability, powers of endurance, and a willingness to work. (See p.32.)

dogs, and toy breeds. This division is appropriate to the purpose of these official organizations, but has no basis in structural formation or anatomy. A classification based on structure and physiology was later developed by C.L.B. Hubbard. This divides the breeds of dog into seven groups: greyhounds, mastiffs, spitz, sheepdogs, spaniels, terriers, and hounds. Hubbard's classification is used in this book.

5 Spaniels This is a large group of dogs, most of which were bred for hunting and retrieving game. It also includes many toy breeds. All have good intelligence. Outward appearance shows great variations. (See p.34.)

6 Terriers Named from the French word meaning earth, the dogs of this group were trained to go to ground after foxes, badgers, etc. Most have a harsh coat, wiry build, and curious nature. (See p.38.)

7 Hounds are often kept in packs for hunting. They are medium to large in size, with short hair. Hounds are noted for their excellent sense of smell. (See p.40.)

8 Crossbreds and mongrels Unlike the other groups described here, these dogs are not distinguished by physical type. Crossbreds result from mating pedigree dogs of different breeds. Mongrels have more mixed ancestry. (See p.42.)

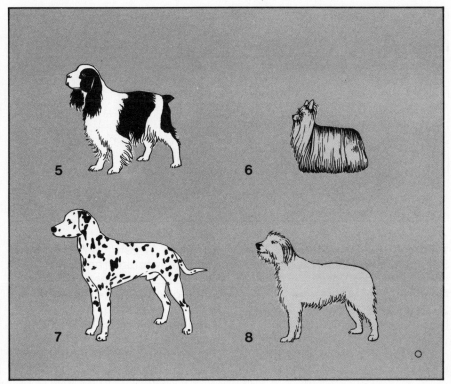

5

6

7

8

Greyhounds

Dogs of this group have a characteristic streamlined appearance. Most were originally bred for hunting large animals, relying in the chase more on sight and speed than on scent and hearing. The greyhound, Afghan, and saluki all have extremely ancient histories; dogs similar to the modern greyhound appear on ancient Egyptian artifacts. Introduced into Britain in Roman times, the greyhound

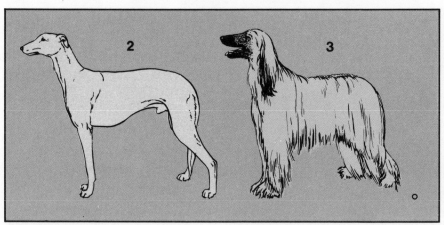

1 Borzoi/Russian wolfhound
Shoulder height 29in (74cm). Long, silky coat. Various colors. Needs large exercise area.
2 Greyhound 28-30in (71-76cm) high. Short, smooth coat in various colors. Usually kept for racing, but also makes a good pet if properly exercised.

3 Afghan 27-29in (69-74cm) high. Long, heavy coat in any color. Strong, fast dog. Needs careful training and a lot of exercise if kept as a housedog.
4 Italian greyhound 10in (25cm) high. Short, thin coat. Unusual high-stepping gait. Not bred as a sporting dog.

type was later modified to produce the Irish wolfhound and Scottish deerhound. The borzoi was a great favorite in pre-revolutionary Russia. Smaller dogs of the group are the whippet, developed for racing in the nineteenth century, and the non-sporting Italian greyhound. With the exception of the latter, all the dogs of this group need a great deal of exercise if kept as pets.

5 Whippet 18in (45cm) high. Short, fine coat in any color. Hardy dog bred principally for racing. Also makes a good pet. Obedient and affectionate.

6 Saluki 23-28in (58-71cm) high. Smooth, silky coat. Very elegant. Bred for speed, needs a lot of space for exercise.

7 Irish wolfhound At least 31in (79cm) high. Rough, harsh coat in various colors. Tallest and perhaps most powerful dog. Needs a lot of exercise.

8 Deerhound At least 30in (76cm) high. Thick, ragged coat in gray, brindle, or wheaten. Needs a lot of exercise.

©DIAGRAM

27

Mastiffs

The group of dogs known as mastiffs descended from a heavily built dog that originated many thousands of years ago, possibly in ancient Assyria. The mastiff was a war dog and was also used for wolf and lion hunting and for bearbaiting. The bull mastiff and the boxer date from the nineteenth century and were bred to combine the strength of the mastiff with a lighter build. Bulldogs are another

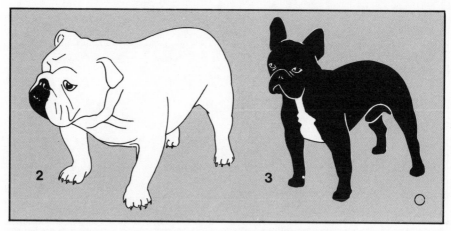

1 St Bernard 25½-29in (64-74cm) high at shoulder. Rough or smooth coat in various colors with patches of white. A large, heavy dog requiring a lot of food and exercise.
2 Bulldog 15in (38cm) high. Short coat in any color except black and yellow. Unique, ugly appearance. Reacts badly to heat. A loyal pet.
3 French bulldog 12in (30cm) high. Short, fine coat in brindle, fawn, or pied. Large bat ears. Used to be very popular in France and the USA.
4 Boxer 21-24in (53-61cm) high. Short, smooth coat in brindle or

offshoot of the mastiff line and were used for bullbaiting. They are renowned for qualities of tenacity and loyalty to their owners. The origins of the Newfoundland and St Bernard are obscure, but both are well known for rescue work. The large dogs of this group are no longer as popular as in earlier times on account of their size and an incorrect reputation for ferocity.

fawn. Cropped ears except in UK. A powerful dog that needs careful training.

5 Newfoundland 28in (71cm) high. Flat, medium-length, water-resistant coat. Usually black. Hardy, gentle, and alert. Excellent water dog.

6 Bull mastiff 25-27in (63-69cm) high. Short, dense coat. Fawn or brindle with dark face. Alert and affectionate. A good house dog, but exercise is vital.

7 Mastiff 30in (76cm) high. Fawn, with short, smooth coat. Powerful and heavy, not noted for speed. Gentle, but makes a good guard dog.

© DIAGRAM

Spitz breeds

Spitz breeds developed in Arctic regions, where they have long been used for pulling sleighs, hunting, and as guard dogs. Many of these breeds are little known outside their countries of origin, but others have won wider popularity as pets and show dogs. Perhaps the best known of the spitz breeds is the husky, originally bred as a sleigh dog in West Greenland and Labrador. Other typical spitz breeds

1 Husky 23-28in (58-71cm) high at shoulder. Long, harsh outer coat with dense undercoat. Makes a good pet, but may be reserved with strangers.
2 Chow chow 18in (46cm) high. Thick coat with ruff and mane. Has a bluish-black tongue and gums. Popular as a show dog.

Also a good pet and guard dog.
3 Schipperke 13in (33cm) high. Harsh, smooth coat, usually black. Bred to guard canal barges. Adaptable and lively.
4 Elkhound 20½in (52cm) high. Coat gray, short on face and front of legs, long on neck, buttocks, backs of forelegs. Bred for

include the chow chow, an ancient Chinese breed, and the Samoyed, with the name of a nomadic people from northern Europe and Asia. The elkhound is a typical spitz from Scandinavia. The Pomeranian is a miniaturized spitz with some popularity as a pet. Also classified as spitz breeds are the schipperke from the Netherlands and the Pembrokeshire corgi. (For Cardiganshire corgi see p.40.)

hunting purposes.

5 Pomeranian 7in (18cm) high. Long, straight, profuse coat that stands out around the neck and shoulders. Various colors. Popular as a lapdog, but needs careful grooming.

6 Welsh corgi (Pembrokeshire) 10-12in (25-30cm) high. Medium-length, smooth, dense coat. Various colors, sometimes with white. Makes an alert and companionable pet.

7 Samoyed 22in (56cm) high. Long, harsh coat with ruff and dense undercoat. White or cream. Careful grooming needed to keep coat in good condition.

©DIAGRAM

31

Sheepdogs

Sheepdogs and shepherds' dogs have been bred over the centuries to herd sheep and to protect flocks from marauders. They are hardy breeds with a high degree of intelligence and good qualities of perception. The German shepherd has been successfully trained to perform a wide variety of tasks. All these dogs show a willingness to work, and need a great deal of exercise if kept as pets.

1

1 Old English sheepdog 22in (56cm) high at shoulder. Shaggy, weather-resistant coat in blue or gray with white.

2 Rough collie 20-24in (51-61cm) high. Dense, harsh coat. (Also smooth-coated variety.)
3 Shetland sheepdog 14in (36cm) high. Resembles small collie. Lively, instinctive herder.
4 German shepherd dog/Alsatian 24-26in (61-66cm) high. Smooth double coat. Very intelligent.

5 Border collie 18in (46cm) high. Long, weather-resistant coat. Intelligent and lively.
6 Bearded collie 18-24in (46-61cm) high. Long double coat. A very old shepherding breed.
7 Pyrenean mountain dog 27-32in (69-81cm) high. Thick outer coat. White, sometimes marked.

©DIAGRAM

33

Spaniels (1)

Spaniels are thought to be of Spanish or at least Mediterranean origin, hence their name. They can be divided into two groups: the "game-finding" dogs such as setters, retrievers, pointers, and spaniels, and the toy breeds, which do not have a typical spaniel appearance. Many of these breeds have been standardized relatively recently, although the Pekingese and Maltese have more

1 Cocker spaniel 16in (41cm) high at shoulder. Flat, silky coat. Various colors. Formerly a sporting dog, but now usually kept as a pet. Intelligent and alert. Check ears for canker.
2 American cocker spaniel 15in (38cm) high. Variation of cocker spaniel, with more profuse coat.

Breed is most common in the USA where it was developed.
3 English springer spaniel 20in (51cm) high. Medium-length, two-color coat. Good hunting dog. Responds well to training. Very active, enjoys working.
4 Cavalier King Charles spaniel 14in (36cm) high. Long, silky

ancient origins. The poodle was originally bred in Germany as a water spaniel, although it is now kept almost exclusively as a pet and a show dog. Apart from the toy breeds, other members of the spaniel group are essentially working dogs and need considerable exercise and careful training if they are to be kept in the home. All of them are intelligent and make good companions.

coat. Differs from King Charles spaniel in size, shape of head, and length of muzzle.

5 King Charles spaniel 11-12in (28-30cm) high. Long, silky coat. Specific markings in various colors. Non-sporting toy spaniel. Active and intelligent.

6 Pekingese 6-9in (15-23cm) high. Long, straight, flat coat with profuse feathering. Plumed tail. Any color. Popular toy breed. Lively and active.

7 Maltese 10in (25cm) high. Long, straight, silky coat, preferably white. Often bred as a show dog. Adapts well to town life. Fairly hardy.

Spaniels (2)

8 Golden retriever 23in (58cm) high. Flat, wavy coat in gold or cream. Hunting dog bred for retrieving game. Easily trained and affectionate family pet.

9 Labrador 22in (56cm) high. Short, smooth coat in black or gold. Most popular breed of shooting dog. Intelligent and easily trained. Good guide dog.

10 Pointer 24½in (62cm) high. Short, smooth coat. White with various colored markings. Bred to "find" game by pointing.

11 Irish setter 23-26in (58-66cm) high. Flat, silky coat. Rich chestnut color. Elegant appearance. Active and playful.

12 English setter 25½-27in (65-69cm) high. Long, silky coat. White with markings in various colors. Stable nature makes it a good family pet.
13 Chihuahua 5in (13cm) high. Fine, close coat in any color. (Also long-haired variety.)
14 Pug 10-11 in (25-28cm) high. Fine, smooth coat in fawn or black. Compact solid body. Originated in the Far East.
15 Miniature poodle 11-15in (28-38cm) high. One of three sizes (see p.23). Profuse off-standing coat, usually clipped. Various solid colors.

Terriers

Terriers are typically small, hardy breeds originally used to force vermin (foxes, badgers, martens, polecats) from their holes. "Terrier" is derived from the French "terre" meaning earth. These dogs are literally "earth dogs," renowned for their ability to go to ground after animals hiding in their lairs. Well-known terrier breeds originated in Yorkshire and the Lake District in England, the Highlands

1 **Airedale** 23-24in (58-61cm) high. Harsh, wiry coat in black and tan. Large terrier breed.
2 **Wirehaired fox terrier** 15½ in (39cm) high. Dense, wiry coat (also smooth-haired variety). White with black or tan.
3 **Schnauzer** Miniature 14in (36cm) high: standard 18-19in (46-48cm) high. Hard wiry coat in white, brown, gray, or black.
4 **Doberman Pinscher** 26in (66cm) high. Short, harsh coat in various colors. "Manufactured" breed from terrier stock.
5 **Boston terrier** 16in (41cm) high. Short, sleek coat. White with brindle or black. US breed.

of Scotland, and parts of Germany and Central Europe. In each of these areas, difficult terrain provides easy cover for foxes and other species that commonly kill sheep. The history of terrier-type dogs dates back to the fifteenth century, but many of the modern terrier breeds are the result of cross-breeding during the course of the nineteenth century.

6 Bull terrier 16in (41cm) high. Short, smooth coat. Predominantly white. Originally developed for dog fighting.

7 Cairn terrier 10in (25cm) high. Profuse, harsh coat. Any color. Fearless, lively nature.

8 Skye terrier 10in (25cm) high. Long, flat coat in gray, fawn, or cream. A good watchdog.

9 Scottish terrier 10-11in (25-28cm) high. Wiry coat in black, brindle, or wheaten. (Name sometimes used to refer to all terriers from Scotland.)

10 Yorkshire terrier 7-8in (18-20cm) high. Long, straight, silky coat in dark gray and tan.

Hounds

Hounds are medium to large dogs developed for hunting, either singly or in packs. Of all dog breeds, hounds have the most highly developed sense of smell. The bloodhound, in particular, is outstanding in its ability to follow a difficult trail. Unlike the Pembrokeshire corgi, which is classified as a spitz (see p.31), the Cardiganshire corgi is considered a true miniature hound.

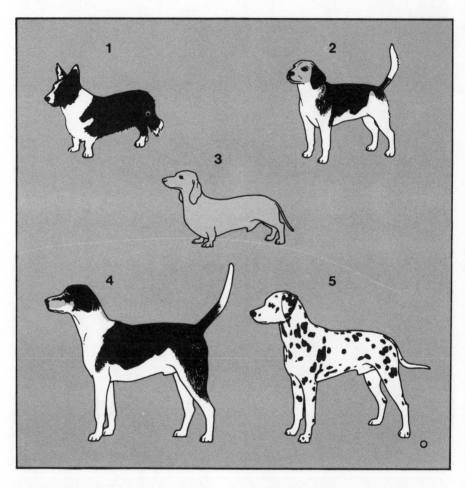

1 Welsh corgi (Cardiganshire) 12in (30cm) high. Short or medium coat in any color except pure white. Tail like fox's brush. Former cattle herder.
2 Beagle 13-16in (33-41cm) high in Europe: smaller in USA. Short, smooth coat. Worked in packs for hunting.

3 Smooth-haired dachshund 5-9in (13-23cm) high. Short, smooth coat in any color. (Also long- and wire-haired varieties.) Loyal, determined, and alert.
4 English foxhound 23in (58cm) high. Short, smooth coat in tan, white, and black. Worked in packs for hunting.

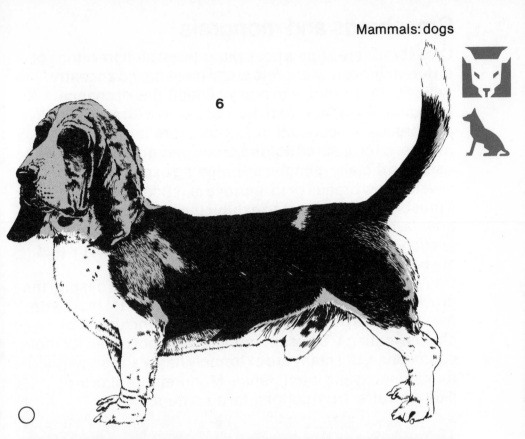

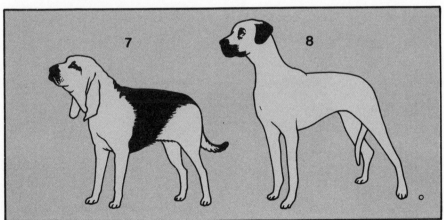

5 Dalmatian 19-23in (48-58cm) high. Short coat in white with black or liver spots. Formerly a coach dog, now usually a pet.
6 Basset hound 13-15in (33-38cm) high. Smooth coat. Very loose skin giving melancholy expression. A French breed.
7 Bloodhound 23-27in (58-69cm) high. Short, glossy coat in "hound" colors. Excellent sense of smell. Often used for tracking.
8 Great Dane 28-34in (71-86cm) high. Short, dense coat in brindle, black, fawn, blue, or with "harlequin" markings on white. A large, active dog that needs a lot of food and exercise.

Crossbreds and mongrels

Crossbreds are dogs whose parents are pedigree dogs of different breeds. Mongrels are of more mixed ancestry, typically the products of many generations of chance breeding. No mongrel can be registered with an official dog-breeders' association, but crossbreds often are. A registered crossbred holds a cross-pedigree and may be used in officially recognized breeding experiments to develop new breeds or to improve existing ones.

Crossbreds often seem to exhibit the best qualities of both breeds in the parentage. The most successful crossbreds are generally those with parents belonging to breeds that are broadly similar in size and structure.

Dogs of mixed ancestry remain popular as pets despite the growth of interest in purebred dogs and the fact that better owner control over dogs has reduced the incidence of chance matings. Typically mongrels are not noted for their appearance, but many are extremely hardy and show good temperament and intelligence. Mongrels are also less likely to suffer from congenital disorders.

5

6

7

1-4 Mongrels Examples chosen to illustrate the great variations in mongrel appearance.
5 Cavalier King Charles spaniel x whippet In this example of a crossbred, the whippet parentage is fairly easy to recognize. The influence of the spaniel parent is seen in the less streamlined line, shorter legs, softer face, and fuller ears.
6-7 Jack Russell terriers The name Jack Russell refers to a particular "strain" of terriers bred for their working ability. Great variations in appearance have so far prevented the Jack Russell's acceptance as a breed.

©DIAGRAM

Feeding dogs

Dogs are carnivores, but, like their wild counterparts, should not feed exclusively on meat. Wild dogs eat the stomach contents of their herbivore prey to gain all the necessary vitamin, mineral, and vegetable constituents of their diet. Feeding a dog is no longer a very complicated process now that many commercial compound foods are available. Dry dog chow is most nutritious and helps to

Puppy diet
1 Milk with baby cereal.
2 Lukewarm milk, glucose, and beaten egg.
3 Meat meal consisting of scraped or raw ground meat with added vitamins and minerals.
Adult diet
4 Dog chow. Contains cereal, meat and fish meals, dry milk

solids, vitamins, and minerals.
5 Canned dog meat. Add to chow.
6 Dog biscuits. Use to reward.
7 Bones. No chicken, fish, or chop bones, which may splinter.
8 Beaten egg. One a week.
9 Fresh meat — liver, kidney, spleen, tripe, heart. Add to chow after boiling and cooling.
10 Fresh water.

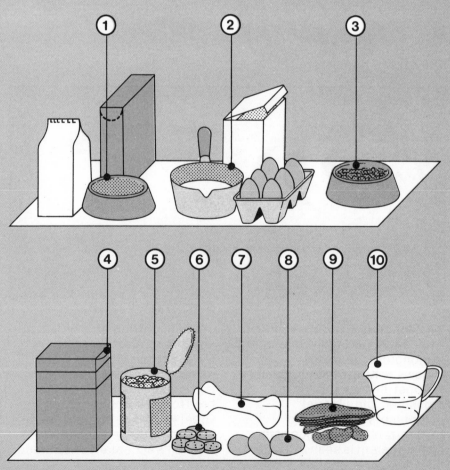

keep teeth and gums in good condition. Some canned dog meat may be added to provide moisture and extra flavor. Dogs must not be overfed or given treats or snacks. Do not make sudden changes in their diet or feeding schedule. Bones are not essential, but a large marrow or leg bone is recommended once a week for valuable chewing exercise. Fresh water must always be available.

Feeding The amount of food that a dog needs will depend on the age and breed of the dog; ask your veterinarian for advice. Puppies require frequent meals — four times a day just after they are weaned. Full-grown dogs do best on one meal a day. Old dogs can be fed twice a day. The diagram (see below) gives an indication of the quantities needed for different sizes of adult dogs, based on their ideal weight. This is not a rigid formula and should be adapted if the dog gains or loses too much weight. It is important to restrain from overfeeding. Fat dogs are prone to many diseases and are unlikely to live their full life.

1lb(0.45kg) of dog food
a Weight of dog in lb(kg)
b Weight of food in lb(kg)

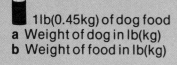

a	5(2.3)	10(4.5)	15(6.8)	20(9.1)	30(13.6)
b	¼(.11)	½(.23)	¾(.34)	1(.45)	1½(.79)

a	50(22.7)	75(34)	100(45.4)	150(68.1)
b	2½(1.14)	3½(1.59)	4½(2.04)	5½(2.5)

©DIAGRAM

45

Housing dogs

Most family dogs now live in the house. Dogs should have a place of their own, free from drafts, somewhere near the center of family life, without being in the way. It is usual to provide a basket or bed, with some bedding for warmth. Outdoor kennels are suitable for working dogs, hunting dogs, or guard dogs, but animals kept outdoors are less likely to respond as pets.

Shelter Dogs kept outside need somewhere to sleep and to shelter from bad weather. Dog houses should be well built, with a sloping, weathertight roof (**a**). They can be raised on bricks to minimize damp. Straw bedding should be provided for extra warmth, and should be replaced regularly to prevent parasites. If several dogs are to be kept outdoors, well-equipped kennel outbuildings will be a great asset.

a

Dog beds are available in a wide variety of designs. No dog needs an elaborate bed, and many will be happy with a folded blanket kept in a designated corner. Straw baskets (**b**) make simple, sturdy beds and are available in a range of sizes. A dog's bed must always be positioned in an area that is both warm and free from any drafts.

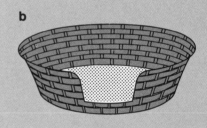

b

Traveling boxes are required for some types of long-distance travel and it is essential that they are properly constructed to ensure an animal's safe arrival. Traveling boxes (**c**) should be lightweight but strong, with adequate ventilation, handles for carrying, and secure fastenings. A box must be big enough for the dog to turn around but small enough to prevent injury from jolts and bumps. Clear labeling is essential.

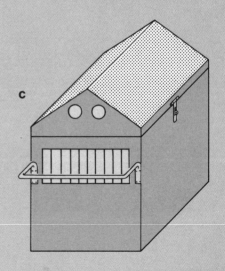

c

Exercising dogs

All dogs need exercise and some need a great deal. Runs and long walks are essential for most large dogs and also for some smaller, highly active terrier breeds. Exercise should be regular, controlled, and in varied locations. It is needed to keep muscles in tone and to provide new interests and surroundings. Ideally it should be one of the more pleasurable aspects of keeping a dog.

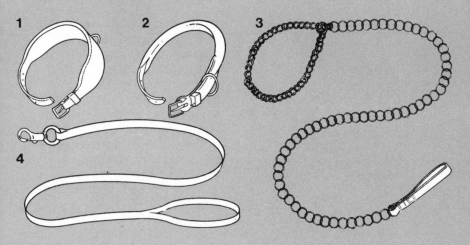

Exercise equipment

1 Flat leather collar. A collar that is too wide or too narrow will cause the dog discomfort.

2 Rounded leather collar.

3 Choke chain and chain leash. A choke chain is a slip collar sometimes used during training. It must be put on so that the chain leading from the loop is at the back of the dog's neck. If used incorrectly, a choke chain will restrict breathing and may damage the throat.

4 Leather leash. Leashes come in different sizes: long for small dogs and short for large ones.

5 Harness. Useful for smaller dogs that are often picked up.

6 Coat. Some shorthaired breeds need protection from the cold. Make sure that a dog coat fits well — covering the chest and abdomen — and is weather resistant and easy to clean.

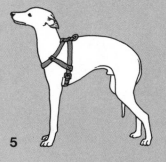

©DIAGRAM

47

Grooming dogs

Grooming is an essential part of dog care. As well as keeping the coat free from dirt and loose hair, it provides an ideal opportunity to check for external ailments such as cuts, insect bites, or parasites. All dogs shed hair, and with longhaired breeds this can cause annoyance if the dog is not brushed on a regular basis. A dog needs to be bathed only if its coat is very dirty.

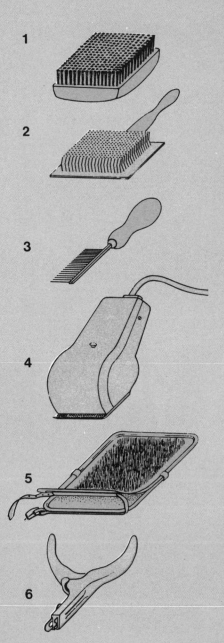

Grooming equipment The type of equipment needed will depend on the breed of dog.
1 Brush for dogs with wiry or medium-length coats.
2 Slicker — wire rakes set in a rubber base — ideal for longhaired dogs.
3 Metal comb for shorthaired dogs and for undercoats.
4 Electric clippers.
5 Hound glove for grooming smooth-haired dogs.
6 Nail clippers.

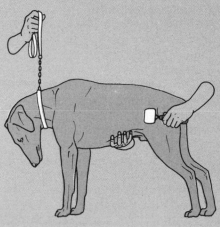

Brushing Brush once or twice a week depending on coat length. If the dog fusses, one person should hold it on a leash while another grooms, keeping his hand under the dog to prevent it sitting down. Gently ease out or carefully cut out any mats of hair. Check for skin problems.

Bathing Bathe a dog only if it is particularly dirty. One person should hold the dog on a leash while another bathes it. Use a bathtub, sink, or basin. Add a few drops of vegetable oil to the dog's eyes to prevent irritation. Wet the dog with lukewarm water, taking care to keep the eyes, ears, and muzzle dry. Apply mild shampoo, never detergent. Rinse carefully. Dry with a towel, then keep the dog in a warm place until quite dry.

1 Pitcher for rinsing.
2 Towels.
3 Mild shampoo.
4 Vegetable oil and eyedropper.

Coat clipping It is customary to clip the coats of some types of dog. Poodles are clipped in a variety of decorative styles such as the one illustrated below. Wirehaired dogs are often clipped in a utilitarian style to keep their coats tidy and easy to clean. Profusely haired dogs like the Old English sheepdog may benefit from a clip in hot weather. Dogs can be clipped professionally or at home, but great care is needed.

Nail clipping Exercise on hard surfaces keeps nails in trim. If nails grow too long they curve inward, causing sores and later deformity. A vet will trim the nails or they can be trimmed at home with clippers. Avoid the vein (**a**) by clipping only $\frac{1}{8}$in (3mm) off the nail's tip (**b**).

©DIAGRAM

Dog behavior

Dogs are social animals that live in large packs in the wild. Domestic dogs show patterns of behavior also found in wild dogs but now adapted to a different environment. In each case, behavior patterns are to a great extent concerned with establishing a dog's position in the social order and with establishing territorial rights.

The complex behavior patterns found in dogs are largely

1 **Paw-giving** Dogs do not have to be trained to give their paws, only when to do so. This is basically a submissive gesture (puppies press paws against their mother's teats to increase the milkflow).

2 **Nose-nudging** Dogs often nudge their owners with their noses, ears laid back. This is a request for attention originating in a submissive gesture — the rooting reflex of nursing puppies.

3 **Tail-wagging** Tail-wagging shows pleasure and excitement.

4 **Circling** Before a dog lies down it circles several times as if making a bed. The dog is actually giving the correct curvature to its spine so that it can rest in a curled-up position.

5 **Fighting** Puppies learn to fight as a way of testing their strength. Real dog fights are often contests to establish the dominant male. In the wild, these rarely end in serious injury, but domestic dogs may have to be separated.

Facial expressions
a Threatening expression with the ears forward, eyes alert, and jaws wide in a snarl.
b Submissive expression showing fear with smooth forehead, ears laid back, eyes narrowed, and corners of mouth drawn back.

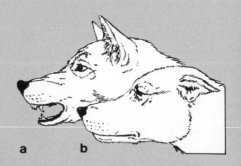

learned during the first weeks of life. If a puppy is taken from its mother and littermates during these crucial weeks it will fail to develop typical responses and may have serious temperamental difficulties.

The fact that only a small proportion of a dog's behavior is instinctive means that dogs generally respond well to training by humans (see p.52).

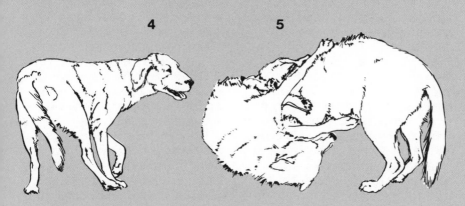

6 Territory Dogs leave a trail of scent in their urine to be picked up by other dogs. This is a means of conveying territorial information and dogs will establish a series of scent posts in their home district.

A new environment is investigated by sniffing, not only for urine, but for the sweat imprints left by other dogs' paws, the only area of a dog's body that sweats.

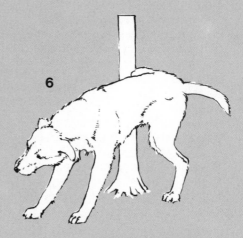

Sounds Dogs make a range of noises that express various states of mind. Yelping signifies submission, barking is a warning or alerting signal, and howling appears to be used to indicate the location of a dog when separated from companions (canine or human). Howling can be heard up to several miles away. Dogs can hear far higher notes than humans. All dogs growl when angry or threatened, and whine when they want something. If injured, they may shriek with pain. Some dogs are mute: greyhounds, Afghans, and borzois are a few of these.

©DIAGRAM

Training dogs

All dogs need to be trained to some extent and most learn easily if the trainer is patient and consistent. Training includes housebreaking (housetraining), which can begin after weaning, and the learning of basic commands, when the puppy is older. Dangerous activities such as chasing cars or livestock should be prevented from the beginning. The best way of training a dog is by the use of rewards.

Housebreaking (housetraining)

1 Confine the puppy to a room or fenced-off area near an outside door and cover the floor with newspaper.

2 After a few days, the puppy should be using one corner, usually the farthest away from the feeding dish. Praise the dog when this place is used.

3 Observe the puppy's schedule, and begin taking it out after each meal and sleep, always to the same area. Praise the dog for using it. Remove the newspaper. Dogs never foul their own area, and when mistakes happen the dog has usually selected an area of the house it considers to be "outside." Do not punish the dog. It is useless to discipline after the event: the dog will not understand. Never rub a dog's nose in its own excrement. The dog will not understand what is meant by this, and may even develop an undesirable appetite. Clean and disinfect the area, and continue to praise for successes.

Training

1 Sit Before dinner, take the dog on a leash to a quiet room. Firmly say "sit" and press down on the hindquarters, forcing the dog to sit. Reward and praise.

2 Down With the dog sitting, press its shoulders, say "down," and pull the forelegs forward. Reward and praise.

3 Stay With the dog on a leash and sitting down, move back away from it while saying "stay." Continue training until the dog will stay without the leash.

4 Come All dogs should be taught to come when called by name. Reward and praise when the dog responds to calling.

5 Heel Take the leash in the right hand, keeping the dog on your left side. The leash should hang slack. Say "heel" and move forward, correcting with the right hand and patting with the left when the dog responds.

6 Fetch Many dogs will retrieve naturally. Before being trained to fetch, a dog should respond to commands to sit, stay, and come.

Training principles

a) The owner should be trainer.
b) Give short daily lessons.
c) Use a consistent tone of voice — firm, but not threatening.
d) Use the same commands.
e) Never punish a dog for not obeying: it will associate the command with punishment.

This strengthens patterns of good behavior, whereas punishment may provoke fear and frustration. At some times, however, the use of a reprimand may be the only way to break a bad habit. Few dogs need more than a harsh word as a punishment: never try to inflict pain. Dogs are easily cowed and may react aggressively as a defensive measure.

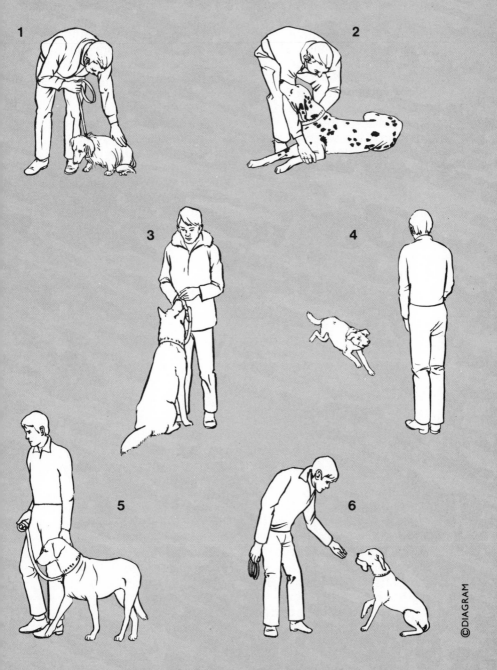

©DIAGRAM

Dog shows and field trials

The first organized dog show was held in Newcastle, England, in June 1859. Field trials began in 1865 in Bedfordshire, England, and the Kennel Club was formed later, in 1873. Today there are many official clubs throughout the world and dog shows are held regularly. These range from local championships to large national shows that attract widespread interest.

Kennel clubs These official organizations exist mainly to supervise and promote the standards of purebred dogs. There are over 500 breeds of dog, but most clubs recognize fewer than one quarter of these. Recognition of a breed depends on the number of dogs of that breed registered with the club. Only when a representative number has been registered will the club draw up a standard of points for the breed.

Showing An owner wishing to show a purebred dog must first obtain pedigree papers and register the dog with a club. Show classes are drawn up according to breed, age, sex, previous showing record, etc. Dogs are judged against the official standard for the breed. Showing owners must pay special attention to the dog's diet, health, grooming, transportation, accommodation, and response to strangers.

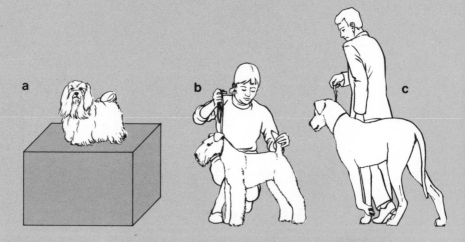

a

b

c

Judging Judges first see the exhibits circling in a ring. Each dog is then closely examined. Judges should have a good knowledge of the breed standard, anatomy, and form. By feeling the coat and checking muscles and bones, faults can be detected that might be hidden by skillful grooming. All points of the dog are considered: stance, appearance, coat, movement, and temperament.
a Small dogs are "benched" for close inspection.
b Dogs must show correct stance.
c Good movement is important.

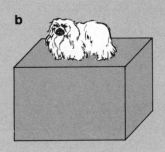

Breed standard Selected points for the Dalmatian (**a**).
Head: fairly long, definite stop.
Eyes: moderately far apart.
Ears: set high, moderate size.
Mouth: tight lips.
Body: deep chest, level back.
Feet: "cat" feet.
Tail: carried slightly upward.
Coat: short, hard, sleek, dense.
Color: spots of liver or black, 1-2in (2.5-5cm) diameter.
General: balanced, muscular, free movement, long strides.

Breed standard Selected points for the Pekingese (**b**).
Head: massive, broad, flat.
Eyes: large, dark, prominent.
Ears: heart-shaped, close to head.
Mouth: level lips.
Body: short, lion-like, level back.
Feet: large, flat, sound.
Tail: set high, curved over back.
Coat: long, coarse, feathered.
Color: any color and markings except liver or albino.
General: small, thickset, alert and intelligent expression.

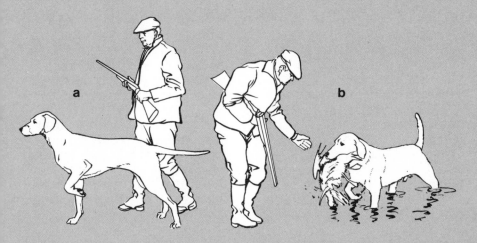

Field trials are events designed to test the obedience, working skills, and endurance of sporting dogs. In most cases such trials are affiliated to a kennel club and subject to official regulation. Tests vary according to the breeds of dog included. Setters, retrievers, and pointers all have their own jobs at a shoot, and their skill at these tasks will be tested. Local conditions also produce variations such as water tests.
a Test for pointers — showing the location of game.
b Test for retrievers — retrieving in various conditions.

©DIAGRAM

Breeding dogs

A large number of unwanted dogs become strays every year. This problem could be reduced if more bitches were spayed — a relatively simple operation that eliminates the inconvenience of the twice yearly "season" when constant vigilance is needed to prevent unsuitable matings. Cross-matings are often successful, but occasionally problems develop when a bitch is carrying puppies that are too large.

Mating Contact the owner of the stud dog as soon as the bitch comes into season. Mating is usually planned for the 12th day from the start of the heat period. Take the bitch to the stud dog. Readiness to mate is shown by the bitch's stance.

Pregnancy Gestation is 63 days. The bitch should have plenty of exercise until the last weeks. Give vitamin and mineral supplements. Worm the bitch in the third week. Notify the vet.

Prepare a whelping box lined with warm bedding and get the bitch used to sleeping in it.

Birth Signs of labor are a drop in temperature of 2-3° down to 98°F (36.7°C), restlessness, and loss of appetite. Stay with the bitch but keep other distractions away. Labor takes 2-20 hours. Puppies are born headfirst in a membrane, which the bitch will eat. Contact the vet if no puppies appear when the bitch strains, or if there is not an afterbirth for each puppy.

Congenital defects Check puppies for congenital defects. Dogs with these defects should not be allowed to breed.
1 Eyelid defects.
2 Elbow dysplasia.
3 Hip dysplasia.
4 Hernia.
5 Undescended testicles.

To breed purebred puppies, a stud dog must be chosen and arrangements made for the mating. A fee is usually charged. A veterinarian will give advice on aspects of caring for bitches during pregnancy and should be notified at once of any difficulties. Professional dog breeding is an expensive occupation, and expert knowledge is an essential ingredient of success.

Growth The four drawings below show the growth of an Afghan puppy from 8 weeks to maturity.

Care of puppies Eight is the maximum number that a bitch should rear unaided. During the first weeks the bitch will take full care of her puppies and the litter should be disturbed as little as possible. If puppies cry a lot there may be nursing problems: consult a vet. Most puppies are wormed at 6 weeks. Try not to overexcite young puppies.

Weaning Begin weaning at 3 weeks, giving twice daily milk meals (cow's milk thickened with baby cereal) when the bitch is away. At 4 weeks add a third meal of raw ground or scraped meat with vitamin or mineral supplements. At 5-6 weeks give four meals a day: two of milk and cereal and two of meat. From 6-8 weeks substitute meat meals for meals of milk and cereal. A fully weaned puppy requires four small meat meals daily (see p.44).

Timetable of development

Loses umbilical cord	2-3 days
Doubles birth weight	9-12 days
Eyes open	12-15 days
Ears open	15-17 days
Stands and crawls	13-18 days
Urinates without stimulation	22-25 days
Teeth in	30 days
Weaning	6-8 weeks
Socializes with humans	8-14 weeks
First heat for bitches	24-52 weeks

Gestation	63 days
Cycle	6 months
Litter	2-12
Weaning	3-8 weeks
Maturity	76 weeks
Lifespan	8-16 years

© DIAGRAM

Dog diseases

The most important aspect of keeping a dog in good health is watching for any symptoms of illness or noting unusual behavior so that veterinary advice can be sought at the earliest opportunity. Diet, exercise, and housing also play a large part in maintaining the health of a dog. Puppies should be vaccinated against some diseases at an early age. Dogs with inherited diseases should not breed.

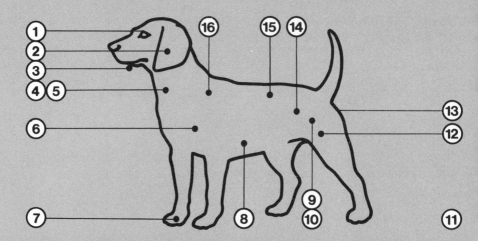

Common ailments Most of these ailments need to be treated by a veterinarian. In some cases, urgent treatment is required.

1 Eye disorders — conjunctivitis, corneal ulcers, eyelid defects. Redness, discharge, puffiness.

2 Inflammation of the ear canal. Head tilt, discharge, odor, pain. Common in longeared dogs.

3 Gum inflammation. Bad breath, swellings in old dogs. Caused by tartar on teeth.

4 Kennel cough. Coughing spasms after exercise. Very contagious.

5 Vomiting. Dogs vomit easily and there are many causes. Seek treatment if the attack is prolonged or the vomit bloody.

6 Heart disease. Most common sign is coughing after exercise.

7 Cysts between toes.

8 Gastric torsion. Distended stomach. Seek urgent treatment.

9 Diarrhea. Many causes. Limit food for 24 hours then see a vet if no recovery. Notice any behavior changes to aid diagnosis.

10 Constipation. Many causes, possibly hernia or obstruction.

11 Fits or hysteria. Comfort dog during attack. Keep dark and quiet. See vet urgently.

12 Cysts, tumors. Common in old dogs. May need surgery.

13 Anal irritation. Caused by accumulation of secretion in glands at base of tail. Dog scrapes rear end along ground.

14 Worms. Various internal parasites cause changes in appetite and bowel movement. Do not attempt home remedies.

15 Kidney disorders. Frequent urination, blood in urine.

16 Skin complaints — eczema, mange, ringworm. Itching, reddened areas, hair loss.

Signs of illness Owners should watch for the following signs of illness in their dogs.
1 Appetite change — either loss of appetite, extreme hunger, or eating odd substances.
2 Sleeping more than usual, lassitude, or withdrawal.
3 Unusual thirst and frequent urination.
4 Unusual bowel movement.
5 Sneezing, coughing, or problems with breathing.
6 Vomiting/excessive salivating.
7 Breathlessness or fainting.
8 Whimpering, crying, or any other indication of pain.
9 Any unusual behavior.

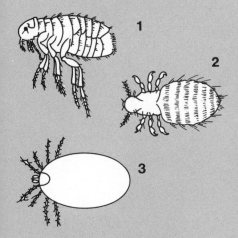

Fleas, lice, and ticks
1 Fleas leave black gritty deposits on the dog's skin. The dog scratches and may get other skin infections as a result. Buy a dog flea powder and follow the instructions carefully.
2 Lice attach themselves to the skin and suck blood. Use lice powder. Disinfect bedding.
3 Ticks are bloodsuckers more common on dogs that roam in fields. Use tweezers to remove the entire tick.

Care of the sick dog Keep the phone number and address of the vet ready for emergencies. When nursing a dog, follow the vet's instructions and administer all medicines correctly. Keep a record of treatment and note changes in the dog's behavior for the vet's information. Sick dogs need extra warmth, isolation from noise and distraction, and sometimes shielding from bright light. Ask the vet if a special diet is required. Keep bedding clean.
Giving medicine
a Pills should be placed as far down the throat as possible. Keep the mouth shut and stroke the throat to encourage swallowing.
b Liquid medicine can be poured into the side of the mouth from a small bottle containing the exact dosage. Hold the mouth shut until the dog swallows.

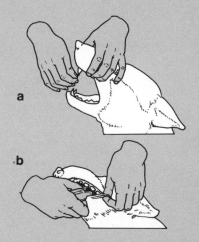

Vaccination First vaccinations are given to puppies at 3 months.
1 Infectious hepatitis vaccine lasts a lifetime.
2 Canine distemper and leptospirosis vaccines need booster shots.
3 Regular rabies vaccination is needed in most countries.

©DIAGRAM

59

History and choosing

Cats were probably first domesticated in Egypt about 5,000 years ago, when wild cats were encouraged to stay around the Egyptians' granaries to catch rodent pests. Unlike dogs, cats have received uneven treatment during their long association with man. The ancient Egyptians revered and mummified them, executing anyone who caused a cat's death. When introduced into China, cats were used mainly to protect silkworm cocoons from rodents. During the Middle Ages in Europe, the cat was thought to be an agent of Satan and thousands of cats were burned and destroyed. Not until the nineteenth century did they again become popular as household pets. Even today superstitions about cats still persist. In North America, a black cat that crosses your path is thought to be unlucky. In England, by contrast, a black cat can symbolize good luck. Cats are much more self reliant than most other domestic animals. In favored circumstances a cat can survive independently of man, and even as pets many cats enjoy the wild world as well as the domestic.

a

b

Cats in art The reverence and awe in which people have held cats can be seen in artistic representations — a statue of the cat goddess of ancient Egypt (**a**), a pottery motif of the Inca cat god (**b**), and a children's book illustration of a witch with a cat on her broomstick (**c**).

c

Ancestry Cats are carnivores and members of the family Felidae which contains nearly 40 species. There is little skeletal difference between wild cats and older types of domesticated cat. It is thought that the main progenitor of the domestic cat (*Felis domestica*) is the Kaffir cat (*Felis libica*) illustrated below. The Kaffir cat is a wild cat of North Africa which will mate with domestic cats to produce fertile half-breeds. Slightly larger than the domestic cat, it has a yellow-buff coat and darker markings that are especially prominent on the tail.

Choosing a kitten Kittens are available from various sources: from breeders, pet stores, or a friend or neighbor whose cat has produced a litter. A home-raised kitten should present few health problems and will usually be free unless it is a purebred. Visit the litter when the kittens are 6 weeks old. Choose a kitten that is neither timid nor aggressive. Pick it up — a kitten that will not relax is unlikely to make a good pet. Kittens should be curious and playful, and should quickly recover their composure after sudden movements and noises. Kittens are ready to leave the litter at 8 weeks. Ask if your kitten has been vaccinated (p.83).

Signs of health
1 Ears are clear and not runny.
2 Nose is clear of mucus.
3 Skin has no rashes, scabs, fleas.
4 Coat is thick and shiny.
5 Body is not skinny.
6 There is no pot belly.

©DIAGRAM

63

Anatomy of the cat

The basic shape of the cat has remained largely unchanged throughout the history of its domestication. The cat is perfectly designed to be a hunter. It is remarkably well coordinated and has a fine sense of balance which usually allows it to land on its feet. Sight, smell, and hearing are highly developed, and there also appears to be an inbuilt sense of time and direction.

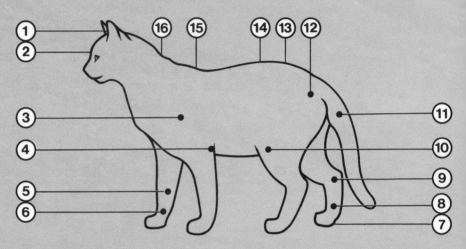

Anatomy All cat breeds are broadly similar in shape. A cat is about 9in(23cm) high at the withers; the hips are slightly higher. Weights range from about 6-15lb(2.7-6.8kg). The hindfeet have four toes, the forefeet five.

Parts of the cat
1 Occiput.
2 Forehead.
3 Shoulder.
4 Elbow.
5 Carpus.
6 Metacarpus.
7 Toes.
8 Metatarsus.
9 Hock.
10 Stifle.
11 Tail.
12 Rump.
13 Hips.
14 Back.
15 Withers.
16 Nape.

Claws The claws of a cat are used for fighting and climbing. They do not get worn down in normal use but must be worn down deliberately by scratching. Cats' claws are retractile — they are pulled up when not needed, enabling the cat to move silently.
1 A muscle (**a**) keeps the claw pulled up when the ligament (**b**) is relaxed.
2 The claw is pulled down when the ligament (**b**) tightens.

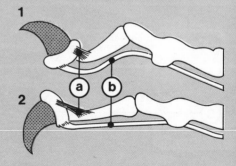

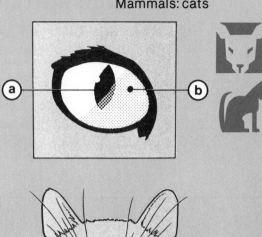

Eyes A cat's eyes are adapted for hunting at night. They are much more sensitive to light than our own. At night the cat's pupils open very wide to let in as much light as possible; during the day the pupils form narrow vertical slits (**a**). On the back of the retina the cat has a layer of light-reflecting cells known as the *tapetum lucidum*. (These cells make the eyes change luster when a light is turned on them.) The cat's eyes are given additional protection by a third eyelid — or nictitating membrane — which slides diagonally across the eye (**b**).

Whiskers A cat's whiskers are important organs of touch and must never be cut. They probably show wind direction and help a cat to gauge whether it can get through narrow openings.

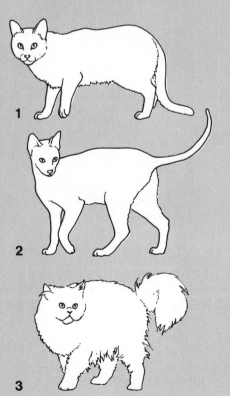

Basic types Cat breeds show much smaller variations in size and shape than dog breeds. Purebred cats are divided into three broad groups according to body type and length of fur. (The characteristics of a mongrel cat obviously depend on its own particular ancestry.)

1 Shorthair (British and American domestic) These cats have broad heads, rounded ears, large, round eyes, powerful bodies, and short, thick tails.

2 Foreign shorthair Cats of foreign type are streamlined in appearance. The head is wedge-shaped, with large pointed ears set well apart. The legs are long and the tail tapering.

3 Longhair Characteristics are a broad, round head with small ears and short, broad nose, a low, well-built body, short legs, and a full tail.

© DIAGRAM

65

British/American shorthairs

The cats illustrated on these pages are pedigree animals classified either as "British shorthairs" or "American domestic shorthairs." They have been especially bred to conform to official breed standards relating to body shape coat color, markings, and eye color.

American domestic shorthairs were originally bred from British stock, and animals in both countries remain

1

1 Tabby May be silver, red, or brown, with dark banded markings. Tabby markings resemble those of the domestic cat's wild ancestors, and often appear in breeds where they are not wanted. Pedigree tabbies are difficult to breed since markings must conform to strictly prescribed patterns.

2 Tortoiseshell Red, black, and cream patches should be evenly distributed over the entire body. Colors must not intermingle. Tortoiseshell males are uncommon, and are usually sterile. (The American blue-and-cream has rather similar

generally similar in type. They have powerful, cobby bodies, thick tails, broad heads, and ears with rounded tips. American domestic shorthairs tend to have larger ears than their British counterparts.

Breeding difficulties make some of these cats quite rare. In certain breeds male cats tend to be sterile, making outcrossing necessary to perpetuate the breed.

markings, although in the British equivalent the two colors should be intermingled.)

3 Tortoiseshell-and-white Also called calico. Resembles a tortoiseshell except for white patches on the face, chest, and legs. Usually female.

4 Bi-colored shorthair May be any solid color and white, with no intermingling.

5 Self-colored Classes for whites (with blue, orange, or odd eyes), blacks, blues, and creams. Colors must be solid with no hairs of any other color. Whites with blue eyes are usually deaf.

©DIAGRAM

Foreign shorthairs

Despite their relatively recent introduction, the group of purebred cats known as foreign shorthairs has acquired tremendous popularity. These cats are distinguished by their build from the other shorthair group — the British and American domestic shorthairs (p.66). Foreign shorthairs have long, lithe bodies, tapering tails, long, well-proportioned heads, and pointed ears. There are some

1 Siamese The colorpoints — mask, ears, legs, and tail — are a darker shade than the rest of the coat. May be seal, blue, chocolate, lilac (frost), tabby, red, and tortie. Siamese have wedge-shaped heads, elegant necks, hindlegs noticeably longer than forelegs.

First introduced into Britain in 1884, the Siamese is now the most popular pedigree breed in many countries. Its origin is unknown, but head and body lines resemble cats worshiped in ancient Egypt. Siamese often demand attention, and are known for their loud and raucous voices.

minor differences in build between the various breeds, but the main variations are in coat and eye coloring.

The names of foreign breeds do not always denote their country of origin. The basic foreign type is believed to have originated in areas of the Middle East and Asia, but some "foreign" breeds like the Burmese were developed by breeding Siamese with other cats of foreign type.

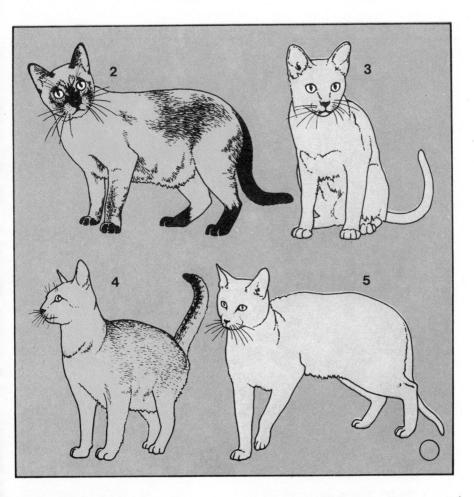

2 Burmese Brown, blue, or champagne, with short, thick, glossy coat. Product of brown foreign-type cat and Siamese.

3 Korat Silvery blue foreign shorthair with dense, soft fur. First brought to North America from Thailand in 1959.

4 Abyssinian An unusual and expensive breed with short, dense, rabbit-like coat. Ruddy brown ticked with darker brown or black. (Also red Abyssinian.)

5 Russian blue Soft, close-lying blue coat. Also called blue foreign type or Archangel cat. Thought to have been taken to England by Russian sailors.

©DIAGRAM

Longhairs

Longhaired cats are perhaps the most beautiful of all the purebreds. Known variously as longhairs, Persians, or angoras, they were apparently first brought to Western Europe from the Middle East toward the end of the sixteenth century. Long hair sometimes appears as a mutation in the litters of shorthaired cats, and in this way a variety of new longhaired breeds has been developed.

1

1 Longhair/Persian Selective breeding has produced color variations corresponding to those for shorthaired breeds. Self-colored longhairs may be white, black, blue, cream, or red. White and black are the oldest varieties, blue is now probably most popular. Blue-eyed whites are usually deaf. Reds and creams are difficult to breed. Smokes have a black coat shading to silver. Specifications for bi-colored cats (illustrated), tabbies, blue-and-creams, tortoiseshells, and tortoiseshell-and-whites are as for shorthairs (p.66-67).

Today, longhairs show all the color variations of shorthaired cats. In addition to a long, flowing coat and full ruff, a longhaired cat should have a broad, round head, small, tufted ears, low, well-built body, short legs, and a full tail. Longhairs require regular grooming to keep their coats in condition and to prevent the formation of hairballs in the stomach and intestines.

2 Colorpoint/Himalayan Bred by crossing the Siamese with various longhair breeds. (The Balinese, another longhaired colorpoint, was developed from longhaired Siamese mutants.)

3 Birman Ancestor of Burmese temple cats. White feet, other points dark. Long nose.

4 Chinchilla White coat tipped with black to give a silvery appearance. Tail bushy, fur on chest and neck shaggy.

5 Van/Turkish White with auburn markings on head and auburn bands on tail. Long nose. Likes to swim in both still and fast-running water.

Other varieties

Grouped together on these pages are a number of cats characterized by a particular unusual feature. In some cases this feature is a mutation of form. The origin of the tailless Manx cat is obscure, but tailless cats have been known in the Isle of Man and elsewhere for many centuries. The sphinx and rex cats with their unusual coats and the Scottish fold with its turned down ears are the result of

1 Manx Tailless cat from the Isle of Man. Has a hollow where the tail should start. May be any color. Fur is soft and dense. Head is large with pointed ears. Powerful, long hindlegs give a rabbit-like gait.

2 Sphinx Light covering of normal-length fur disappears before weaning. Adults have very short, dense hair giving a suede-like feel. No whiskers. Needs protection from cold.

3 Cornish rex (Also other rex varieties.) Short, curly coat in any color. Curly whiskers. Long, slim body. Wedge-shaped head. Developed since the 1950s.

more recent mutations that have been preserved by cat breeders for their novelty value. The Egyptian Mau does not have any mutated features; it is an as yet unrecognized breed reminiscent of cats in ancient Egyptian paintings. The large American Maine coon cat with its medium-length fur evolved over several centuries but is only now gaining recognition as a breed.

4 Scottish fold Distinguished by short ears that fold forward and lie against top of head. Various colors and patterns. Known since early 1960s but not yet recognized as a standard.

5 Egyptian Mau Foreign-type cat marked with spots and bars. Silver (with black markings) or bronze (on pale background). Not yet officially recognized.

6 Maine coon cat Developed in USA over several centuries. Medium-length fur, prominent ruff. Exceptionally large; males may weigh 40lb(18kg). Raccoon coloring is commonest; other colors also occur.

© DIAGRAM

73

Cat care (1)

Cats are sometimes said to look after themselves, accepting human hospitality when it suits them, but basically remaining capable of surviving alone. Although there may be an element of truth in this statement, there is certainly no justification for failing to provide the basic needs that cats, like all other household pets, require. Cats that hunt mice and birds should still be given regular,

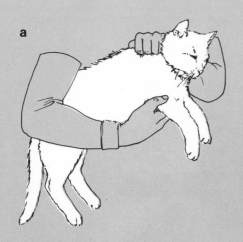

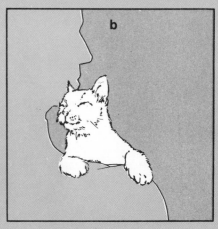

Handling Never pick up a cat by the scruff of its neck. Cats should be handled gently and carried so that the entire weight of the body is supported.

One good way of carrying a cat is to rest the animal on your forearm with your hand turned up to support its foreparts (a). The cat's body is held gently between your arm and body.

Other cats prefer different methods — many like to be carried over the shoulder (b).

Grooming Cats keep themselves very clean, but longhaired breeds need extra brushing with a wire slicker (a) to prevent matted fur and hairballs.

Cats dislike water and should be bathed only if unusually dirty. Use a mild shampoo and a minimum of water.

If necessary, a cat's claws can be trimmed in the same way as a dog's (see p.49), but press upward between the toes (b) to keep the claws unsheathed.

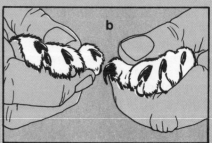

balanced meals. Those allowed outdoors require some supervision, especially in urban areas where the risk of accidents is greater. Although the cat is a very clean animal, additional grooming is needed for longhaired breeds. Caring for a cat also includes handling, playing, and training — cats are often unsociable simply because they do not receive attention.

Feeding A very nutritious basic diet for a cat is ⅔ dry cat chow together with ⅓ canned meat or fish for added flavor and moisture. Fresh meat or fish will also be appreciated, but make sure that the diet is balanced or the cat may develop such serious disorders as malnutrition or kidney disease. Water should always be available. Milk is usually enjoyed, but if given in large quantities may cause diarrhea or encourage worms.

Growing grass is needed for nibbling. Feed kittens four times daily, adults once or twice. Required amounts vary with size, age, and activity. Do not allow your cat to become overweight.
1 Dry cat chow.
2 Canned meat or fish.
3 Fresh meat (liver or muscle).
4 Fresh fish (lightly boiled).
5 Milk.
6 Water.
7 Growing grass.

Catnip The plant commonly known as catnip (*Nepeta cataria*) is a strong-scented type of mint containing a substance that cats find extremely attractive. A cat will appreciate catnip in the garden, and it is also possible to buy simple toys made from dried catnip leaves.

©DIAGRAM

75

Cat care (2)

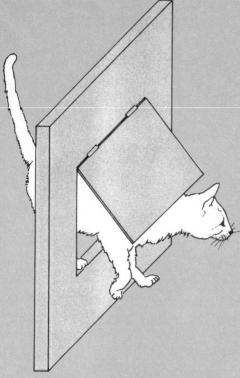

Housing Pedigree or city-dwelling cats are often kept entirely indoors. Many cats, it seems, can be quite happy with no access to the outside world. Problems are, however, common if a cat has previously been accustomed to outdoor living. Keeping two cats in the home may help reduce boredom and possible destructiveness. Cats kept indoors will need a litter box. A scratching post may reduce damage to furniture. Most cats live both indoors and out. A cat flap (see left) allows free entry and exit. A cat allowed outdoors faces many risks — among them traffic accidents, poisoning, injury in fights, straying, and theft. It is advisable to keep cats indoors at night. A cat that hunts should be wormed twice a year as both mice and birds are sources of parasites.

Housebreaking Cats are easily housebroken (trained) and will readily use a litter box once they know where to find it. Boxes should be large and deep for adults, shallow for kittens. Use an enamel or plastic tub (**a**) containing commercial litter (**b**), sand, or wood shavings. Place it on newspaper. Feces and soiled litter should be removed daily and more litter added. Clean thoroughly once a week, washing the box and supplying new litter.

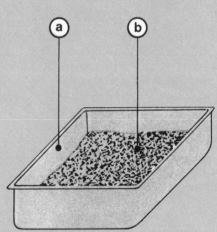

Collar and leash A collar with an identity tag is useful if an outdoor cat can be persuaded to wear one. It should be light, narrow, and elasticated.
A few cats, notably Siamese, can be accustomed to walking on a leash. Use a lightweight leash and allow time for training.

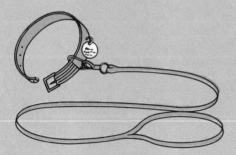

Beds Cat beds should be warm, filled with bedding that is easily washed, and placed in an area that is free from drafts. A cardboard box (**a**) makes a good bed. Many cats, however, prefer to select their own sleeping area. A washable cover in this place will protect upholstery.

Carriers Since many cats do not accept being led on a leash, cat carriers are useful for journeys. These should be secure and well ventilated, and should open from the top for easy access. Wicker carrying baskets are commonly used: others have a transparent lid (**b**).

a

b

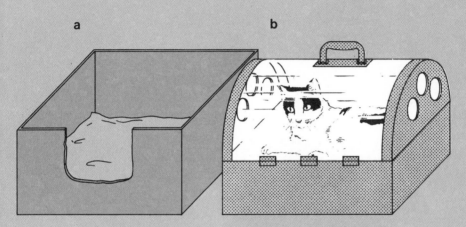

Training For cats, training consists mainly of preventing undesirable activities such as scratching furniture, walking on kitchen surfaces, or stealing food from plates. "No" plus a gentle tap on the rump is enough of a reprimand. It is impossible to train a cat not to hunt — even a bell on its collar may not be effective. Some cats will learn to play games, but most are not as receptive to training as dogs.

Play Kittens are naturally playful and adults will often enjoy a game if encouraged. A routine period for toys and games gives indoor cats extra exercise, prevents boredom, and makes them more sociable and responsive. Toys should be simple and nontoxic. Avoid any that can be taken apart and swallowed. Good ones include: string (**a**), table tennis ball (**b**), empty spool (**c**), crumpled paper (**d**), catnip mouse (**e**).

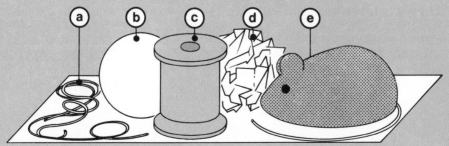

Cat behavior

Cats have a reputation for being aloof and unresponsive to the wishes of others. Certainly they are characteristically harder to train and more independent than dogs. A possible reason for this difference is to be found in the behavior of cats and dogs in the wild: cats hunt singly, but dogs hunt in packs under a leader.

It is sometimes argued that cats are more attached to

Sounds Cats make a variety of sounds. Purring is a sign of contentment, mewing is a request signal, and growling or spitting shows anger and alertness to danger. Cats are more vocal at certain times. During the breeding season both males and females may yowl and caterwaul. Mother cats make a series of calls when training kittens. Some breeds are noisier than others: Siamese are noisy, Abyssinians quiet.

1 Greeting The cat adopts a bowing posture, its tail held up.
2 Head rubbing Scent glands on the forehead, lips, chin, and tail are used to mark objects, people, and other cats. Head rubbing is a sign of affection.
3 Scratching This is the way cats keep their nails in trim. It is also thought to be a territorial marking showing the cat's size. (To protect furniture, encourage the cat to use a scratching post.)

Facial expressions In general, facial expressions are less differentiated than in the dog.
a Aggressive expression — with pupils constricted, ears alert.
b Submissive expression showing fear — with pupils dilated, ears flattened.

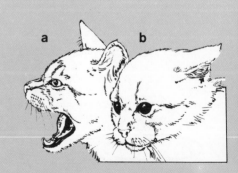

places than to people. Whether or not this is true, territory is important in cat behavior and cats often prove very sensitive to changes in environment. But they are also responsive to human contact. A cat raised from a young kitten with affection and attention will develop quite differently from one that has been deprived of all association with people.

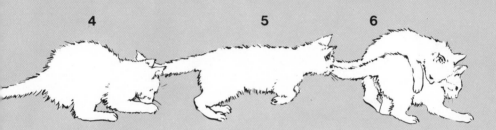

4 Stalking is the instinctive first stage in hunting, perhaps triggered by hearing prey.
5 Pouncing is also instinctive. The cat lands hind feet first.
6 Killing bite is the final stage of hunting, and must be learned from the mother. The teeth must find a gap between the prey's neck vertebrae. The bite is often practiced (with no ill effect!) on littermates. A cat without this skill appears only to play with its prey.

Territory Territorial behavior is most evident in male cats. Males defend their territory by threatening other cats — adopting the threatening posture of the cat shown below on the left (**7**) — and by fighting. They mark the limits to their area by spraying urine, even in the house. If a male is neutered, spraying, fighting, and wandering — territorial behavior related to breeding instincts — will usually no longer be a problem.

7

©DIAGRAM

Breeding cats

Cats breed very efficiently, and problems are unlikely except in the case of certain purebreds. An unfortunate consequence of this efficiency is that many millions of unwanted cats and kittens have to be destroyed each year. The owner of any cat should seriously consider the advantages of having it neutered. Unneutered males are prone to wandering and fighting, and spray urine even in

Mating Before mating, female cats should be vaccinated and wormed. Any unneutered female that is unconfined during estrus (heat) will probably find a mate. Signs of estrus are calling, an arched back, holding the tail up, treading the hindlegs, and rolling on the ground. Mating is not advised at the first estrus.

Pregnancy Gestation is 58-70 days. Increase food to double rations. Provide a nest box. A few days before the birth the cat will start spending more and more time in the place she has chosen to have her kittens.

Birth Keep an eye on the cat's progress. Call the veterinarian at once if a kitten is stuck or an afterbirth missing. If the mother fails to tear open the amniotic sac in which a kitten is born, do this with scissors and dry the kitten's head.

Sterilization Neutering is recommended before sexual maturity — at about 6 months for females and 7 months for males. (Later than this a male will only partly change his habits.) In female cats, the ovaries (**a**) and uterus (**b**) are usually removed. In males, the testicles (**c**) are removed. Both these operations are simple and fairly inexpensive. Females may be kept overnight at the surgery; males can be released.

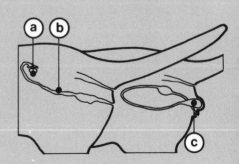

the home. Unneutered females have frequent heat periods when they become anxious and noisy if unable to find a mate. If allowed out of the home they are almost certain to become pregnant, and finding homes for kittens can prove extremely difficult. Neutered cats of both sexes tend to be calmer and more affectionate. There is a tendency to put on weight, but this can be curbed by diet.

Growth The illustrations below show the growth of a kitten from birth to six months.

Care of kittens Cats usually have litters of 4-6 kittens. Weak or defective offspring are often destroyed by the mother at birth or abandoned by her later. During the first weeks the mother will take care of all her kittens' needs — nursing them, keeping them clean, and disposing of their waste. The mother should receive double rations of food throughout this time. (If a kitten has to be hand-reared, consult a veterinarian.)

Weaning Kittens are fully weaned at 8 weeks, by which time they are ready to leave the litter. A newly weaned kitten will require feeding 4-5 times daily. Feed 3 times daily from about 3 months old, and twice daily from about 6 months.

Before leaving the litter a kitten should be examined by a vet, vaccinated, and dewormed.

Timetable of development

Loses umbilical cord	2-3 days
Eyes open	7-12 days
Temporary teeth	30 days
Weaning	8 weeks
Permanent teeth	6 months
Neutering (female)	6 months
Neutering (male)	7 months
Maturity (female)	6-8 months
Maturity (male)	7-12 months

Gestation	58-70 days
Litter	4-6
Weaning	8 weeks
Maturity	6-12 months
Lifespan	14 years

Cat diseases

Some of the most virulent diseases affecting cats can now be controlled by vaccination. To reduce the spread of infection every cat owner should ensure that his pet is vaccinated. Although it may be possible to treat minor ailments at home it is always wise to consult a veterinarian as soon as a cat shows signs of ill health. Attention to diet (p.75) helps keep cats healthy.

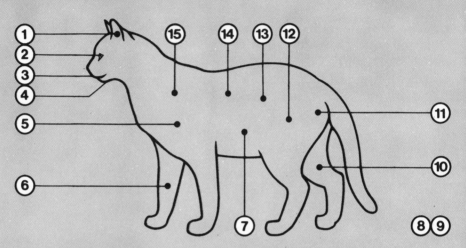

Common ailments Always contact a veterinarian. There is a risk of complications even with comparatively minor ailments.

1 Ear inflammation (irritation, brown, scaly crust in ears).

2 Eye disorders. Conjunctivitis (inflammation, discharge). Prolapsed third eyelid — will go back without treatment.

3 Gum inflammation — caused by build-up of tartar.

4 Feline acne — infection of large skin glands on chin. Requires urgent treatment.

5 Skin disorders. Dermatitis (red eruption), ringworm (red circular patches), eczema, mange (caused by mites).

6 Abscesses — often caused by cat or rat bites (deep puncture wounds that become infected). Drainage required.

7 Intestinal obstruction — usually caused by accumulation of hairballs in longhaired cats.

8 Fits. Comfort cat during attack. Other symptoms may reveal underlying cause.

9 Anemia (pale paw pads, gums, tongue, listlessness). Commoner in cats than in any other animal.

10 Skin parasites — fleas, lice, ticks, mites. (See dogs, p.59.)

11 Diarrhea or constipation — many causes, possibly dietary.

12 Urinary tract disorders (frequent urination, lack of urination, straining to urinate). Urgent treatment needed to prevent uremic poisoning.

13 Cysts and tumors — may be removed surgically.

14 Worms (change in appetite or bowel movement, pot belly). Do not attempt home remedies.

15 Respiratory disorders. Colds, asthma, pneumonia. Symptoms similar to humans.

Signs of illness Many cat diseases develop rapidly; prompt treatment by a veterinarian may save a pet's life. Never ignore the following warning signs.

1) Listlessness.
2) Poor coat condition.
3) Hiding in dark corners.
4) Change in temperament.
5) Running eyes or nose.
6) Cough.
7) Vomiting or drooling.
8) Loss of appetite or extreme hunger.
9) Weight loss or unusual weight gain, distended stomach.
10) Change in bowel movement.
11) Fits.

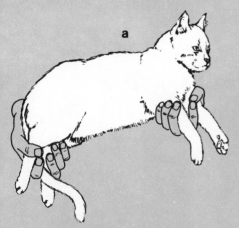

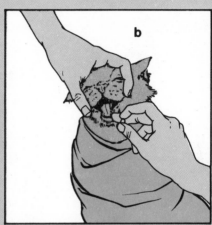

Giving medicine Two people may be needed: one to hold the cat, the other to give the medicine. To prevent scratching, restrain the cat as illustrated (**a**). Place pills at the back of the cat's throat (**b**). Hold the mouth shut and stroke the throat to encourage swallowing. Pour liquid medicine into the side of the cat's mouth from an eyedropper (**c**). Hold the cat's mouth shut until the medicine has been swallowed.

Care of a sick cat Contact the veterinarian as soon as symptoms appear. Keep a record of the progress of the disease to aid diagnosis. Provide warmth, quiet, and, unless directed otherwise, whatever food the cat is able to manage. Keep bedding clean. Make sure the cat's eyes and nose are kept clear of mucus.

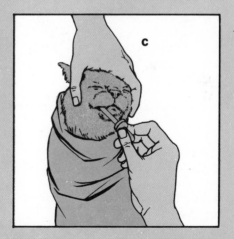

Vaccination
1 All cats require vaccination against panleukopenia (feline distemper). Give after weaning.
2 Vaccination against upper respiratory infections is needed if cats are boarded or shown.
3 Rabies vaccination is needed in most countries.

©DIAGRAM

Mustelids

Ferrets

The ferret is a domesticated descendant of the wild
European or North African polecat. It is a member of the
Mustelidae or weasel family — the most primitive family of
mammalian carnivores. Raised in captivity in Europe since
Roman times, domesticated European ferrets were first
imported into the USA in the 1870s. Although ferrets are
now sometimes kept simply as pets, their historical

Ferret *(Mustela putorius)* 2ft
(61cm), including 8in (20cm) tail;
yellowish white, or brown and
cream; long, furry body; short
legs; flattened, triangular head;
small, sharp eyes; short, furry
tail; lifespan 4-7 years.
Handling Test for tameness by
offering back of closed fist (**a**). If
no attempt is made to bite, run
the hand gently over the ferret's
back (**b**), grasp the back of its
neck (**c**), and lift it to be carried
with both hands (**d**).

Behavior Naturally nocturnal,
ferrets can be switched to a day
schedule. Most become very
tame if acquired early and
handled often. They keep
themselves well groomed and
like to bathe occasionally in a
basin of water. A strong odor is
emitted from the anal musk gland
if a ferret is hurt or very
frightened. Males smell in the
breeding season. Females
generally do not smell and
usually make better pets.

importance is as hunting animals. The ferret is trained to go into holes to drive out pests such as rats, mice, or rabbits, which can then be captured as they attempt to escape. Ferrets require careful handling but most become extremely tame. In some parts of the United States a permit is needed to keep ferrets because of the danger to poultry if they escape.

Keeping indoors Some people like to keep pet ferrets indoors. A simple cage with a dark sleeping box containing bedding will still be needed. The cage door can be left open to allow the ferret freedom in the home. Since ferrets always choose to eliminate in the same places it is quite easy to get them to use a litter tray.

Cleaning Cages and litter trays must be kept clean. Remove all food hidden in sleeping boxes.

Keeping outdoors Ferrets are usually kept in an outdoor cage. A cage suitable for two ferrets is shown below.
1 Hinged door for access.
2 ½in (1.3cm) wire mesh run, 6ft ×18in × 18in (2m × 50cm × 50cm).
3 Short wood legs.
4 Weather-resistant sleeping box with two compartments. Hay or straw bedding is needed.
5 Hole for access.
6 Sloping roof, hinged and covered with roofing felt.

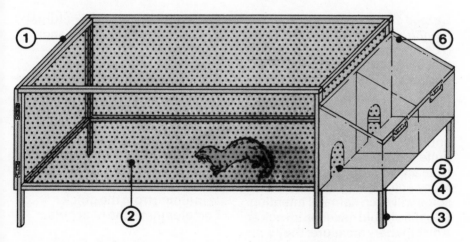

Feeding Ferrets used to be fed mainly on bread and milk, but a meat diet is much better. Canned dog or cat food is ideal if sometimes supplemented with chicken parts, eggs, mink feed, extra vitamins, and milk. Water should always be available, ideally in a gravity-flow bottle.

Diseases Ferrets are hardy and generally healthy. They should be inoculated at an early age against distemper and — in most countries — against rabies. Inoculations for ferrets are also available against influenza and cat pneumonitis.

Skunks

Pet skunks have become increasingly popular in North America over the past ten years. It is important never to take a skunk from the wild: epidemics of rabies are common in wild populations. Skunks for pets can now be obtained from breeders and some pet stores.

Skunks vary in temperament but are often affectionate and docile. They can be easily housebroken. Skunks are

Striped skunk *(Mephitis mephitis)* North America; 30in (76cm), including 7in (18cm) tail; black with two white stripes on body that join to form a broad white stripe on head; long bushy tail; sharp claws; life 5-6 years.

Handling Although never to be entirely trusted, skunks become quite tame if handled regularly from an early age (5-6 weeks). Many enjoy being stroked and some will even demand attention. Skunks should never be struck as a disciplinary measure: they will not understand your action and may never trust you again. For exercise a skunk may be taken outdoors on a leash. Use a light harness that fastens behind the forelegs (as illustrated right) rather than a collar that can easily slip over the skunk's narrow head. A lightweight leash should be used.

Behavior Skunks are nocturnal and may be difficult to change over to a day routine.

In the wild, skunks go into semi-hibernation during the winter; to prepare for this, food intake is increased in the fall. Pet skunks tend to be sleepy and sluggish in winter. Skunks are burrowing animals and have long claws that should be kept trimmed to a length of ¼ in (6mm) from the quick. Females make the best pets.

members of the Mustelidae family and are well known for their natural defense: a strong smelling musk which they emit from two anal glands. Pets are sometimes descented, but a pet skunk is in any case unlikely to use its defense on its owners. Local health authorities should be consulted before obtaining a skunk as they are forbidden as pets in some areas because of the threat of rabies.

Housing Skunks require a washable box or basket that can act as a substitute den. A cave-like wicker dog basket — with disposable cloths or hay for bedding — is ideal. Two skunks can share a large basket.

Housebreaking (training) Skunks select one corner away from their basket for elimination. Put newspaper in this favored spot and change it often. (A litter tray is not recommended as skunks will try to burrow in it.)

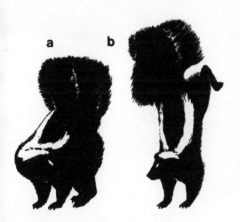

a   b

Smell A skunk can be descented by removal of its anal glands — an operation best carried out at age 6-8 weeks. Many people, however, prefer to leave their pet skunks intact. Accidents are rare if the animal is handled correctly, and clear warning is given before spraying — the skunk raises its tail and lifts its hindquarters (a) or stands on its front legs (b). Tomato juice, detergent, and water will help remove odor.

Feeding Skunks are omnivorous. They do well on a basic diet of canned cat food with fresh fruit and vegetables. They should be fed once a day in the evening. Feed only moderate amounts as skunks tend to overeat. Fresh water should be constantly available.

Breeding Skunks do not breed readily in captivity.

Diseases Pet skunks require regular vaccination against rabies. Vaccination is also sometimes recommended against canine distemper and feline enteritis. In case of illness, consult a veterinarian.

©DIAGRAM

Rabbits

Characteristics and choosing

Although rabbits were raised by the Romans for meat, true domestication of the rabbit does not appear to have taken place until the Middle Ages. The development of pedigree rabbit breeds is a still more recent occurrence — only a handful of breeds were known at the start of the twentieth century. Today there are over 60 pedigree breeds — all descended from the European wild rabbit.

Rabbits belong to the zoological order Lagomorpha, which also includes the hare and the pika, a small, short-eared, rabbit-like animal found in the Himalayas and the Rockies. The jack rabbits of North America are in fact hares, and even the cottontails are not true rabbits.

Domestic rabbits make excellent pets. They are docile, attractive, and fairly simple to look after. Wild rabbits and hares, however, do not make good pets even if they are hand-reared. They remain highly nervous, defend themselves by kicking and biting, are potential disease carriers, and generally react badly to life in captivity.

Characteristics The wild rabbit (**1**) and the hare (**2**) can be easily distinguished by their appearance and behavior.
The rabbit is smaller and lighter — up to 18in (46cm) long and 3lb (1.4kg) in weight, compared with the brown hare's 27in(68cm) and 10lb(4.5kg). Body proportions and typical stance of the two animals differ as illustrated. Wild rabbits are sociable, burrowing animals. Hares are solitary and do not burrow. Hares have a great capacity for running and jumping — making them unsuitable for domestication.

Lagomorphs Rabbits and hares belong to the order Lagomorpha, distinguished from rodents by a second pair of incisors (**a**) in the upper jaw behind the first pair (**b**).
Ancestry The European wild rabbit *(Oryctolagus cuniculus)* — depicted below — is the ancestor of all today's domestic breeds.

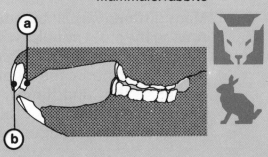

Obtaining a rabbit A great variety of breeds (see p. 94) can be obtained from pet stores or from breeders. Before making a choice it is a good idea to go to a rabbit show and to learn about the characteristics of various breeds. Young rabbits are ready at 8-12 weeks.
Selecting for health
1 Ears should be clean.
2 Eyes should be bright but not wild, free from mucus, and with no ingrown eyelashes.

3 Nose should be free from mucus.
4 Lower front teeth should fit neatly onto small upper incisors. Gums and teeth should be clean.
5 Skin should be clean and free from cysts or abscesses.
6 Coat should be thick and glossy and with no trace of scurf.
7 Body should feel solid without being fat.
8 No signs of diarrhea.
9 Rabbit should move freely with no soreness of the hocks.

© DIAGRAM

93

Rabbit breeds

Many different rabbit breeds are now widely available. Among the most popular with petkeepers are the Dutch, the English, and the New Zealand white.

For showing purposes rabbits are divided into two broad groups — "fur" and "fancy." The New Zealand white is an example of a "normal fur" breed, with an underfur interspersed with longer guard hairs. In rex rabbits,

1 Dutch 4-5lb (1.8-2.3kg). Small and sturdy. White and colored as shown (several colors). Gentle, easy to handle. Excellent pets.
2 English 6-8lb (2.7-3.6kg). Medium-sized. White with darker ears, flank spots, and markings on spine, nose, and around eyes.
3 Polish 2-2½lb (0.9-1.1kg). Tiny and compact. Usually white, black, or chocolate. Lively.
4 Belgian hare 8-9lb (3.6-4.1kg). Not a hare. Distinctive shape and stance. Red, tan, or chestnut.
5 Lop As large as possible. Drooping, soft, broad ears may measure 26in (66cm) from tip to tip. Principally black or fawn.

selective breeding has shortened or eliminated the guard hairs to produce a velvety coat. Satins, the third category of fur breed, have flattened hair scales that give a sheen to the coat. The Dutch, English, Polish, Belgian hare, lop, Flemish giant, and angora are examples of fancy breeds, indicating the great variety of shapes, sizes, colors, and patterns of today's pedigree rabbits.

6 Flemish giant 15-20lb (6.8-9.1kg). Largest breed. White, fawn, sand, blue, gray, or black.
7 Rex 6-8lb (2.7-3.6kg). Medium-sized. Short, velvety coat. Some 30 different self-colored, shaded, and patterned varieties.
8 Angora 6-8lb (2.7-3.6kg). Fine, soft fur — called "wool" — may grow to 6in (15cm) long. Usually white, but also various other colors. Coats require a great deal of grooming.
9 New Zealand white 9-12lb (4.1-5.4kg). Medium to large, with solid body. Albino. Prolific breeders and good mothers. Make excellent pets.

©DIAGRAM

95

Rabbit care

Rabbits will be healthy, gentle, and longlived pets as long as they are properly cared for. The provision of suitable housing is extremely important. Rabbits are usually kept in outdoor hutches, where they can remain throughout the year provided there is adequate protection from bad weather or hot sun. Each rabbit should have its own hutch, which must be large enough for the breed of rabbit, well

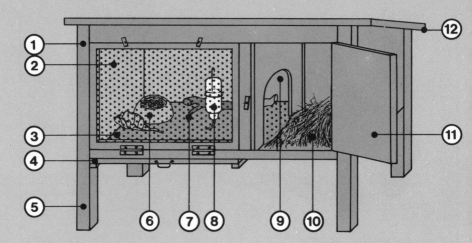

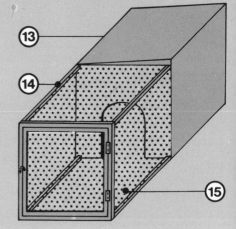

Popular all-year hutch
1 Wood hutch. Dimensions for medium-sized rabbit: 2ft × 4ft × 2ft (60cm × 120cm × 60cm).
2 Wire mesh door (downward opening, with secure fastening).
3 Wire mesh floor allowing droppings to fall through. (Or a wood floor with bedding.)
4 Removable litter tray. (Or newspaper under the hutch.)
5 Legs to keep out drafts.
6 Heavy dish for food.
7 Hardwood for gnawing.
8 Water bottle (or heavy dish).
9 Entrance to sleeping area.
10 Sleeping area with bedding (straw, hay, or wood shavings).
11 Wood door.
12 Sloping, weathertight roof.
Portable warm-weather hutch
13 Shelter, with wire floor.
14 Wire-covered run.
15 Open bottom to allow grazing — move hutch daily.

Hutch cleaning Remove droppings and stale food daily. Clean thoroughly once weekly (if possible remove rabbit to a safe place). Remove droppings, food, and old bedding. Scrub surfaces with warm, soapy water (no detergent). Provide new bedding when hutch is fully dry.

ventilated, and kept clean. Portable hutches with wire runs allowing grazing on the lawn may be used in spring or summer. Some people keep rabbits in an open enclosure, with weatherproof shelters and a deeply sunk protective surround. Rabbits may even be kept in the home — they can be housebroken (trained) quite easily and with careful handling will become very tame.

Handling A rabbit will become very tame if it is gradually accustomed to regular handling from an early age.
Never pick up a rabbit by its ears as this can cause injury. Support the rabbit's weight with one hand, and with the other hand hold onto the loose skin behind the rabbit's ears (a).
A rabbit that is wrongly handled will defend itself by biting, scratching, and kicking out with its hind legs.

a

Grooming Most rabbits keep themselves well groomed by licking. But long-haired rabbits should be given additional grooming because of the risk of internal obstruction from matted, swallowed fur. Gently use a fine-toothed metal comb or soft brush (b) once a week, or more often during molting.
Nails The nails of a rabbit kept in a wire-floored hutch may grow too long and require clipping, preferably by a veterinarian.

b

Outdoor exercise A tame rabbit can be allowed outdoor exercise provided that certain safety precautions are taken.
1 Make sure that the rabbit cannot escape from the yard.
2 Make sure that all dogs and cats are well out of the way.
3 Watch the rabbit constantly.

Freedom indoors A rabbit can be housebroken (trained) quite easily since it will naturally always choose the same place for its droppings. Provide a shallow box with cat litter. Harder to cope with is an indoor rabbit's tendency to gnaw on furniture or electric wires.

©DIAGRAM

97

Feeding rabbits

Rabbits require a healthy, balanced diet and are generally fairly easy to feed. Rabbit pellets can form the bulk of their nourishment as these have been produced both to include necessary vitamins and to provide protection against disease. A range of other foods may be used as supplements, but sudden food changes are to be avoided. Do not overfeed rabbits — they are prone to overeating.

Feeding Feed once daily in the late afternoon. Wash all fresh foods carefully, and never use greens treated with insecticides. Amounts will vary according to the size of the rabbit. Suitable foods include the following.
1 Pellets — forming the bulk of the diet. Place in a heavy dish.
2 Fresh, raw carrots.
3 Clover — small amounts.
4 Oats, bran, barley, wheat.
5 Fresh, raw cabbage.
6 Clean, fresh water — a constant supply. In a heavy dish or a gravity-flow bottle.
7 Dandelions — small amounts.
8 Boiled potatoes.
9 Hay — best in a rack.
10 Fresh, raw parsnips.
11 Lettuce — small amounts.
12 Fresh, raw kale.
13 Well-baked brown bread for gnawing — 2-3 times weekly.
14 Salt disk. Leave in hutch.

Coprophagy (feces eating) Rabbits produce two types of feces — hard and soft. The latter are the product of a predigestion process, and to obtain complete nourishment the rabbit will eat them as they emerge.
Poisonous plants Rabbits — like many other animals — must never eat poppy (**a**), buttercup (**b**), foxglove, (**c**). Other poisonous plants include hemlock, aconite, belladonna, mustard, anenome, primula.

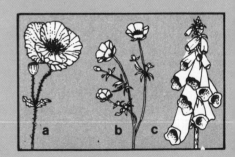

Rabbit diseases

Only when many rabbits are kept are infectious diseases likely to be a problem. A pet rabbit may, however, have picked up an infection before it was acquired. In general, pet rabbits suffer few illnesses provided they are properly housed and fed. If a rabbit does show signs of illness it is always wise to consult a veterinarian at once, since different illnesses may produce similar symptoms.

Signs of illness
1 Listlessness. Hunched position.
2 Fever or lowered temperature.
3 Ears drooping, swollen, encrusted, or causing irritation.
4 Eyes dull, swollen, running.
5 Sneezing or coughing. Nasal discharge. Labored breathing.
6 Abscesses, cysts, sores.
7 Loss or matting of fur.
8 Poor appetite. Loss of weight.
9 Constipation (caused by wrong diet or balls of swallowed fur).
10 Diarrhea (diet or infection).
11 Inflammation of or discharge from genitals.

Problems and symptoms
a) Ear mites cause canker — irritation, encrusted ears.
b) Mange mites — irritation, scaly crust, loss of hair on face, chin, and at base of ears.
c) Fleas and lice — irritation.
d) Ringworm — circular bare patches. Fungal infection.
e) Tapeworm — poor coat, mucus or blood in droppings, diarrhea.
f) Coccidiosis — difficult breathing, diarrhea, pot belly, rough coat, failure to grow.
g) Pasteurellosis (snuffles) — cold symptoms, inflammation of genitals, abscesses. Highly contagious. Often fatal.
h) Pneumonia — fever, difficult breathing, listlessness, diarrhea.
i) Mucoid enteritis — rough coat, drooping ears, closed eyes, listlessness, diarrhea, difficult breathing.
j) Hutch burn — infected sores. Caused by contact with urine in dirty, damp hutches.
k) Eye infection — discharge from eyes, irritation.
l) Middle-ear infection — head tilted to one side.
m) Heatstroke — warm, dry skin, panting, vomiting, blue tongue.

© DIAGRAM

Breeding rabbits

Breeding pet rabbits is interesting, rewarding, and generally fairly easy. Problems at birth are rare and most rabbits make good mothers. Sometimes, however, a doe will eat her young, and to reduce the risk of this it is essential to disturb the mother as little as possible for several days before and after the birth. Separate hutches will be needed if the young are to be retained.

Nest box Provide a nest box well in advance of the due date.
1 Wood box — approximately 12in (30cm) wide by 20in (50cm) long for a medium-sized rabbit. Sides 12in (25cm) high.
2 Bedding of straw, hay, or wood shavings. Rabbit will add fur.
3 Entrance to box about 6in (15cm) high, giving easy access to mother but keeping small babies inside.
4 Hinged mesh lid.
5 Drainage holes in base.

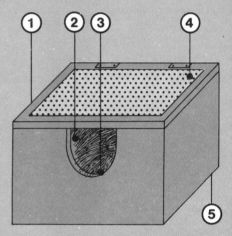

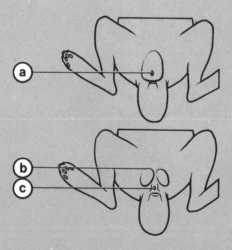

Sexing Pressing gently behind the urogenital opening of a young rabbit will reveal a slit in a doe (female) and a circular shape in a buck (male). In older rabbits (see above), the doe's vulva (**a**) and the buck's testicles (**b**) and penis (**c**) can be distinguished more easily.

Selection for breeding Only rabbits that are in good condition should be mated. Do not mate rabbits until they reach full size (5-9 months). Only mate rabbits of the same breed.
Timing There is no regular reproductive cycle in rabbits. A mature young doe can produce four or five litters in a year. Ovulation is stimulated by mating. Does are receptive to bucks a great deal of the time. The best method of finding out whether a doe is in heat is to put her with a buck.
Mating For mating, the doe should always be introduced into the buck's hutch. If fighting occurs the doe should be removed at once. If the rabbits are to mate they will do so within a few minutes. The doe should be removed immediately after mating.

Pregnancy The normal gestation period is about 31 days. Nest-building 17 days after mating means a pseudo-pregnancy; remate the doe. By the 17th day it is possible to confirm a pregnancy by gently feeling for the marble-like fetuses in the doe's abdomen. Food should be gradually increased up to double rations by the end of pregnancy.
The doe will normally make her nest 3-4 days before the babies are due. She should be supplied with fresh bedding in time for this. Do not disturb her once nest-building begins.

Birth The doe will retreat to her nest. Do not disturb her for 2-3 days. Then persuade her to leave the box and remove her from the hutch before quickly checking the litter. Remove deformed or dead babies. Return the mother.

Litter The number of young in a litter may be as few as two or as many as 18. Litters of five or six are commonest. A doe's first few litters tend to be largest. Newborn rabbits are blind and covered only with fine down (**a**). Eyes open at 10 days and rabbits are fully furred by 4 weeks (**b**).

Care While nursing, a doe needs three times her usual food and plenty of water. Young can leave the nest at 3-4 weeks and start nibbling solids. Limit handling before this time. Separate doe from litter at 8 weeks. Young can stay together until put in individual hutches at 12 weeks.

Gestation	31 days
Litter size	5-6
Weaning	3-8 weeks
Maturity	5-9 months
Lifespan	10 years

Rodents

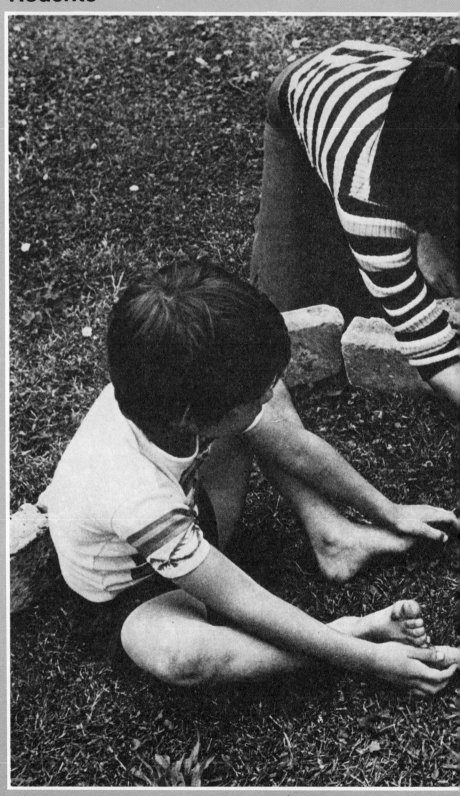

Characteristics and choosing

The order Rodentia is named from the Latin verb to gnaw. It contains some 3,000 species distinguished by the presence of only a single pair of incisors in the upper and lower jaws. These typically small, gnawing animals are found in all continents in many different types of environment. Most have shown themselves well able to survive despite their many predators. Rapid reproduction is the key to their success, maintaining populations and allowing timely adaptation to changes in environment. Several rodent species are now extremely popular as pets. Most of these were first domesticated for use in laboratory experiments — for which they have the advantage of being relatively clever for their size. Domesticated rodent pets give their owners few problems: cages are widely available from pet stores or can be made by a handyman; feeding is simple and inexpensive; and handling is generally easy once an animal has been tamed. Keeping wild rodents as pets is a very different matter. A few species can be kept, but they require specialized care (see pages 166-169).

Obtaining a rodent Rodents are available from pet stores, from breeders, and sometimes from research laboratories. Avoid animals that have been kept in dirty, overcrowded conditions. Avoid animals that look poorly fed. Avoid the weakest in a litter. Always see animals handled before buying. Avoid nervous or bad-tempered individuals. Baby rats will normally come to investigate: mice, gerbils, hamsters, and chinchillas will scramble away. See that animals for breeding are properly sexed.

Signs of health
1 Clean ears, without blemishes.
2 Bright eyes.
3 Nose free from mucus or blemishes.
4 Free movement.
5 Soft, silky coat, no hair loss.
6 Strong, solid body.
7 No signs of diarrhea (check under tail).
8 Tail not blemished or swollen.

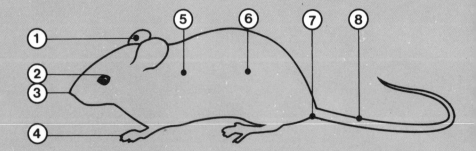

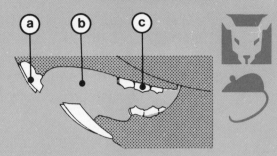

Teeth Rodents' teeth are adapted for gnawing. The two prominent incisors (**a**) at the front of the upper and lower jaws have sharp chisel edges. Behind the gap or diastema (**b**), the premolars and molars (**c**) have grinding edges. Teeth grow continually to cope with wear.

Rodent pet guide

1 Mice Numerous fancy types available. Naturally timid but can be tamed. Cages need frequent cleaning. (See p.110.)

2 Rats With proper handling, domesticated rats make good pets. Intelligent and playful; soon learn tricks. May be destructive. (See p.112.)

3 Gerbils Curious, sociable, and easily tamed. Keep in pairs or groups. Virtually no cage odor. (See p.114.)

4 Hamsters Naturally nocturnal. May bite if awakened during day. Handle regularly to keep tame. Keep singly to avoid fighting. (See p.116.)

5 Cavies/Guinea pigs Docile but not typically playful or responsive. Longhaired cavy varieties require regular grooming. (See p.118.)

6 Chinchillas Lively and attractive. Formerly raised mainly for fur. Sometimes kept as pets. Expensive. (See p.120.)

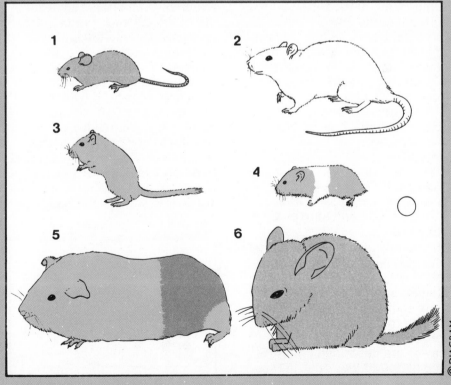

© DIAGRAM

Caging rodents

Most rodent pets spend virtually their entire lives inside their cages. Obviously a healthy environment is essential. Cages may be bought or made, but make sure that they are large enough to allow sufficient exercise and to provide separate areas for sleeping, eating, and eliminating. Cages must be cleaned regularly, and kept out of drafts, damp, and direct sunlight.

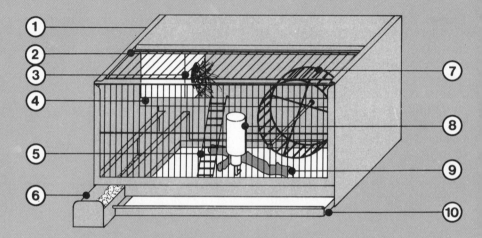

Cage for small rodents
1 Dimensions 2ft × 1ft × 1ft (60cm × 30cm × 30cm) — walls of metal or stout wood to stop drafts and gnawing damage.
2 Slide-out wire lid and front for access and observation.
3 Nest box with bedding of wood shavings, hay, or paper.
4 Shelf.
5 Ladder.
6 Pull-out food tray.
7 Wheel for exercise.
8 Gravity-flow water bottle.
9 Unpainted hardwood or stick for gnawing.
10 Removable floor tray for easy cleaning — covered with litter (sawdust or peat with sand).
Caging other rodent pets
Rats should have a metal cage, similar to the one above but larger. The requirements of cavies are described on p.119, and of chinchillas on p.121.

Exercise Tame pets can be let out of the cage for exercise, but take great care to prevent escapes, especially with mice.
Cleaning Cages need thorough cleaning every 2-3 days for mice, 3 days for rats, 5-7 days for hamsters, and 7-10 days for gerbils. Put animal in a secure, ventilated box or holding cage (see below). Dispose of litter and bedding. Wash surfaces with warm, soapy water, rinse, and dry.Give new litter and bedding.

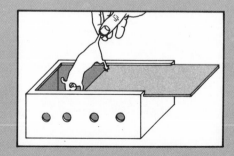

Rodent diseases

Rodent pets generally remain healthy provided they are properly housed and fed. Failure to provide proper care, however, soon takes its toll. Select new animals carefully (p.104), and quarantine them for 3 weeks before mixing with existing stock. Observe pets closely and isolate any animal showing signs of illness. Consult a veterinarian if any problem persists more than 24 hours.

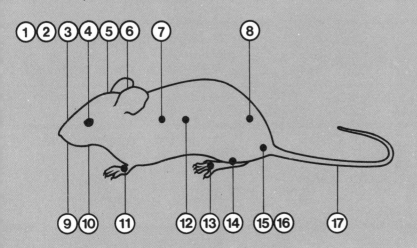

Signs of disease
1 Lethargy. Reluctance to move.
2 Staggering. Poor coordination.
3 Sneezing, nasal discharge. Coughing. Difficult breathing.
4 Eyes dull, discharging, or swollen. Constant, rapid side-to-side movements of eyes.
5 Head tilted (ear infection).
6 Ears encrusted (mange).
7 Fur dull and ragged.
8 Sores, cysts, or tumors.
9 Slobbering (malformed teeth).
10 Hair loss on face or body.
11 Sores on feet. Ingrowing toenails (especially cavies).
12 Loss of weight.
13 Dragging hind legs.
14 Stiff joints.
15 Diarrhea or constipation (infection or poor diet).
16 Abnormal swelling or protrusion of rectum.
17 Tail swollen, encrusted, or with sores.

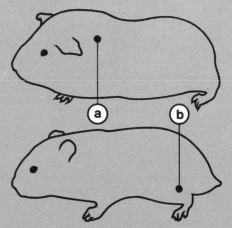

Specific problems Easy to diagnose problems confined to single pet species include:
a vitamin C deficiency in cavies — stiff joints, severe loss of weight, hair loss;
b wet tail in hamsters — diarrhea stains, protrusion of rectum, difficult breathing.

©DIAGRAM

Breeding rodents

Rodents are renowned for their prolific breeding ability. In captivity, this is likely to cause caging or disposal problems if owners keep their pet mice, rats, or gerbils in breeding pairs or groups. A pair of mice, for example, can in theory be responsible for some 30,000 offspring in a single year. Hamsters are more difficult to breed in captivity as they will very often fight when introduced.

Mice

Mating and pregnancy Breeding pair or one male to two females. Remove male during pregnancy. Provide nesting materials. Two females may make a joint nest.

Rats

Mating and pregnancy Can be kept in breeding pairs. Male may remain with female during pregnancy and weaning. Provide materials for nest building.

Gerbils

Mating and pregnancy Form into breeding pairs if kept in a colony. Keep males with females throughout. Provide suitable nesting materials.

Hamsters

Mating and pregnancy Obtain expert advice before mating hamsters (fighting is common and may cause serious injury). Provide nest box and bedding.

Cavies

Mating and pregnancy One boar to two or more sows. (More in commercial breeding). Breed females by 1 year. No need to remove male. Provide nest box and hay.

Chinchillas

Mating and pregnancy Pairs (or one male to several females in commercial breeding). No need to remove male. Give nest box and hay. No baths in last 2 weeks.

With cavies and chinchillas, too, there is unlikely to be an overpopulation problem since gestation periods are longer and litters typically small.

During pregnancy and lactation additional food should be provided. A few days before the birth, clean the cage thoroughly and provide suitable nesting materials. Avoid disturbing the mother in the days after the birth.

Litter Born hairless with eyes closed. Remove mother after weaning. By 6 weeks separate sexes. Bucks should not be kept together after 9 weeks.

Gestation	20 days
Typical litter	6-8
Weaning	3-5 weeks
1st mating (male)	10 weeks
1st mating (female)	12 weeks

Litter Young born hairless with eyes closed. Except when overcrowded, young can stay with parents until maturity.

Gestation	21 days
Typical litter	7-8
Weaning	2-3 weeks
Puberty	10-12 weeks
1st mating	16 weeks

Litter Born hairless with eyes closed. May remain in colony with parents, but separation of new pairs is advised once breeding starts.

Gestation	24 days
Typical litter	4-5
Weaning	3 weeks
1st mating	10-12 weeks

Litter Young born hairless and with eyes closed. After 20-30 days remove mother to prevent bullying. Put young in individual cages at 5 weeks.

Gestation	16 days
Typical litter	7
Weaning	3 weeks
Puberty	6-8 weeks
1st mating	10-12 weeks

Litter Young born fully furred with eyes open. Can nibble hay at 1 day old. Separate young to prevent early breeding (females can breed at 5 weeks).

Gestation	70 days
Typical litter	3
Weaning	2½ weeks
Puberty	5-10 weeks
1st mating	5 months

Litter Born furred and with eyes open. Dust is dangerous; no baths for lactating mother. Nibble solids at about 10 days. Can be separated when weaned.

Gestation	111 days
Typical litter	2
Weaning	60 days
Puberty	8-12 months

Mice

Mice have lived with humans for some 10,000 years — ever since early man first began to store grain. Since then the mouse has been hunted as a pest, worshiped as a god, used in laboratory experiments, and kept as a household pet. "Fancy" breeds were first developed in Japan in the seventeenth century. Today, breeding exhibition mice is a popular hobby in many countries. The well-known white

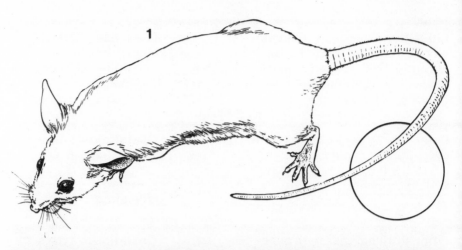

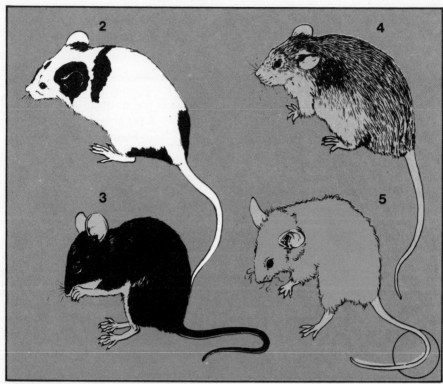

mouse has now been joined by many other varieties showing differences in color, markings, and coat quality. In all, some 40 different varieties have so far been officially standardized. Most wild mice are unsuitable as pets. They are often diseased, can be destructive, and are not easily tamed. Deermice and dormice are kept occasionally (see pages 166-167 for details).

Domestic mouse *(Mus musculus)* 8in (20cm), including tail; various colors (see below); long slim body; head long but not too pointed; ears large and tulip-shaped; eyes large, bold, and prominent; tail long and tapering. Lifespan 3-4 years.

Examples of varieties

1 White self May have pink or black eyes. Selfs (all one color) are also black, blue, chocolate, red, fawn, champagne, silver, dove, and cream.

2 Broken marked Marked mice are white with colored markings that may be broken (uneven), Dutch (like Dutch rabbits), even (uniform pattern), or variegated (color splashes).

3 Black-and-tan Tans have top color as for self varieties and a tan belly. (Foxes are similar but with white bellies.)

4 Chinchilla Pearl-gray ticked with black — an example of the various color ticked and shaded varieties now being bred.

5 Astrex With wavy coat. (Long-haired mice are also bred.)

Behavior Mice are by nature timid and although they can be tamed will bite if frightened. Care is needed to stop escapes. Mice become dormant if food is scarce and the temperature low. They are naturally nocturnal. Frequent cage cleaning is needed to minimize odor.

Feeding Food should always be available because mice have a high metabolic rate and soon use up eaten food. Under ¼ oz (5g) of food is needed per day. Oats or wheat and seeds should form the bulk of the diet, together with nuts, brown bread, some greenstuff, and milk. Water should be provided in a gravity-flow bottle.

Caging See p. 106.
Diseases See p. 107.
Breeding See pp. 108-109.

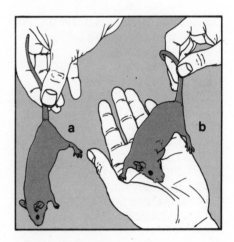

Handling Mice are tamed by short, frequent periods of handling. Food is a useful lure at first. The correct way to pick up a mouse is to grasp it near the base of the tail (**a**) and then transfer it at once to another support (**b**). Mice must never be squeezed.

©DIAGRAM

Rats

Domestic rats are easy to tame, affectionate, playful, and intelligent. They make excellent pets — quite unlike their wild relatives to which many people feel a natural and well-founded aversion. The domestic or "fancy" rats now kept as pets are descended from an albino strain of the brown rat which has been widely used in scientific research over a

Domestic rat *(Rattus norvegicus)* 16in (41cm), including tail; lifespan 4-5 years.

Characteristics

1 Tulip-shaped ears.
2 Long, tapered head.
3 Large, prominent eyes.
4 Long whiskers.
5 Long, slender body.
6 Short, sleek coat.
7 Tail shorter than body.
8 Tail sparsely haired.
9 Produce less odor than mice.
10 Become dormant when cold.

Varieties As with mice, a number of different varieties of fancy rats can be obtained. Selfs (one color) may be white, black, gray, tan, red, blue, or chocolate. Marked rats (white with a color) include the Japanese hooded rat (shown above), the capped rat (with a colored head), and the Irish black (with four white feet and a triangle on its chest). There are also brown and fawn agouti rats (fur with dark ticking).

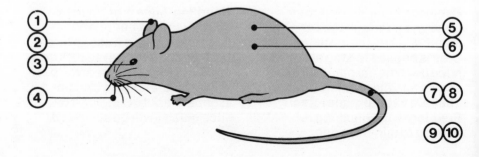

long period of time. In addition to the original white, fancy rats are now available in a variety of different colors. Wild rats, however, deserve their bad reputation. There are five billion of them, spreading disease, and destroying property. Do not keep wild rats as pets. They carry disease, are rarely tamable, and often savage. In some places it is an offense to allow a captive rat to escape.

Handling Most pet rats have been bred from gentle strains and are unlikely to bite once they are used to handling. It is, however, essential always to take care since a bite will be deep if given. The correct way to pick up a rat is shown (**a**). The animal is grasped gently from above, and lifted onto the palm of the other hand for support. A rat must never be picked up by the tail as this will pull away the skin.

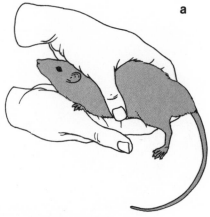

a

Behavior Rats are much less timid than mice. They respond quite readily to the human voice and with proper handling become affectionate pets. The intelligence that makes rats so useful in laboratory work means that a pet rat will soon learn entertaining tricks. Females are often recommended as nonbreeding pets as they tend to be livelier than males. However, males may live longer.

Feeding Food and water should be constantly available. Rats require 1¼ -1½ oz (30-40g) of food each day. Feed oats or wheat, seeds, nuts, green vegetables, apples, carrots, and occasionally mealworms or brown bread soaked in milk. Remove uneaten food daily. Supply bones or hardwood for gnawing.

Diseases See p. 107.

Breeding See pp.108-109.

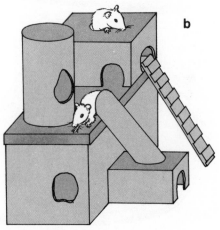

b

Caging See basic cage on p.106, but a rat's cage must be bigger.

Exercise See p. 106 for in-cage exercise. Rats will also benefit from exercise outside their cages — perhaps in a playground made from boxes (**b**). Tame rats will not try to escape — but watch out for gnawed furniture!

©DIAGRAM

113

Gerbils

Gerbils are comparative newcomers to the pet scene. First imported into the United States in 1954 for use in medical research, these tiny desert animals were soon found to make ideal small pets. Within a decade they had gained wide popularity in the United States and elsewhere. Mongolian gerbils were the first to be imported and are still the most usual gerbil pets. More recently, Egyptian gerbils

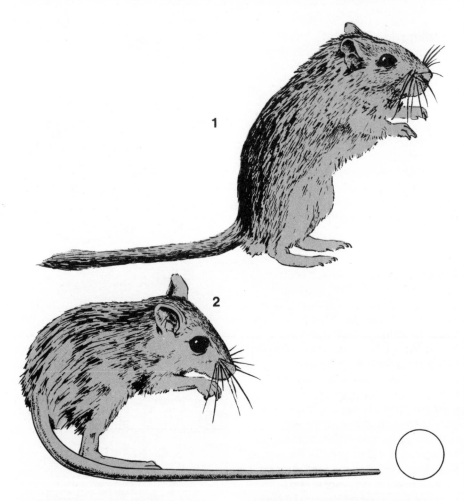

1 Mongolian gerbil *(Meriones unguiculatus)* E. Asia; 8in (20cm) long, including tail; gray-brown fur on body and tail, light gray on belly (also albino); head is broad and eyes large. Long tail and long hind legs allow "kangaroo" stance. Lives 4-5 years in captivity.

2 Egyptian gerbil *(Gerbillus gerbillus)* Middle East; 9in (23cm) long; gray-brown with light gray belly; body slimmer and nose more pointed than in Mongolian gerbil; tail proportionately longer and only sparsely covered with fur. Lives 4-5 years in captivity.

have also become popular with petkeepers.
Gerbils are easy to look after and do not smell. Their big, bright eyes give them an attractive appearance, and they are intensely curious, sociable, and easily tamed. They can, however, move very quickly and the risk of their escaping and becoming a crop pest has led them to be banned as pets in some American states.

Handling Gerbils respond well to frequent handling. They rarely bite and then only when frightened. Naturally curious, they will soon eat from your hand. A gerbil should be picked up by the base of the tail (not the tip as this causes the skin to pull away), and then transferred to the free hand and held securely as shown (**a**) to prevent jumping. Sudden movements must be avoided as they may bring on convulsions.

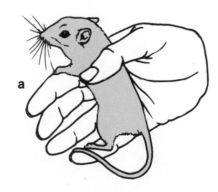

Behavior Gerbils are sociable animals and should be kept in pairs or in groups. They keep the same mate for life. Short sleeping and waking periods occur during both day and night. In the wild, burrowing is a major activity; cages should contain nesting material. Gerbils use water extremely efficiently — resulting in a lack of cage odor since feces are dry and urine scant.

Feeding A gerbil will eat about ½ oz (15g) of food each day. Mouse, rat, or hamster chow can form the bulk of the diet, together with seeds and small quantities of fruit and green vegetables. Greens must always be carefully washed and dried. Fresh, clean water should be constantly available.

Diseases See p.107.

Breeding See pp.108-109.

Caging A cage suitable for gerbils is shown on p.106. They may also be kept in a cage made from an aquarium tank.

Exercise Wheels for gerbils should be made of solid plastic (**b**). Wheels with bars are unsuitable as gerbils' tails are easily trapped and damaged.

©DIAGRAM

115

Hamsters

Although there are several other species, the golden hamster is the one most usually kept as a pet. All today's pet golden hamsters are descended from 13 discovered in the Middle East in 1930 by a professor researching a reference to "Syrian mice" kept as caged pets by children in ancient Assyria. Golden, or Syrian, hamsters are now much more numerous in captivity than in the wild.

Golden hamster *(Mesocricetus auratus)* 4½ in (11cm); originally red-brown with gray belly, now also white, tortoiseshell, banded, etc; some have velvety fur; average lifespan 3 years.

Characteristics
1 Stout, furry body.
2 Stumpy tail.
3 Short legs.
4 Small ears.
5 Blunt nose.
6 Large cheek pouches.
7 Hand-like front feet.

Behavior Hamsters are nocturnal; they may be noisy at night or may bite if wakened by day. They are antisocial, and adults should be kept singly or they will fight. A temperature of 65-75°F (18-24°C) is needed — below this they may become dormant. Adequate provision for exercise is required to prevent paralysis. Hamsters are poor climbers, and need protection from heights. They are natural burrowers; nesting material should be supplied.

In addition to the original reddish-brown, they are now available in a range of colors and with different types of fur. They are clean, odorless animals that need roomy cages and a constant, warm temperature. Generally easy to care for, they suffer from few illnesses provided they are given a healthy, fresh diet and adequate facilities for exercise.

a
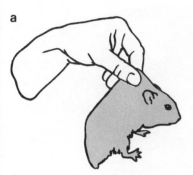

b
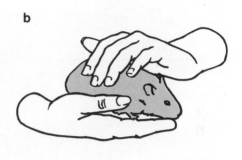

Handling Hamsters should be handled daily to keep them tame. To pick up: before hamster is tame, lift by loose skin behind head (**a**); when tame, pick up by gently placing hand right around hamster (**b**). Avoid any sudden movement that may cause alarm. Never let a hamster fall from a height of more than 9in (23cm) as serious injury is likely.
Caging See page 106.
Diseases See page 107.
Breeding See pages 108-109.

Feeding Hamsters survive best on a diet of hamster food, wheat, crushed oats, peanuts, dog kibble, carrot, apple, lettuce, cabbage, cress, and occasional meat scraps. Fresh, clean water should always be available. Be careful to wash greens, and to introduce new foods gradually. Feed ⅓oz (10g) each evening. Hamsters store surplus food in cheek pouches. The illustrations below show a hamster before feeding (**a**) and after feeding (**b**).

a

b

Cavies/Guinea pigs

The cavy or Guinea pig is a native of the Peruvian Andes and was first domesticated by the Incas who raised these animals to eat. The name cavy is derived from the Peruvian Indian name, and is now gaining favor in preference to Guinea pig (which is a misnomer on two counts since these animals are not pigs and do not come from Guinea).
A few wild cavies remain in their natural habitat, and in

Cavy/Guinea pig *(Cavia porcellus)* 11in (28cm); stocky body; short legs; petal-shaped ears; lifespan 4-5 years.
Examples of varieties
1 Tortoiseshell-and-white A shorthaired variety. (Also one-colored selfs, Himalayans, Dutch, and ticked agoutis.)
2 American crested Various colors, with crest on forehead.
3 Abyssinian Rough-coated cavy, hair grows in rosettes.
4 Peruvian Longhaired cavy with hair-concealed face. (The silkie or sheltie is a longhaired cavy with visible face.)
Behavior Cavies are diurnal but they are not playful or particularly responsive. They can be kept singly or in groups, but do not put males together as they will fight. Cavies are odorless. Sounds made range from a squeak to a whistle.

Peru cavies are still raised for their meat. In North America and Europe, however, this docile, furry animal is known for its popularity as a children's pet. Today cavies are available in a variety of colors in addition to the original light brown agouti. Fancy-coated varieties like the Abyssinian and Peruvian are popular for showing purposes but do need regular grooming.

Housing Rabbit hutches (p.96) can be used — 18in × 2ft × 18in (45cm × 60cm × 45cm) for one cavy. Hutch floor should be wood not wire. Use wood shavings and hay for bedding. Clean out thoroughly once weekly.

Movable hutch and run
1 Wire mesh run.
2 Pipes for shelter.
3 Hinged doors for access.
4 Weatherproof shelter.
5 Wood floor with bedding.
6 Mesh floor allowing grazing.

Handling Cavies must have frequent handling to prevent nervousness. Hold gently around body when picking up.

Grooming Longhaired cavies need frequent grooming with a fine comb or bristle brush.

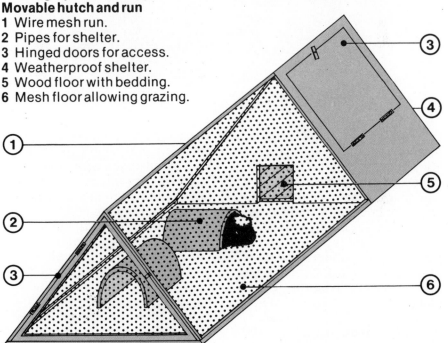

Feeding Cavies are unable to synthesize vitamin C so care is needed to provide it. Cavies thrive on vitamin-enriched cavy chow, good quality hay, and supplements of green vegetables, grass trimmings (unsprayed), carrots, turnips, fruit, and occasional bran mash and wheat germ oil. If oats or rabbit chow are given in place of cavy chow, a vitamin C supplement will be needed. Fresh water must always be available. Beware overeating — feed about a handful of food daily.

Diseases See p.107.
Breeding See pp.108-109.

©DIAGRAM

Chinchillas

Once found in large colonies in the South American Andes, the chinchilla is now rare in its natural habitat. High prices for its fur — one of the loveliest of all animal pelts — resulted in heavy trapping and brought this attractive animal to the verge of extinction in the wild. The raising of chinchillas in captivity became for some years a popular and profitable activity on ranches and

Chinchilla *(Chinchilla laniger)* Andean regions of S. America; 10in(25cm) excluding tail; soft, dense fur, usually silver-gray but also beige, cream, or white; large, rounded ears; large eyes; long whiskers, bushy tail; lifespan 6-7 years.

Fur In the chinchilla numerous fine hairs grow from a single hair follicle (as shown below). This makes the chinchilla's coat so dense that it is difficult to see the skin beneath it.

Behavior Chinchillas are agile climbers and as pets are best kept in tall cages with branches. They are naturally nocturnal and not easily switched to a daytime schedule. They are able to survive a temperature range of 40-75°F (4-24°C). Chinchillas can be kept singly or in pairs or groups, but males will fight if caged together. With careful handling, these attractive animals can become extremely tame.

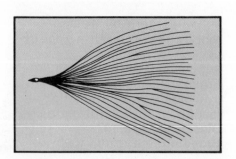

Feeding Chinchillas should receive 2-3oz(60-85g) of food daily. Feed good quality hay, commercial pellets, apple, turnip, green vegetables, seeds, and twigs (unsprayed). Fresh water should be constantly available, although only a little will be drunk.

farms in North America and Europe. More recently, falling fur prices have brought a major cutback in this activity. One result of this is that chinchillas have become available to the petkeeper. A chinchilla remains more expensive to buy than other common rodent pets, but once purchased this interesting and responsive animal is no more costly or difficult to keep than a cavy.

Handling Chinchillas are naturally friendly and alert, and respond well to frequent, brief periods of gentle handling. A chinchilla should be held as shown in the illustration (right), with one hand over the animal's shoulder and the other giving support to its rump. Avoid any sudden movement that might scare the chinchilla and provoke a sharp bite.

Diseases See page 107.

Breeding See pages 108-109.

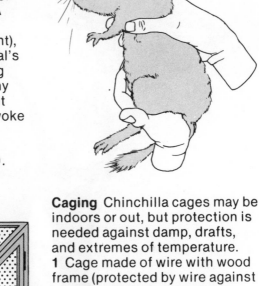

Caging Chinchilla cages may be indoors or out, but protection is needed against damp, drafts, and extremes of temperature.

1 Cage made of wire with wood frame (protected by wire against gnawing). Size: 3½ft × 2½ft × 4ft (75cm × 75cm × 120cm).

2 Raised wood nest box.

3 Large branch for exercise.

4 Gravity-flow water bottle.

5 Heavy food dish.

6 Wood floor with sawdust or wood shavings. Or a ½in (1cm) gauge wire floor, with removable litter tray beneath.

7 Dust bath.

Bathing A dust bath should be provided at least once a week. In a bath 12in × 8in × 4in (30cm × 20cm × 10cm) supply 1in (2.5cm) depth of Fuller's earth or very fine, powdered clay or sand. Place bath in the cage for 30 minutes before feeding.

©DIAGRAM

Horses, ponies, donkeys

History and uses

Horses are members of the family Equidae, which also includes donkeys, zebras, tapirs, and rhinoceroses. All are perissodactyls — hoofed animals whose weight is supported by the third toe. Przewalski's horse — a wild horse from Mongolia — is the only member of the species not to have been domesticated. The horse's distribution worldwide is mainly due to man. Man and horse have been associated since prehistoric times. The horse was first hunted for food, and then later used for riding and various types of work. Ancient Egyptian murals record the use of the horse from 2000BC. Horses retained their economic and historical importance until the beginning of this century. Even today the horse is an essential source of agricultural power in those parts of the world where mechanization is limited. In Western countries, the horse's popularity declined sharply during the early twentieth century. Since the Second World War, however, there has been a widespread renewal of interest in horses for use in a variety of enjoyable leisure activities.

Evolution of the horse Although disputed, it is widely thought that the modern horse evolved along the following lines.
1 *Eohippus* is the earliest likely ancestor, from 60 million years ago. Terrier-sized, it had four toes on the forefeet and three on the hindfeet.

2 *Mesohippus*, dating from 30 million years ago, and
3 *Pliohippus*, dating from 5-2 million years ago, are probable later stages in development. They illustrate the evolution of the foot into a single hoof.
4 *Equus caballus*, the modern horse, appeared c. 2 million years ago.

Working horses

1 Heavy breeds were developed to carry knights in armor to war.

2 Horses and hardy ponies have been used as pack animals from earliest times.

3 Teams of horses have been used to draw heavy vehicles such as stagecoaches.

4 The horse as a draft animal was important in both agriculture and industry. Farm horses were used for centuries to pull all types of agricultural machines.

5 Today the working use of the horse has been eclipsed by the engine, but horses are still important in many police forces.

Anatomy of the horse

The modern horse is adapted for swift movement. Breeds showing variations in height and weight have been developed to suit a range of different tasks. Ponies belong to the same species as horses, but differ in conformation and temperament. Ponies are smaller than horses — with a maximum height of 14.2 hands (see p.128 for measuring details). They also tend to be hardier.

Points of the horse

1 Forelock.
2 Muzzle.
3 Windpipe.
4 Elbow.
5 Forearm.
6 Knee.
7 Cannon.
8 Fetlock joint.
9 Hoof.
10 Pastern.
11 Chestnut.
12 Flank.
13 Stifle.
14 Shannon.
15 Hock.
16 Gaskin.
17 Tail.
18 Thigh.
19 Dock.
20 Croup.
21 Loins.
22 Back.
23 Withers.
24 Shoulder.
25 Crest.
26 Mane.
27 Poll.

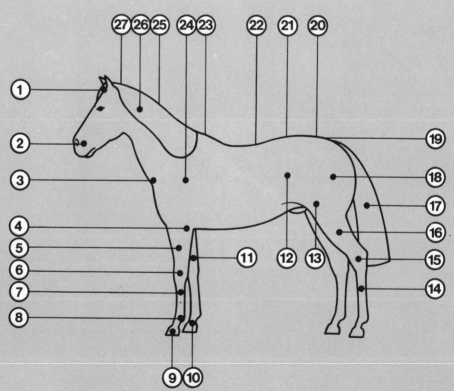

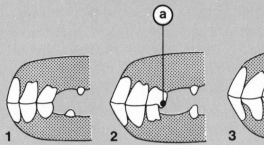

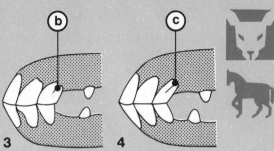

Teeth

Teeth help show a horse's age.

1 At 5 years all permanent teeth are present. Before this there are up to 24 temporary teeth; age is assessed according to the number present.

2 At 7 years a hook (**a**) appears on the upper corner incisors. This disappears by 8 years.

3 At 10 years Galvayne's groove (**b**) appears on the upper corner incisors.

4 By 15 years this groove goes halfway down the tooth (**c**).

Feet

Feet The horse's feet are structured, like the legs, to be shock-absorbent and also to be strong, durable, and elastic. Because the full weight is sometimes taken on only one foot, the horse's feet are vulnerable to injury. Shoeing, necessary for work on roads, has the disadvantage of reducing the natural elasticity of the feet. The plan of the foot (**1**) and rear view (**2**) show the frog (**a**), sole (**b**), and wall (**c**).

Eyes

Eyes The horse can see to the front, but mainly to the side, and has relatively poor eyesight. In order to see properly the horse must move its entire head, and for this reason, should not be closely reined in face of obstacles.

1 The head is lowered for distance vision.

2 The head is kept straight to see objects at normal distance.

3 The head is raised to see close objects.

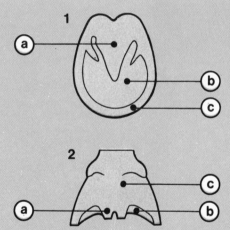

©DIAGRAM

Choosing a horse

Before choosing a horse or pony consider very carefully the full implications of ownership. The purchase price — expensive enough in itself — represents only the start of a heavy and continuing financial outlay. Stabling, pasturing, feedstuffs, tack, and veterinary bills can all be expensive items. In addition, care and exercise require a lot of time and effort. For many people, it is definitely

Sources Horses and ponies can be bought from dealers, at auctions, from riding schools, or from individual owners. Unless you know a lot about horses, always seek the advice of someone who does. Buying from a dealer or at an auction is particularly risky for the inexperienced. If buying from a riding school, take care that the mouth is sensitive. Many good buys are made privately; local knowledge is invaluable.

Suitability Great care is needed to make a good purchase. Watch very carefully as the animal is handled and ridden; try to assess temperament as well as action. Make sure that the animal matches the riding ability of the person for whom it is intended — not every small pony, for example, is suitable for a young and inexperienced rider. Also bear in mind any individual riding preferences such as for jumping or hunting.

b

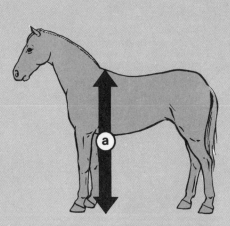

Measuring The height of a horse or pony is measured to its withers, as shown (**a**). Height is expressed in "hands" (hh). One hand is 4in(10cm), the average width of a person's hand. Height is given to the nearest inch — a pony measuring 50in(127cm) is said to measure 12.2 hands.

Height Illustration (**b**) shows a young rider on a pony of suitable size. The following table may help potential buyers.

Pony's height	Child's age
11-12hh	7-9 years
12-13hh	10-13 years
13-14.2hh	13-15 years
14.2-15.2hh	15-17 years

preferable to attend a riding school.
The choice of a horse or pony will depend very largely on the potential owner's particular requirements. The animal's height, conformation, age, temperament, health, and soundness are all important considerations. Careful examination is essential before any purchase, and a veterinarian's certificate should always be obtained.

Health The following points should all be considered.
1 The seller's premises should be clean and well cared for.
2 The animal should have an alert, intelligent expression.
3 Assess the age of the horse or pony by examining its teeth (see p.127 for details). In general, choose an animal aged between 5 and 12 years.
4 There must be no cough or other respiratory trouble.
5 Avoid animals with a narrow chest or flat ribs — these generally lack stamina and are prone to foreleg interference.
6 Check that the legs are sound, and there is no lameness.
7 Check that the feet are sound.
8 The horse or pony should be neither too thin nor too fat.
9 If buying a gelding, check that it was properly castrated.
10 Coat and skin must be in good condition.
11 Check that there are no saddle sores.

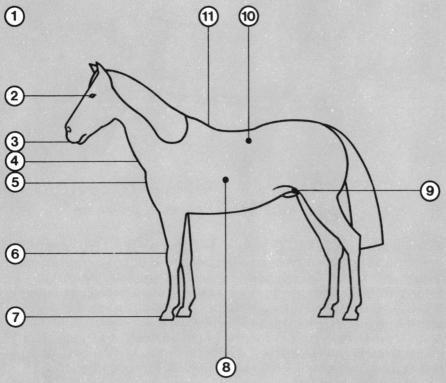

©DIAGRAM

Arabs and related breeds

Horses of arab type have an extremely ancient history, and examples can be seen in drawings and carvings dating back thousands of years. The purity of the arab stock was jealously guarded during many centuries of breeding in the Middle Eastern deserts; today, arab horses are bred in countries all over the world. The characteristic beauty of this fine breed is matched by a

1 Arab Height 14.2-15hh. Small, refined head with concave profile and small muzzle. Arched neck. Broad, deep chest. Strong legs. Tail carried high. Action free, fast, and floating. Very hardy. Great endurance.
2 Barb Height 14-15hh. Native of North Africa. Profile similar to arab, but head longer. Flat shoulders. Rounded chest. Tail set lower than in arab.
3 Anglo-Arab Considerable variations in height. Composite breed from crossing arabs with English thoroughbreds. Many combine best qualities of both lines. Make good hunters.

1

4 Andalusian 15.2-16hh. Breed developed by crossing Iberian horses with barbs. Gray or bay. Strong. Good temperament.
5 Lipizaner 16-17hh. Austrian breed with Spanish, Italian, and arab blood. Usually gray. Strong, elegant, intelligent. Used by Spanish Riding School, Vienna.
6 Trakehner/East Prussian 16hh. Developed by crossing E. Prussian with arab horses. Thoroughbred blood added later. Excellent constitution and stamina.
7 Australian waler Developed from Spanish and Dutch stock with the addition of arab and English thoroughbred blood.

sound constitution, great endurance, and an ability to thrive in harsh conditions. The qualities of the arab, together with a pronounced ability to pass on these qualities to its progeny, have made the arab invaluable in the development and upgrading of other breeds. Arab influence is found in all the other breeds on these two pages, as well as in the English thoroughbred (p.132).

British horses

For several centuries the British Isles have enjoyed a worldwide reputation for horsebreeding. To a large extent this reputation rests on the excellence of the English thoroughbred, the champion of the racetrack. Originally developed from oriental stock, all examples of this fine breed can be traced back to three famous stallions of the 17th and 18th centuries — the Darley Arabian, the

1 Thoroughbred Height 14.2-17hh. Refined appearance. Fairly small head, arched neck, comparatively short back, sloping shoulders, long, lean legs. Extremely fast, with long, striding action.

2 Cleveland bay 15.2-16hh. Bay with black points. Body wide and deep. Legs short and muscular. Used in agriculture and to draw carriages. Now often crossbred.

3 Hunter Not a breed but a range of types. Show hunters classified as light, medium, or heavy. Good legs, generous body. Must jump boldly.

1

4 Hackney Usually 14.3-15.3hh. Compact body, powerful shoulders, short legs. Harness horse with high-stepping gait.

5 Cob Up to 15.2hh. Not a breed but a distinctive type. Short, very wide body, large hindquarters, short legs. Placid. Excellent horse for heavy or elderly riders.

6 Clydesdale Usually 16-17hh. Bay, brown, or black with white on face and legs. Draft horse combining size, weight, strength, stamina, and activity.

7 Shire Height 16.2-17.3hh. Largest British draft horse. Strong, steady worker. Docile. Now often exported.

Godolphin Arabian, and the Byerley Turk. The oldest established British breed is the Cleveland bay, now often crossed with the thoroughbred to produce excellent hunters. The cob, like the hunter, is a type not a breed. The hackney was developed as a fancy harness horse, while the Clydesdale and Shire are great draft animals now only rarely seen outside the show ring.

©DIAGRAM

North American horses

The horse is thought to have been reintroduced into the Americas by the Spanish explorers of the fifteenth and sixteenth centuries. Later, settlers continued to import horses from Europe both for their own use and to improve native stock. The result has been the development of a number of excellent North American horse breeds. Notable among these are the Morgan descended from a

1 Morgan Height 14-15hh. Compact, very muscular, elegant. Good temperament. Fine general purpose breed.
2 American quarter horse Around 15hh. Very powerful hindquarters, wide chest. Agile. Fast starter, good sprinter. Equable temperament.

3 Standardbred Average 15.2hh. Similar in type to thoroughbred but more robust, with heavier limbs and longer body. Developed for harness racing.
4 American saddle horse Height 15-16hh. Light and elegant. Head and tail carried high. Three or five show gaits.

famous stallion owned in the 1790s by Justin Morgan, the American quarter horse developed for quarter-mile racing, the standardbred developed for trotting and pacing, and the American saddle horse and Tennessee walking horse both developed for their distinctive gaits. The pinto, Appaloosa, and palomino are recognized as breeds in the USA but generally elsewhere only as colors.

5 Tennessee walking horse
Usually over 15hh. More robust and less elegant than American saddle horse. Named for special gait — the running walk.
6 Pinto White with black, bay, or brown markings. Known for toughness. Famous Indian horses of the "wild west."

7 Appaloosa Height 14.2-16hh. White with black or brown spots on body and legs. Arab blood has increased refinement.
8 Palomino Gold coat with almost white mane and tail. White markings permitted only on face and legs. Arab or barb type but larger and more solid.

135

Pony breeds

Ponies are horses not exceeding 14.2 hands in height. There are, however, other characteristic distinguishing features. Pony breeds are native to regions with harsh climates and difficult terrain, and natural selection over long periods of time has made them typically hardy, strong for their size, sure-footed, and intelligent. They are, in fact, often crossed with horses to promote these

1 Shetland Smallest pony breed: average 10hh. Well shaped head. Profuse mane and tail. Double winter coat. Very strong for size. Some have a reputation for stubbornness.

2 Exmoor Up to 12.3hh. Bay, brown, or dun with black points. Mealy muzzle. Strong, fast, courageous. Britain's oldest pony breed. Good for children.

3 New Forest Height 12-14.2hh. Big variations in type. Hardy, intelligent, dependable. Larger sizes make good family ponies.

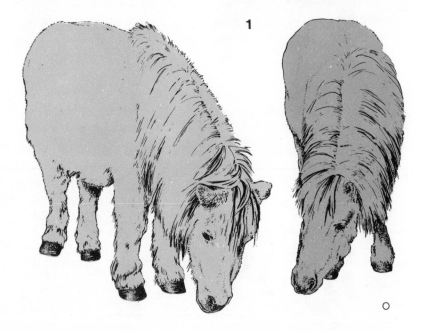

1

4 Welsh mountain pony Average 12hh. Dainty but strong. Hardy and intelligent. Excellent for children. Jumps well. Often used in crossbreeding.

5 Connemara Height 13-14hh. Grays now predominate; dun original color. Irish pony with native, Spanish, and arab blood.

6 Criollo Height 14-14.2hh. Usually dun. Argentinian pony evolved on pampas from animals from Spain. Used as cattle horse and pack animal.

7 Timor Native pony of East Indies, now established in New Zealand and Australia. Strong and eager. Used by stockmen.

qualities. Many pony breeds are native to Northern Europe, and Great Britain has no fewer than eight native pony breeds. Other hardy ponies have evolved in Asia. For centuries ponies have been used for a variety of work purposes. Today they are most commonly ridden for pleasure. They are extremely popular with riding schools, particularly as mounts for children.

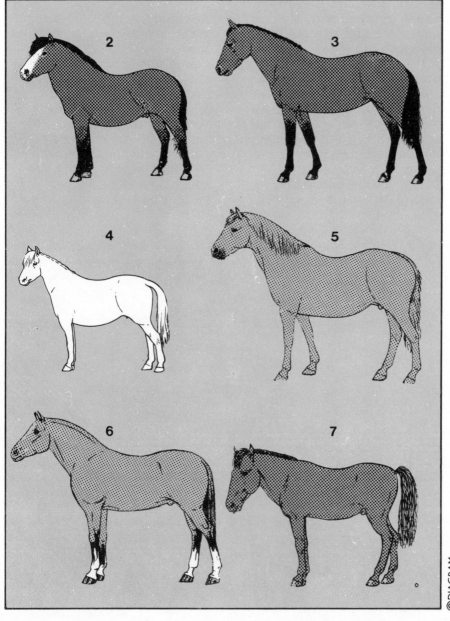

©DIAGRAM

Keeping outdoors and in

The decision to keep a horse or pony outdoors or in depends on the climate, the facilities available, and the hardiness of the animal in question. In general, ponies are hardier than purebred horses. No matter where a horse or pony is kept, health problems and lameness will be avoided only if constant attention is paid to the animal's diet, water supply, and feet.

Keeping outdoors If you have insufficient land of your own it may be possible to make arrangements to keep your horse or pony on the land of a local farmer. Ideally, two fields or paddocks should be available in order to allow the land to rest after heavy grazing. Fields must be well drained and free from poisonous shrubs such as yew, hemlock, or ivy.

1 Large field — at least 1½ acres (0.6 hectares) per horse or pony.

2 Secure fencing — post and rail is excellent, wire fencing is dangerous.

3 Gate with secure fastening — a five-barred gate will prove strong and long-lasting.

4 Trough for fresh water. Fill once a day or install a self-filling mechanism. Clean often.

5 Shed facing away from the prevailing wind to give shelter from cold weather and sun.

6 Horse box for transporting.

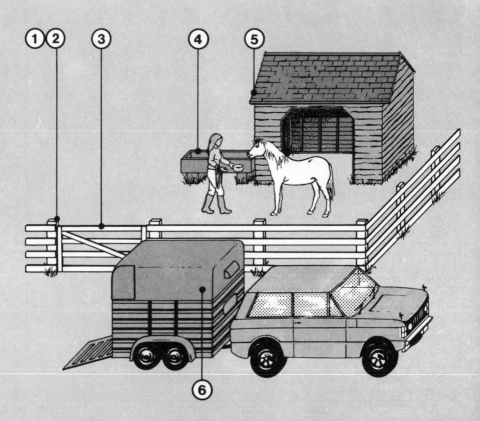

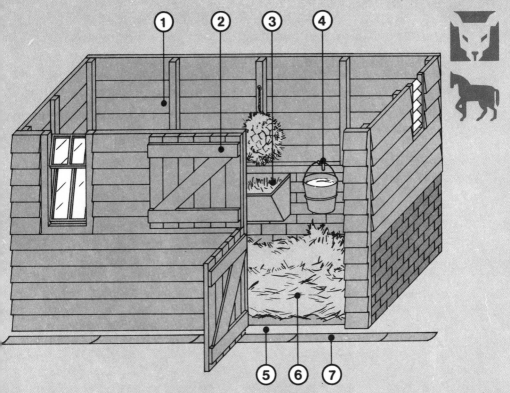

Catching To catch a horse in a field, approach the animal from the front with the bridle or halter over one arm and a treat of chopped apple or pony nuts in a bowl in the other hand (see illustration, left). Many horses learn to respond to whistles or calls. If an animal is difficult to catch, try to win its confidence by making regular visits to the field with treats. If absolutely necessary, always keep the horse in a head collar.

Transporting Horses are transported in trailers (horse boxes) pulled behind cars or trucks (see illustration, left). During transportation, drive slowly and try to avoid sudden stops. After use, always clean out the horse box to keep its fittings in good condition.

Stabling Any form of stabling must be well ventilated (but not drafty), and free from damp. There should be a separate room for storing feed and equipment. Horses are kept in loose boxes or tethered in stalls — loose boxes are generally preferred as they allow lying down.
1 Loose box (roof removed for illustration).
2 Wide double door.
3 Manger 3ft (1m) high, with rounded or covered edges.
4 Securely held bucket.
5 Solid floor (ideally concrete).
6 Deep bedding — straw, peat, sawdust, or wood shavings.
7 Outside drain (with box floor sloping toward it).
Mucking out Clean out all soiled bedding daily and add clean straw. To prevent disease, check that the drain is clear and the box floor dry.

Feeding horses

Each horse must be treated as an individual with respect to feeding. Amounts and type of feed will depend on size, age, temperament, health, work, and breed. Horses should be fed small quantities often. Water should be offered before meals, and animals should not be worked hard immediately after eating. Sudden changes in feeding routine may provoke digestive disorders such as colic.

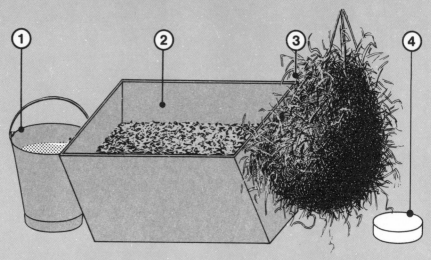

Feeding Individual needs vary, but the following information should act as a useful guide. A stabled 16hh horse in regular work will require 25-32lb (11-14 kg) of food daily, of which 12-14lb (5-6kg) should be hay. Feeds should be given at least three times a day, and the bulk of the hay should be given at night. A horse kept at grass will need supplementary hay and 4-5lb (1.8-2.3kg) of oats daily in the winter when the grass is poor.

Basic diet items

1 Water — 9-11gal (41-50l) per day. Change three times daily.
2 Short feed — given for extra energy. Give oats, pony nuts, boiled barley, beans, and maize.
3 Hay — important for bulk. Give long in a hay net, or chopped (chaff) mixed with short feed.
4 Salt block for licking.

Poisonous plants Horses must never eat poisonous plants like yew, laurel, hemlock, or bracken.
Mashes Bran mash, made by boiling bran and allowing it to cool, can be given once weekly as a laxative. Linseed mash is a restorative and laxative.
Treats such as apple, carrot, or turnip are useful during training or catching. As shown below, treats should be given in an open hand with the fingers kept straight to prevent injury.

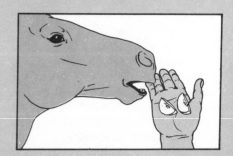

Grooming horses

Daily grooming is an essential part of caring for all horses kept indoors. Grooming helps to clean the skin, to prevent parasites, and to improve the animal's general appearance. Full grooming should take about an hour. Horses that are kept outdoors should be groomed less often as the accumulation of natural grease on the coat helps to keep them warm and dry in bad weather.

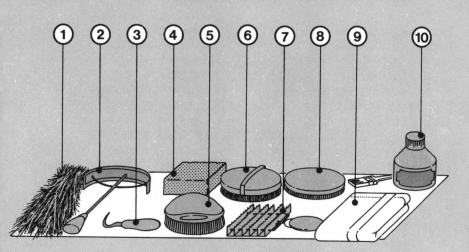

Grooming routine Cool off the horse by walking. Use a handful of straw (**1**) to restore circulation on the saddle mark and behind the ears. If necessary, use a sweat scraper (**2**) to remove sweat from the head and neck. Carefully clean out the feet with a hoof pick (**3**). Wash the eyes and nostrils with a sponge (**4**). Begin brushing with a dandy brush (**5**) to remove dirt. Then use a body brush (**6**) all over the body, leaving the legs until last. At the same time use a curry comb (**7**) to clean out the body brush as it accumulates dirt and loose hair. Brush the face and head with a dry water brush (**8**), then wet it for use on the mane, tail, and feet. Rub down the horse with a stable rubber (**9**). Finally, if the hooves are brittle or broken use a small brush to apply hoof oil (**10**).

Technique Always brush with the lie of the hair, using wide circular movements. Groom with the entire body weight not just with the strength of the arm.
Clipping Horses grow two coats each year — winter and summer. Horses kept in stables are sometimes clipped in the fall to prevent overheating and to make them easier to groom. In cold weather, a New Zealand rug (see below) is sometimes used to keep clipped horses warm.

Horse diseases

Horses that are well cared for and vaccinated regularly are unlikely to suffer serious disease. But be sure to call the veterinarian promptly if a horse shows any signs of illness. Colic is one of the more common problems that always requires urgent attention. Horses are particularly prone to lameness — for which man must be very largely held responsible.

Prevention Careful attention to living conditions and diet will reduce the risk of illness. Regular vaccination should be given against tetanus and equine encephalitis. Vaccinate pregnant mares against rhinopneumonitis. Strangles vaccination may also be needed.
Treatment Seek veterinary advice at the first signs of illness. Keep the horse warm and dry. Isolate it if infectious disease is suspected.

Signs of illness
1 Refusal to eat or drink.
2 Coughing.
3 Discharge from eyes or nose.
4 Shivering or sweating.
5 Temperature over 103°F(39.4°C).
6 Dull coat.
7 Skin blemishes.
8 Loss of balance.
9 Change in temperament.
10 Lying down, rolling, or groaning — signs of digestive disorders (colic); horses are unable to vomit.

Lameness Horses are prone to lameness largely because they are not naturally adapted to carrying a rider. Shoeing — necessary in modern conditions — also impairs the legs' natural shock absorbing mechanisms. In addition to injury, causes of lameness in the foreleg (a) and hindleg (b) may be as follows.
1 Thoroughpin — hock swelling.
2 Spavin — excess fluid on joint.
3 Curb — sprained ligament.
4 Splint — lump on splint bone.
5 Windgall — painless swelling.
6 Interference — one leg striking another in action.
7 Ringbone — bone deposits.
8 Quittor — abscess on foot.
9 Sandcrack — split in hoof.
10 Navicular disease — lesions on bone, caused by jarring.
11 Laminitis — foot engorged with blood.
12 Thrush — infection of frog.

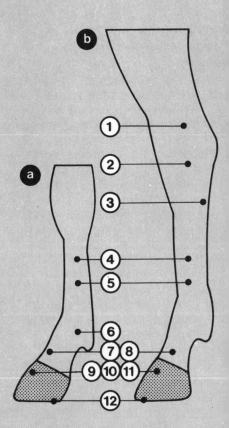

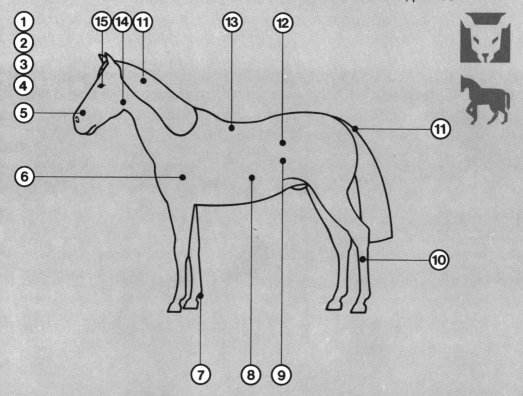

Ailments and symptoms To avoid complications, always consult a vet without delay.

1 Tetanus (poisoning of central nervous system) — stiff limbs, inability to open mouth. Bacteria enter through wounds.

2 Staggers — sudden loss of balance for no apparent reason. Horse normal between attacks.

3 Anthrax — swollen head, high fever, colic. Highly contagious.

4 Equine infectious anemia (swamp fever) — high fever, weakness, poor coordination.

5 Respiratory problems. Broken wind — shortness of breath. Roaring (paralyzed vocal cords) — noise on breathing in. Equine influenza. Pneumonia. Strangles — nasal secretion, cough, fever, swollen and then abscessed lymph glands under and between jaws.

6 Lice — gray parasites visible, itching, bald patches. Treat with louse powder.

7 Cracked heels (eczema at back of pastern).

8 Colic (stomachache) — restlessness, sweating, groaning, rolling. Call vet at once to avoid internal injury.

9 Worms (tapeworms, roundworms, red worms) — horse does not thrive, eggs found at base of tail or in feces.

10 Bot fly infestation — horse bares teeth. Eggs laid on legs reach stomach via mouth.

11 Sweet itch — irritation of tail and mane. Possible allergy.

12 Polyps, warts, cysts, tumors.

13 Galls — raw, open wounds from ill-fitting saddle or girth.

14 Mange — itching, crusty scabs. Caused by mites.

15 Eye disorders (blocked tear duct, conjunctivitis) — eyes swollen and discharging.

©DIAGRAM

143

Breeding horses

Novice owners are not recommended to try breeding their horses or ponies. It is an expensive and time-consuming activity, and even with expert management a great many things can go wrong. Because many faults are hereditary, only healthy animals with good conformation should be used for breeding. A foal will need three to four years of care and training before it can be worked.

Mating Mares are usually taken to a stud farm for mating; arrangements should be made 3 months in advance. Mares come into season every 3 weeks during the spring and summer. To avoid fighting, it is usual to test the mare's receptivity by showing her the stallion while keeping him at a distance.

Pregnancy A veterinarian will certify that the mare is in foal. Pregnant mares kept outdoors need additional protein; stabled mares need double food rations (but less hay than usual).

Birth Make sure a veterinarian is on hand. Signs of labor are discharge, sweating, kicking, and restlessness. In a normal birth, the legs appear first, followed by the head and body; prompt help will be needed otherwise. The afterbirth should be expelled 4 hours later.

Care of foal Mares need double rations while nursing. At 5 months, the foal should be weaned and separated from its mother. It should be eating 7lb (3.2kg) hay and 5lb(2.3kg) oats daily by this time. Foals should be wormed and vaccinated as the veterinarian directs.

Training The foal should wear a head collar and be accustomed to gentle handling for short periods daily from the first week. "Breaking" a horse or pony — preparing it for riding or harnessing — is a skilled job needing expert attention.

Gestation	11 months
Typical litter	1
Weaning	5 months
Puberty	15-24 months
Lifespan	20 years

Riding equipment

Many styles of bridle, bit, and saddle have been developed to meet individual needs. Careful choice of equipment is crucial to the comfort of both animal and rider. Ill-fitting saddles produce painful sores, while use of the wrong bit can completely ruin an animal's mouth. Equipment should be cleaned regularly. Bridles and saddles are best stored on hooks or racks.

1 Typical bridle Parts are: browband (**a**); noseband (**b**); head piece (**c**); cheek piece (**d**); throat latch (**e**); reins (**f**).

2 Bit The bit illustrated is a simple plain ring snaffle — a popular, fairly mild design. Also commonly used are curb bits — with a single metal bar.

3 Spring tree saddle This popular modern design of saddle is suitable for many types of riding activity. Its chief advantage is a flexible frame allowing maximum contact between rider and mount.

Parts of the saddle are: pommel (**a**); seat (**b**); saddle flap (**c**); girth (**d**); cantle (**e**); stirrup leather (**f**); stirrup (**g**).

4 Western saddle Originating in the Western United States, this heavier style of saddle was developed for hard wear.

Shoes Horses should be shod every few weeks. Different shoe styles are available and good fit is essential to prevent the animal becoming lame. Before nailing the shoe in place, the blacksmith files the hoof down to the level of the last growth.

Riding clothes A full set of riding clothes is not essential, but a hard hat should always be worn to protect the head from injury in a fall. Boots or shoes should have heels high enough to prevent the foot from slipping through the stirrup.

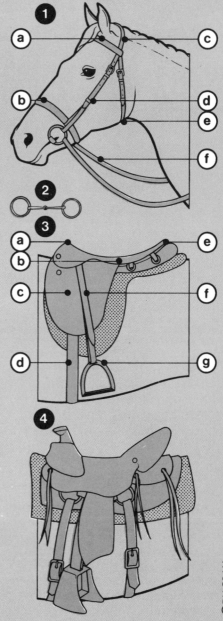

©DIAGRAM

145

Horse riding

Most horses and ponies are now kept for riding purposes. Riding combines exercise for the animal with enjoyment for the rider. The more skilled the rider, the more comfortable and safe the horse will be. Good riding schools provide novices with all the necessary training. The essence of good riding is the rider's "seat" — a combination of balance, grip, and control.

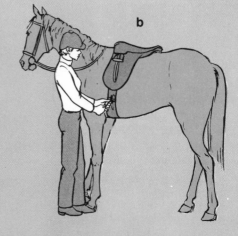

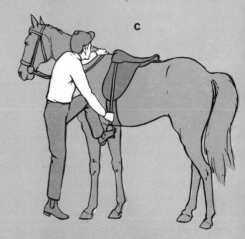

a Bridling Move quietly, calmly, and quickly. Stand on the horse's near side, with the bridle prepared to go on in one piece. Put the reins over the horse's head and remove its head collar. Quickly run the bridle up the horse's face and pass the head piece over its ears. Hold the bit against the teeth and gently prise open the horse's mouth by pressing on the corner of the lips. Finally, fasten the bridle's throat latch.

b Saddling First place the saddle on the horse's back, forward of the withers. Then slide it back into position so that it rests behind the withers but in front of the loins. Next fasten the girth, tightening it gradually and taking care not to pinch the horse's skin. The girth may need to be readjusted after the horse is mounted.

c Mounting Stand on the near side, holding the reins in the left hand. Shorten the offside rein to keep the horse's head turned away. Put the left foot in the stirrup, take hold of the pommel, and swing gently into the saddle. Adjust girth and stirrup leathers if necessary.

1 Walk Used to warm up the horse when exercising begins.
2 Sitting trot When trotting, the horse's legs move on alternate diagonals. For a sitting trot, the rider grips tightly with his knees and stays well down in the saddle.
3 Rising trot The rider lifts himself slightly out of the saddle on the first beat of the pace and returns on the second.
4 Canter A fast 3-time pace comfortable for horse and rider.
5 Gallop The fastest pace — and difficult to sustain.
6 Jump Horses can be trained to jump over a cavaletti.

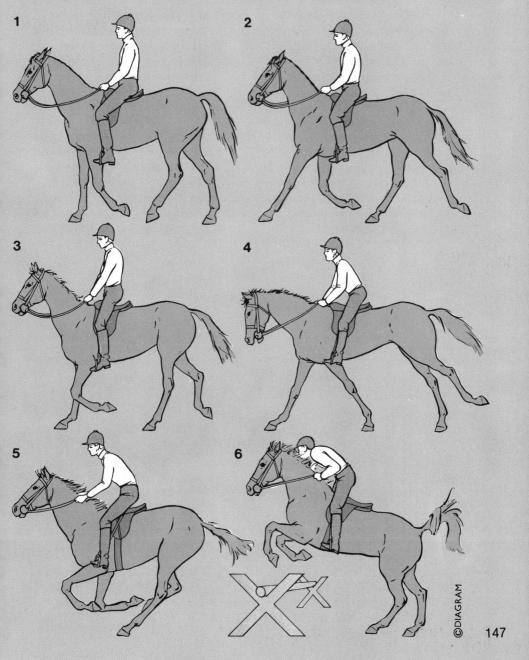

©DIAGRAM

Riding events

Equestrian sports have greatly increased in popularity in recent years. They range from simple games in children's gymkhanas to Olympic sports requiring a high degree of skill and coordination from horse and rider alike. For the participant, riding events are both challenging and rewarding. For the spectator, they provide entertainment as well as possible hints for improving technique.

Riding events The following give an indication of the great variety of equestrian sports.
1 Show jumping — events at all levels to Olympic. Errors result in lost points ("faults").
2 Dressage — events up to Olympic. Marks are awarded for set figures and movements.
3 Three day event — Olympic sport combining dressage, endurance, and show jumping.
4 Gymkhana — races and games, eg potato race.
5 Showing — classes judging conformation and action.
6 Hunting — riding to hounds.
7 Driving — races or displays of driving ability with horses pulling a variety of vehicles.
8 Polo — horseback ball game for two teams of four players.
9 Racing — either flat or over jumps (steeplechase or hurdles).
10 Harness racing — horses driven from a two-wheeled "sulky" at either trot or pace.
11 Rodeo — popular event from the American West. Skills tested include catching a steer.

1

©DIAGRAM

Donkeys and their relatives

The donkey is derived from the wild ass of north-east Africa, which was domesticated as a beast of burden at least 5,000 years ago. Other asses or ass-like animals — of which the kiang and the kulan are examples — are found in mountainous parts of Asia. Also included on this page is the mule — a useful ass-horse hybrid.

In tropical and semi-tropical countries the donkey

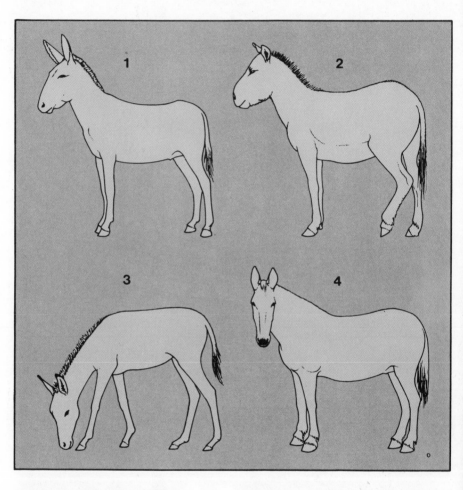

1 African wild ass *(Equus asinus)* From Sudan and Somaliland. Wild ancestor of the domestic donkey.
2 Kiang *(Equus hemionus kiang)* From Tibet and Sikkim. Largest wild ass: 51in(130cm) at withers.
3 Kulan *(Equus hemionus hemionus)* Wild ass from

Mongolia. Smaller and lighter than the kiang.
4 Mule Infertile hybrid from crossing a male ass with a female horse. (The offspring of a female ass and a male horse is called a hinny.) They combine the ass's resistance to heat with the horse's greater strength.

remains invaluable as a working animal. It is reliable and sure-footed over difficult terrain, and has the additional advantages of being easier to care for than a horse and of being better able to work in high temperatures. In cooler countries, donkeys are most often seen as children's pets. They are typically gentle and affectionate — and great fun to ride.

5

5 Donkey *(Equus asinus)* Height 28-50in at withers. Coarse coat, usually slatey gray with some black but also beiges and whites. Other characteristics include: rather large head; long ears; short, upright mane; flat withers; box-like feet; tail with only a tuft of hair; loud, braying voice. Lifespan 20-25 years.

Behavior Donkeys have often been ill-treated because of their reputation for being stubborn. In fact, their "stubbornness" derives from an instinct to freeze when in danger. Provided they are well treated, most are gentle, affectionate, and willing.

Housing Donkeys do not need elaborate housing, but in cooler, wetter climates some form of weatherproof shelter with dry bedding is essential. In hot countries, donkeys should have some access to shade.

Feeding Each donkey should have ½ acre (0.2 hectares) of land for grazing. In the winter, additional hay, bran, pony nuts, and oats should be provided. Fresh water should always be available, and a salt block is also needed. Carrots and apples can be given as treats.

Handling Donkeys make ideal first mounts for children. They can also be trained for driving, dressage, and even hunting!

Breeding As with many other animals, expert advice should always be sought before breeding is attempted. In general, care is similar to that for ponies. Gestation takes 11½-12½ months.

Disease Donkeys are rarely ill if they are kept warm and dry. Consult a vet at the first sign of illness. Deworm regularly, and trim hooves every 5-6 weeks.

© DIAGRAM

Artiodactyls

Characteristics and choosing

Mammals with cloven hooves make up the zoological order Artiodactyla. In these animals, weight is rested equally on the third and fourth toes of each foot. Other toes may or may not be present depending on the species. There are three suborders; the Ruminantia (including goats, sheep, cows, deer, antelopes, giraffes); the Tylopoda (llamas and camels); and the Suiformes (pigs and hippopotamuses). Most artiodactyls are herbivores; members of the Ruminantia and Tylopoda have complex stomachs and chew the cud. Many artiodactyls, particularly the males, have horns. Goats, sheep, cows, and pigs all have a long history of domestication. For over 5,000 years man has tended and raised these animals for their wool, milk, or meat. Today all these animals are most commonly kept in fairly large numbers on farms. If you have sufficient land and proper housing facilities it may be possible to keep one or two of them as interesting and useful pets — but first be sure to check with your local authorities.

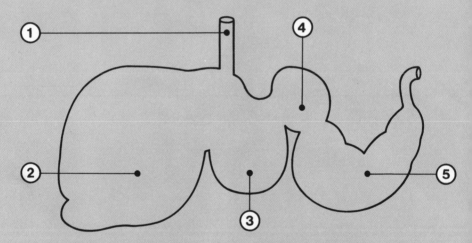

Ruminant digestion Many of the artiodactyls ruminate (chew the cud). This process allows them to digest large quantities of cellulose occurring in grass and hay. Animals that ruminate have complex stomachs, such as the four-chambered stomach of a cow shown in the diagram above. Food passes down the esophagus (1) to the rumen (2), where it is partly broken up and returned to the mouth to be rechewed as cud. The cud is then swallowed and passes from the reticulum (3) and omasum (4). Further digestion takes place in the abomasum (5).

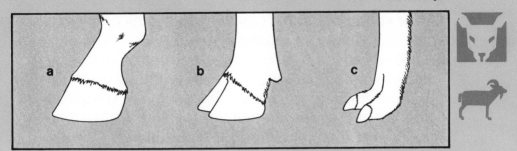

Feet Animals with hooves are sometimes called ungulates. They include artiodactyls and perissodactyls, differentiated by the number of functional toes. The horse, a perissodactyl, has one functional toe encased in a horny hoof (**a**). The cow, an artiodactyl, has two functional toes covered by a hard hoof (**b**). The llama, an artiodactyl with specialized feet, has two fleshy toes with hard nails (**c**) that allow it to walk on soft ground.

Farm animal pet guide First check that there are no laws against keeping any of these animals in your area.
1 Goats Good milk producers. Some make affectionate pets.
2 Sheep Docile but unresponsive pets. Defenseless against dogs.
3 Llamas Sometimes kept as unusual pets. Need a lot of room.
4 Cows Too large and difficult for most people to keep.
5 Pigs Intelligent and easy to train. Size often prohibitive.

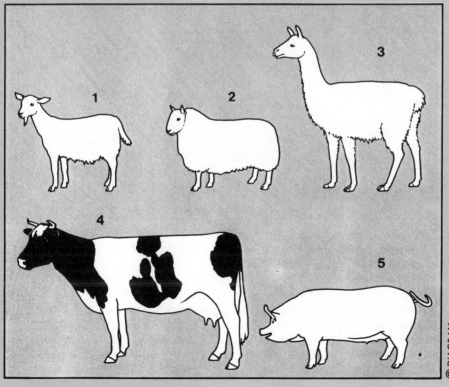

© DIAGRAM

Goats

The goat *(Capra hircus)* has been raised by man since prehistoric times as a source of milk, wool, skin, and meat. Goat-keepers today have two categories of specialized breeds to choose from: those kept primarily for their milk, and those kept for their wool. Saanens and Toggenburgs dominate milk production in Europe and North America. Angoras are the most important wool breed.

1 Saanen Swiss milk breed. Average weights: females 160lb (73kg); males 210lb(95kg). Big-bodied. Short, white coat.
2 Toggenburg Swiss milk breed. Females 120lb(54kg); males 175lb(79kg). Brown with white legs, ears, and stripe on face. Coat curly or smooth.

3 Angora Mohair-producing goat from Turkey. Females 80lb(36kg); males 150lb(68kg). Long white fleece.
4 Anglo-Nubian Milk breed. Females 160lb(73kg); males 210lb(95kg). White, black, or tan, with or without markings. Drooping ears. Roman nose.

Goats are attractive animals to keep. Provided there is sufficient space for grazing and exercise it is best to keep two or more goats, since they are sociable animals and enjoy company. Females generally make the best pets. They are typically inquisitive, lively, and affectionate. Males are larger, smell strongly, and may be aggressive and even dangerous in the breeding season.

Pasture and housing Allow 1 acre (0.4 hectares) per goat. A dry, windproof shelter is needed to give protection from bad weather. Goats are expert climbers and jumpers; paddocks should have a robust fence at least 5ft(1.5m) high.

Tethering Some goats can be tethered as an alternative to providing strong fencing. Tethering is also used to stop goats damaging young trees or eating poisonous vegetation such as yew, rhododendron, laurel. Use a 12ft(3.6m) chain and a metal stake. Move the stake several times daily, and always leave water within reach.

Handling Goats are responsive and affectionate. Many bleat noisily to attract attention. Handling must always be calm and gentle.

Breeding To produce milk, does must breed every 2 years. It is advisable to delay the first mating until a doe is 18 months old. Gestation is 145-155 days.

Feeding A basic diet of hay and succulents (green leaves, twigs, young bark, short grass, clover, lucerne, kale, sprouts, root vegetables, apples, etc) should be supplemented with concentrates (crushed cereals, dairy nuts, oil cakes). Goats require feeding twice or three times daily. Amounts depend on the goat's size, milk yield, system of management, and the nutritional values of the foods given. Seek expert advice. Clean water and a salt block should always be available.

Milking Goats require milking once or twice daily (depending on how recently the goat kidded). Hand milking is easily mastered after a practical demonstration. Stand the milk can in cold running water to cool. Sterilize equipment after each milking.

Disease Goats generally stay healthy if well cared for. Call a vet if a goat shows signs of illness, eg listlessness, dull coat, loss of appetite, diarrhea, constipation, distended body, failure to chew the cud, sudden drop in milk yield, coughing.

Lifespan 12-15 years.

© DIAGRAM

Sheep

With the exception of hand-reared lambs, sheep are not particularly responsive to humans. For the petkeeper, however, they do have the advantages of thriving on rough land, manuring the ground, cropping the grass, and providing wool. Some breeds adapt better than others to backyard life. In general, amateur sheep owners are advised to keep a breed common in their own locality.

Sheep *(Ovies aries)* Domestic; height at shoulder varies with the breed, average 3ft(91cm); coat dense and woolly, usually white; face and legs white, black, or brown; narrow mouth and thin lips; long tail usually docked; lifespan 17 years.

Breeds There are numerous domestic breeds. Names often refer to places of origin or to prevailing distribution, in some cases also with an indication of fleece or body type.

Feeding Hand-reared orphan lambs must be fed every few hours. Use a bottle and a special lamb teat. Feed commercial ewe milk substitute, or goat's milk. Adult sheep need at least ½ acre (0.2 hectares) of well-drained grazing land. To reduce the risk of parasitic infection, do not graze one field continuously. Give supplements of grain or sheep nuts if the grass is poor. Provide a salt lick. Fresh water must always be available.

Protection Sheep must be given protection from other animals, particularly dogs. Provide good fencing, and take care not to leave gates open.

Shearing Sheep are shorn in the early summer. Novice owners should hire a professional or take instruction.

Disease Sheep are susceptible to bacterial diseases such as braxy and lamb dysentery, to certain metabolic disorders, and to parasitic infestation. Seek a vet's advice on vaccination. Antiseptic dips (compulsory in some cases) give sheep vital protection against parasites.

Llamas

The domesticated llama is a descendant of the wild guanaco, a South American relative of the camel. Used principally as pack animals, llamas have been bred in captivity in South America for centuries. They are now also being raised in the southern USA. Care is similar to that needed by sheep. Most llamas remain good tempered if handled properly and given enough exercise.

Llama *(Lama glama)* S. America; domestic; 45in(114cm) at shoulder; white, brown, black, piebald, skewbald; long woolly coat; long neck; short tail; erect ears; narrow feet; live 20 years.

Care The basic care and feeding of llamas is similar to that for sheep, but each llama needs at least 1½ acres (0.6 hectares) for grazing and exercise.

Shearing Llamas are generally shorn for their wool. They produce about 5lb(2.3kg) of long, coarse hair a year.

Behavior Llamas are responsive and affectionate when young. Males become more aggresive with maturity. Llamas are likely to refuse a load they consider too heavy, and have an unpleasant habit of "spitting" when displeased. They should be halter-broken at an early age.

© DIAGRAM

Cows

Cows were among the first animals to be domesticated, and they remain an important source of meat and milk. Most commonly kept in large herds on farms, they are sometimes kept singly by families attracted by the idea of meeting their own milk needs. A permit is often required. Cows are fairly demanding in their care and need a lot of land. They do not make responsive pets.

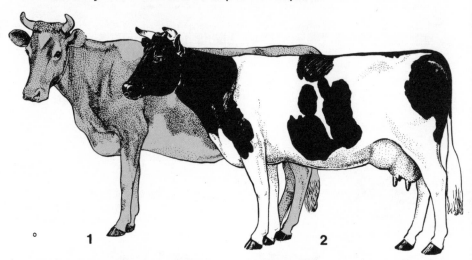

1 2

Cow *(Bos bovis)* Sizes and weights vary with the breed; a typical milker may weigh 1500lb (680kg). Milking breeds are generally wedge-shaped with fine limbs, neck, and head. Examples of good milking breeds include the Guernsey (**1**) and Friesian (**2**).

Pasture and housing A cow needs at least 5 acres (2 hectares) of good, fenced pasture. A warm shelter must also be provided.

Feeding Cows need 3lb(1.4kg) of dry food — hay, silage, grass — per 100lb(45kg) of body weight daily. Milkers need 4lb(1.8kg) of special concentrates such as dairy cubes for each gallon produced daily. Mineral supplements are also needed. Provide a salt block and water at all times.

Disease Consult a vet promptly if a cow shows signs of illness. Certain diseases can be passed on to humans either directly or in milk. Tetanus and brucellosis vaccinations may be utilized.

Milking To produce milk, a cow must calve annually. Gestation is 270 days. Cows require milking 2-3 times daily. Hand milking is easily mastered after a practical demonstration. As shown below, the milk is squeezed gently from the teats.

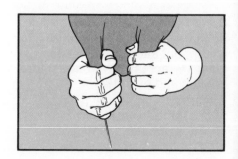

Pigs

Pigs are most often reared for their meat. Unlike other artiodactyl pets, they do not have the advantage of providing milk or wool to offset the expense and trouble of caring for them. They grow to a considerable size and make rather impractical companions, but they are intelligent and can even be trained to do tricks. Their reputation for dirtiness is largely undeserved.

Pig *(Sus domestica)* Size at maturity varies with the breed, from 100-500lb(45-225kg) or more; long, stout body with bristle covering; short legs; snout with gristle disk for rooting; large ears; small eyes; curly tail. Examples of breeds:
1 Large white Unusual pricked ears. Sometimes rough.
2 Wessex With saddle marking.
3 Large black Good breeder.
4 Landrace White, long-backed breed from Scandinavia.

Housing Pens should be 2-4 times the pig's length, with a sleeping box filled with fresh straw. It is essential to provide pigs with shelter from cold and damp. Given enough space, they will use one corner for elimination. Pigs enjoy wallowing in mud or straw.
Feeding Feed once daily 1lb (0.4kg) of food for every 30lb (13.5kg) of body weight. Give commercial pig feeds and fresh table scraps. Check local laws before feeding swill. Provide fresh water at all times. Pigs never overeat to the point of becoming ill. They are often obese as a result of breeding.
Disease Seek veterinary advice at the first sign of illness. Swine erysipelas and swine fever are serious diseases of pigs for which vaccination may be needed; consult a vet.

©DIAGRAM

Keeping wild mammals

Most of the species of domesticated or semi-domesticated mammals that are kept in captivity are animals which adapt well to confinement, and may even thrive in human company. This is not necessarily true of wild mammals, for a variety of reasons. Animals that are endangered, large and aggressive, or for behavioral reasons miserable when confined, must never be kept as pets. This applies to many of the large carnivores and higher primates that were once popular in fashionable homes. The remaining species that are possible to keep tend either to be closely related to domestic types, or to be smaller and more primitive and hence easier to care for. Even so, the problems of keeping a wild animal are usually immense. To begin with, there is often a lack of information or of experienced supportive services like veterinarians to help with care. Diet may be a problem, and housing needs are often specialized. Patient and informed care is essential to be genuinely successful in keeping any wild mammal as a pet.

General principles First check local laws. Remember, too, that the responsibility of keeping a wild animal as a pet may last many years. A tame young animal raised in captivity may prove too hard to handle as an adult, but by this time it is unlikely to be able to fend for itself in the wild. Some wild animals can be tamed as free-roaming "pets."
Learn about the animal's diet, feeding habits, and normal activities in the wild. Prepare a substitute environment that allows as much expression of natural behavior as possible. Avoid diseased animals. Any illness that develops in captivity may be a sign of poor or improper care. Taming will depend on the age, species, and habits of the animal. Nocturnal animals rarely tame well.

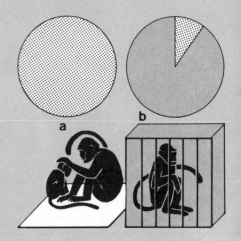

Species unsuited to captivity include those that never adapt happily to confinement. Monkeys may live 20 years in the wild (**a**), but rarely survive 2 years as pets (**b**). Other reasons for unsuitability are shown in the table opposite, with the animals to which they apply.

Table showing reasons for not keeping wild mammals as pets

 Some species

 All species

	Endangered	Disease-carrier	Dangerous
Wild canids include wolves and foxes. Some species are now endangered in the wild. Canids carry rabies. All are dangerously aggressive and are not trustworthy when adult.			
Wild felines include many species now endangered, such as tigers and cheetahs. These animals are both aggressive and destructive in captivity, and can inflict serious wounds.			
Bears include many North American species whose numbers are dwindling. Many have parasites. Even if taken as cubs, bears do not remain trustworthy as adults.			
Beavers and otters are not necessarily destructive or aggressive, but some species are protected. There is no satisfactory substitute for their natural environment.			
Primates rarely adapt well to confinement. Many are endangered, and some carry diseases that affect humans. Many, such as chimpanzees, can be dangerously aggressive.			
Deer are protected in many areas. They cause serious damage to vegetation. Males, with their sharp antlers, can be extremely dangerous in the breeding season.			

Wild rodents (1)

Rodents account for over 50% of living mammals, and large populations are found worldwide. They are generally small to medium-sized animals, chiefly vegetarian and not aggressive. Some wild rodent species can be kept relatively easily in captivity, with certain reservations. Wild rodents need larger accommodation than most domestic species, to allow for individual habits

Kangaroo rat *(Dipodomys spectabalis)* North American deserts; 1ft (30cm) including tail; brown; long hindlegs for jumping; long tufted tail; cheek pouches; nocturnal; burrower.
Care All kangaroo rats move by jumping and need more room than domestic mice and rats. Cages should be 4 x 3 x 2ft (120 x 90 x 60cm) with at least 1ft (30cm) of damp, sandy soil packed down on the floor to allow burrowing. Add dry plant material for bedding. Feed a mixture of seeds with leafy green vegetables. Water should be made available in a gravity-flow bottle, but like most desert animals, kangaroo rats absorb most of their water needs from their food. To prevent fighting, never keep more than one kangaroo rat in the same cage.

Jerboa (family Dipodidae) 25 species found in desert and arid areas from North Africa through Asia; 13in (33cm) including tail; extremely long hindlegs; short forelegs; light brown and white; nocturnal; burrower.
Care Cages should be a minimum of 6 x 4 x 4ft (1.8 x 1.2 x 1.2m) to allow ample room for exercise. The bottom should be covered with closely packed sand to a depth of 18in (45cm) to allow burrowing. Supply stones and rocks for shelter. Jerboas need a dry atmosphere and a minimum temperature of 65°F (18°C), or they will become torpid and inactive. Feed a dry seed diet with added insect food, such as cockroaches and mealworms. These should be buried just under the surface of the sand. Provide water in a bottle.

like jumping or climbing. Cages must be secure and tough — rodents' teeth will gnaw through any wood container. For gnawing purposes, all rodents need fresh supplies of woody material. Many are nocturnal and timid, and not very interesting in captivity. Larger rodents, like squirrels and woodchucks, are best kept in some form of semi-captivity, or tamed as free-range "pets."

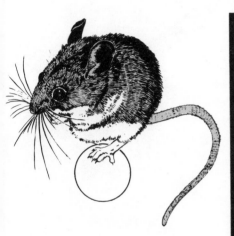

Deermouse *(Peromyscus leucopus)* N. America; 8in (20cm) including tail; dark to sandy brown, white belly and feet; ears slightly larger than *Mus musculus;* timid; lifespan 4-5 years in captivity.

Care Deermice can be raised in the same way as fancy mice (see page 106 for caging, and 110-111 for general care of mice). The main difference is that deermice are fond of nuts, and should be fed a selection of these in addition to a normal mouse diet. Deermice are generally much more timid than their domesticated relatives, and must be handled very carefully. Patience will ensure some degree of taming. Deermice are free breeders in captivity, particularly in summer months, although if kept warm, will breed all year round.

Dormouse *(Glis glis)* Europe, North Africa, Asia; 12in (30cm) including tail; gray to brownish gray, dark ring around each eye; thick soft fur; bushy tail; very active; climbs and jumps; social animal; nocturnal; hibernates.

Care Cages must be at least 4ft (1.2m) square and 4ft (1.2m) high. Add twigs and branches for climbing, and dry grass or straw in a covered corner for a nest. Dormice become very active at night and need the largest possible accommodation. Feed a mixed diet of seeds, nuts, fruit, and occasional mealworms. Water must always be available. Dormice should be allowed to feed up in the summer and hibernate normally out of doors in the winter. Always keep in small groups, as these are sociable animals.

Wild rodents (2)

a Fox squirrel *(Sciurus niger)*
United States; 24in (61cm); buff,
gray, or black; bushy tail; small
ears; tree squirrel.
b Prevost's squirrel *(Sciurus
prevosti)* Malaya; 24in (61cm);
black, red, cream, and fawn;
tropical tree squirrel.
Care Most squirrels become
pets through being abandoned
as young animals. (First check
local laws.) When full grown,
they will remain tame, even as
free-range pets. Cages must be
large: 10x6x7ft (3x1.8x2.1m),
containing branches and a nest
box 1ft (30cm) square and 1½ft
(45cm) deep, with a 3in (7.5cm)
hole on the underside. Place
nest box high in one corner, and
cover the floor with leaves and
straw. Clean regularly. Tropical
squirrels need a minimum of
65°F (18°C). Feed nuts, chopped
fruit, corn, and fresh twigs.

Southern flying squirrel
(Glaucomys volans) North
American pine forests; 12in
(30cm) including tail; brown with
white belly; large eyes; small,
flat ears; long tail, less bushy
than those of typical squirrels;
webs of skin from wrists to
ankles allow extensive gliding or
"flying"; nocturnal.
Care Cages should be at least
4ft (1.2m) square, and 4ft (1.2m)
high, with a rotten tree stump
providing holes for sleeping.
The floor should be covered with
leaf litter. Place the cage inside
a larger fenced-off area, such as
a spare room, attic, or porch, and
add branches. At night the cage
door can be opened, and the
squirrels will climb and glide.
They should be fed a diet of
seeds, nuts, and a regular
supply of mealworms. Water
should always be available.

a Spotted ground squirrel
(Citellus suslicus) Eurasia; 11in
(28cm); black with pattern of
pale spots; short ears; short tail;
terrestrial; may bite.
b Eastern chipmunk *(Tamias
striatus)* Eastern North America;
11in (28cm); gray coat with black
and white dorsal stripes;
terrestrial; sociable.
Care Chipmunks and ground
squirrels are sociable and best
kept in small groups. Cages
must be at least 6x5x4ft
(1.8x1.5x1.2m), with hollow logs,
tree stumps and a 1½ft (45cm)
covering of leaf litter. Cages
should be weathertight and
placed in an outdoor pen of wire
netting sunk 1½ft(45cm) in the
ground. Feed seeds, fruit, and
freshly chopped greens, plus
occasional live insects, eg
grasshoppers and beetles.
Water must be available.

Woodchuck *(Marmota monax)*
North America; 2ft (61cm) in
length; 40lb (18kg) in weight;
small ears; large, typical rodent
incisors; stout body covered in
thick fur; reddish brown;
extensive burrower; hibernates.
Care Woodchucks make better
free-roaming pets than caged
ones, but it is possible to pen
them if a lot of space is
available. They need at least a
10ft (3m) square chain-linked
cage sunk 3ft (90cm) in the
ground. The soil should be light
to allow burrowing. Feed rabbit
pellets, vegetables, and
unshelled nuts. Woodchucks
destroy vegetation and are often
aggressive when adult. They
spend most of their time in their
burrows, and hibernate below
ground for up to 8 months. In the
wild, burrows may be 30ft((9m)
long and 5ft (1.5m) deep.

169

Wild carnivores (1)

Most wild carnivores make unsuitable pets, either because of their size or their hunting instincts, which make them aggressive and destructive in captivity. Many are also endangered. Three carnivore groups, however, do contain animals of manageable size and behavior. These are the procyonids or predogs, including raccoons, the viverrids, including genets and mongooses, and

Raccoon *(Procyon lotor)* North America; 30in (76cm); gray-brown, ringed tail, black mask over eyes; fox-like appearance; adept forefeet or "hands"; often lives close to man; washes food before eating; nocturnal.
Care Cages must be 10ft (3m) square with strong branches, a nest box, logs, and stones. The floor should be damp earth, covered with sawdust. Hygiene is important. Supply a diet of fresh fish, eggs, chicken heads, crusts of bread, and vegetables. Do not feed red meat or spicy food. Provide a deep container filled with clean water for drinking and for washing food. Young raccoons are interesting and inquisitive, but adults tend to be irritable and are best returned to the wild. Give as much exercise outside the cage as possible.

Cacomistle/ringtail *(Bassaricus astutus)* C. and N. America; 13in (33cm) with 17in (43cm) tail; gray-brown, black and white banded tail; large eyes ringed with white fur; slender; short legs; strictly nocturnal; arboreal.
Care Cages of wood and wire are required, at least 6ft (1.8m) square by 5ft (1.5m) high, with a sleeping box and branches. Feed mainly meat (ground horsemeat, chicken necks, and mice) mixed with bonemeal, and fruit. Do not overfeed. Cacomistles are intelligent and curious. They demand plenty of attention, but remain strictly nocturnal. Taming is a slow process and requires regular handling. In the southwestern areas of the United States, where they occur in the wild, cacomistles are best tamed as free-range pets only.

the mustelids. All of these animals are active and intelligent and require a great deal of care. As young animals they are often appealing and readily tamed, but inevitably revert to more suspicious and unpredictable behavior when adult. Any home area should be used just as a base, as simple caging is too confining. Great effort will be needed to train them from destructiveness.

Coatimundi *(Nasua narica)*
South America; 50in (127cm) including tail; brown with white patch on nose; long, mobile snout; banded tail carried up; diurnal; sociable; very active.
Care A wood and wire cage 6ft (1.8m) square, and 5ft (1.5m) high is needed, with a sleeping box, branches, non-destructible toys. Coatis are essentially tropical and need a constant temperature above 65°F (18°C). Feed a mixed diet of ground meat, bone meal, eggs, and green vegetables. Allow plenty of exercise outside the cage, but be prepared for a great deal of destructiveness. Young coatis are playful and interesting. Adults are often hostile and difficult to handle, and may inflict serious bites without warning. Coatis often breed freely in captivity.

Kinkajou *(Potos caudivolvulus)*
Central and South America; 36in (91cm) including long, prehensile tail; golden brown; resembles monkey in form and habits; nocturnal; arboreal.
Care Kinkajous need cages similar to those for coatimundis, with branches, and a sleeping box placed high in one corner. Draft-free conditions are essential, with a constant temperature of over 70°F (21°C). Feed fruit, vegetables, eggs, chopped meat, insects, and plenty of water. Kinkajous are fond of honey and are sometimes called "honey bears." Wash all food carefully, as they are susceptible to insecticides. Kinkajous may be docile when mature, but are strictly nocturnal. They need a lot of exercise, and may be destructive. May live 20 years.

171

Wild carnivores (2)

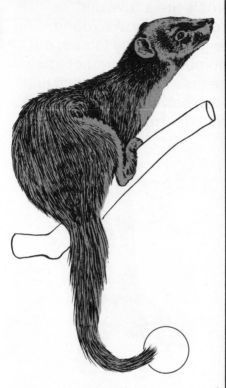

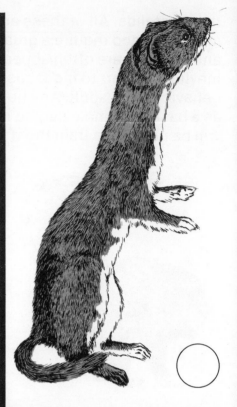

Tayra *(Eira barbara)* South America; 12in (30cm); gray-brown; weasel-like appearance; slender body; long tail; diurnal.
Care Cages should be 6x5x5ft (1.8x1.8x1.5m), with stout branches for climbing, and a secure sleeping box at the back of the cage. Feed a mixed animal and fruit diet. Tayras appreciate as much natural food as possible and will eat mice and dead birds. Like most carnivores, tayras are best reared from young animals, but even so, they become aggressive when mature and are capable of administering sharp bites. Always wear strong gloves when handling, or inspecting the cage. Tayras are extremely active throughout the day, and have a strange habit of emitting clicking noises as they move about.

American weasel/stoat *(Mustela erminea)* Europe, North America, North Asia; 12in (30cm) including tail; upperside red-brown, underside cream in summer; completely white in winter except tip of tail which is black; strong smell emitted from anal glands; nocturnal.
Care All types of weasel are extremely fierce. They are best obtained when young, but still never become fully tame. Keep in an outdoor cage 6x4x4ft (1.8x1.8x1.2m), made of fine mesh netting, with a hard floor and a double door to prevent escapes. Provide two weathertight nest boxes, and drainpipes to allow tunneling. Weasels should be fed as much fresh meat as possible — dead birds, rats, mice, with the occasional egg. Fresh water is essential.

Small spotted genet *(Genetta genetta)* Southern Europe, Africa; 44in (112cm) including tail; yellowish-gray fur with rows of dark spots; long tail ringed black and white; resembles cat but with slender body, pointed muzzle, long neck; arboreal; nocturnal.
Care If genets are obtained when young, they remain quite tame when adult, although they are nocturnal. If not captured when young, adult genets resent handling and may inflict a serious bite. Unless taming is complete, genets must be housed in a large cage, with branches for climbing, and a sheltered sleeping area. Genets are true carnivores and need as much fresh meat as possible. Feed dead birds, mice, and insects, and supply fresh drinking water.

Eyptian mongoose *(Herpestes ichneumon)* Southern Europe, Africa; 42in (107cm) including tail; gray, speckled appearance; short legs; long, pointed tail; chiefly nocturnal; active, brave, and agile.
Care House in an outdoor wire run 5x3x3ft (150x90x90cm), with a weathertight sleeping box at one end, filled with fresh straw. Keep at a minimum temperature of 65°F (18°C). Feed raw meat, chicken heads, mice, and dead birds. Fresh water is essential. It is best to obtain young mongooses and then to train them to live indoors. Once familiar with their owner, they become dedicated companions and require a lot of affection. It is even possible to train a mongoose to walk on a leash. Mongooses tend to be jealous of other household pets.

© DIAGRAM

173

Other wild mammals

Included on these two pages are four other wild mammals sometimes kept in captivity. They belong to four widely different mammalian groups. The opossum is a marsupial, a primitive order characterized by the development of immature young in an external pouch. Bushbabies are the only primates considered suitable for inclusion in this chapter, and even they have habits and

Virginia opossum *(Didelphis marsupialus)* Eastern North America; 36in (91cm); gray, coarse fur; opposable hind toe; hairless, prehensile tail; shams death when threatened by attackers; nocturnal.
Care Keep in an outdoor cage 6x5x5ft (1.8x1.5x1.5m), with branches, and a hollow stump placed high up in a sheltered area for sleeping. Dry grass should be provided for bedding. The opossum's diet in captivity must contain as much natural food as possible. This should include small fish, dead birds, insects, fresh greens, fruit, milk, and supplies of fresh water. Feed in the evening, as the opossum is nocturnal. Opossums are hardy in captivity, but tend to become irritable when mature.

Senegal bushbaby *(Galago senegalensis)* Africa; 18in (46cm); brown; thick, soft, silky fur; long, bushy tail; short muzzle; large eyes; large naked ears that can be folded over; long hindlegs; good climber and jumper; nocturnal.
Care Cages should be large, with plenty of branches, shelves, and planks, as well as nest boxes supplied with wool, straw, and dry grass. Feed a mixed diet of meat, fruit, and vegetables, given in small amounts at frequent intervals. Guard against overfeeding. Keep indoors and give extra heating if the temperature drops drastically. Although appealing to look at, bushbabies rarely become tame enough to handle. Bushbabies urinate on their hands and feet, and can be messy if let out of their cages.

requirements that make them unsuitable for any but the most dedicated owner. Fruit bats belong to the order Chiroptera; small ones make interesting but rather smelly pets. Hedgehogs are an asset to a European garden, but they are best considered as only temporary pets. None of these four animals is particularly responsive, and all have the disadvantage to the petkeeper of being nocturnal.

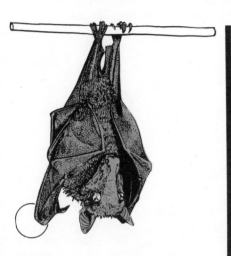

Fruit bat (genus *Pteropus*) Old World tropics and subtropics; 150 types; up to 60in (1.5m) wingspan; large ears; pointed muzzle; large membranous wings; clawed feet; nocturnal.
Care Small fruit bats can be kept in a large indoor aviary 15x8x12ft (4.5x2.4x3.6m) at a minimum temperature of 65°F (18°C). Cover a top corner of the cage and fix a branch underneath where the bats can sleep hanging upside down in the day. At night feed a mixed diet of freshly chopped bananas, apples, pears, and grapes, placed in a feeding trough well up the side of the cage. Water should be supplied in a gravity-flow bottle. Cover the floor with newspaper and replace it regularly. Fruit bats are best kept in groups, and squeak noisily when excited.

Northern hedgehog *(Erinaceus europaeus)* Europe; 9in (23cm); body covered with dark spines tipped with white; head and belly covered with brown, stiff hairs; pointed muzzle; curls up when in danger; hibernates; nocturnal; insectivore.
Care Keep in an outdoor cage in the garden, surrounded by a pen of wire netting. Feed at dusk on a diet of live prey — worms, beetles, slugs, snails, and large insects. Hedgehogs also eat bread and milk, raw egg, and vegetables. Once tame, the netting around the cage can be removed, and the hedgehog will accept the cage as its home and return to it. Hedgehogs must be allowed complete liberty in the fall, so that they can increase their food intake sufficiently to go into hibernation.

2

Fish

Swimming fish are among
nature's most graceful sights.
These finned, gill-breathing,
aquatic vertebrates come in a
dazzling variety of shapes, sizes,
and colors. There are some
30,000 different species living in
inland pools, rivers, estuaries, or
seas. No other backboned
creatures are so numerous.
Most fish lay eggs, but some
bear live young. Some eat
plants, but many are carnivorous.
These delightful animals have
been kept for many centuries
either as pets or for food. Until
comparatively recently it was
only possible in temperate
climates to keep hardy
freshwater fish in outdoor pools.
But the invention of cheap glass
tanks, electric water heaters, and
salt mixtures has changed all
this. Millions of people are now
able, in the comfort of their living
rooms, to watch fascinating
fish from every type of water.

Right Proud new owner of a pet
goldfish (Photo Margaret Murray).

Fish characteristics

Fish are cold-blooded, backboned animals superbly built to breathe, move, feed, and breed in water. Body temperature varies with that of their surroundings; cold makes most fish sluggish and kills tropicals. Fish breathe by drawing water in through their mouths and passing it across their gills — folded, fleshy pockets that absorb the oxygen dissolved in water. Most fish have bodies streamlined for easy movement through water, and swim with muscles that waggle the tail fin rather as a man with one oar sculls a rowboat. Other fins serve as brakes and balancers. Most fish control their level in the water by altering the volume of the air bladder — a gas-filled bag inside the body. Some use it to make sounds, or as a kind of lung. Mouth shape and size are geared to the food a fish eats. Fish are keenly sensitive to odors and vibrations, but have poor hearing. Their eyes can detect colors though some have weak sight; others are blind. Most kinds of fish lay eggs but in some groups the females bear live young.

Anatomy of a fish
1 Body shape varies with habits or habitat.
2 Nostrils sense smell keenly.
3 Eyes lack lids.
4 Gill covers conceal gills that absorb oxygen from water.
5 Air bladder controls buoyancy.
6 Dorsal fin keeps body upright.
7 Lateral line's nerve endings sense vibrations.
8 Mucus coating the scaly skin keeps out infection.
9 Tail (caudal fin) provides propulsion.
10 Mouth shape varies with food.
11 Some fish have barbels: "whiskers" bearing taste buds.
12 Pectoral fins help steer and brake.
13 Ventral fins help steer and brake.
14 Anus.
15 Anal fin keeps body upright.

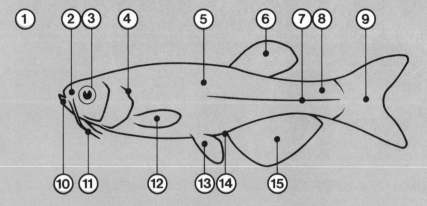

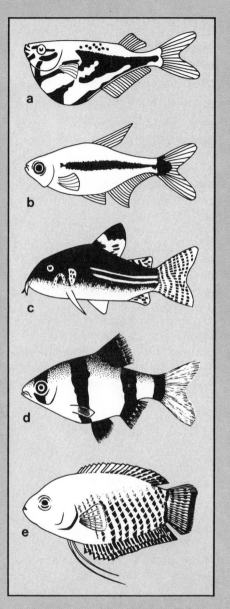

Shapes and coloring

Surface-swimming fish like the hatchetfish (**a**) tend to have flat backs, more or less convex bellies, and upturned mouths. Mid-depth fish like many characins (**b**) typically have convex backs and bellies, and mouths directed forward. Bottom-dwellers include catfish (**c**), with convex backs, concave bellies, downturned mouths, and barbels to find food in mud. Other fish adapted to life on the bottom are the snake-like eels (p.196, 211), and flatfish such as rays and plaice (p.215).

Torpedo-shaped fish like the zebra danio (p.202) are able to swim fast in open water.

Tall, narrow fish like angel fish (p. 208) are adapted to swim between plants and rocks.

Mouth shapes reflect feeding habits. The Chinese algae eater (p.205) has a sucker mouth to rasp algae off plants and stones. The long-nosed butterfly fish (p. 218) uses its snout to tweak coral polyps from stony cups.

The tiger barb (**d**) is a fish with camouflage. It is counter-shaded dark above and light below and has vertical bars to disrupt its shape optically.

Other fish, eg the dwarf male gourami (**e**), are distinctively shaped and colored to attract mates and to deter rivals.

Water flow

Water flows from a strong to a weak solution. The body fluids of a freshwater fish (**a**) are saltier than the water: the fish absorbs water, losing the surplus via the kidneys. Sea water is saltier than the body fluids of a marine fish (**b**): the fish loses water, drinks to replace it, and excretes surplus salts through gills and kidneys.

⇨ Water ➡ Water/salts

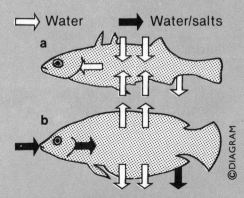

©DIAGRAM

179

Choosing fish

When starting to keep fish the first choice is between four groups with different needs: coldwater and tropical freshwater fish, and coldwater and tropical marine fish. Generally speaking, the first of these groups needs the least equipment, the last is costliest and most demanding, but outranks all others in splendor. Many novices succeed with freshwater tropicals, which include a great

Choosing for health

1 Eyes of a fish should be bright and not sunken.
2 Body should be free from tiny white blobs, cottony patches, or signs of erosion.
3 Fins should be free from tiny white blobs, cottony patches, or signs of erosion.
4 Most kinds should hold the dorsal fin well up, not clamped to the body.
5 Most kinds should swim upright on an even keel; but note the unusual attitudes of, for example, the upside down catfish (p.204) and striped anostomas or headstander (p.211).
6 Most kinds should swim smoothly, without making jerky movements or "shimmying" (swimming but making no progress).
7 Avoid fish with a hollow, caved in appearance (but note the concave bellies of some catfish).
8 Avoid fish with scales missing.
9 Avoid fish with badly torn fins.

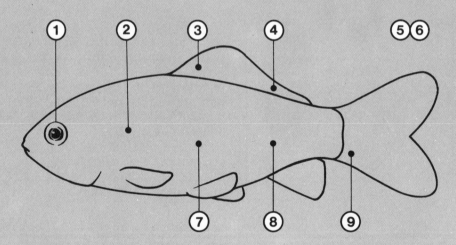

Quarantine Even apparently healthy fish may introduce infectious disease to your home aquarium. Diseases may be spread from tank to tank by use of the same net. A healthy fish caught by a contaminated net can acquire and spread diseases in this way. Before you buy, check that your dealer uses a separate net for each tank. To play safe, quarantine new purchases for 6 weeks in a special tank before putting with other fish. Keep a net and other aids for that tank only. Before ending the quarantine, study the fish closely in a good light.

many cheap, colorful, and undemanding species. Before you buy any fish check that it appears to be healthy and that the pet store's other tanks seem to be free from disease. Avoid the temptation of buying more fish than your bowl or tank can comfortably hold (see pages 183, 190, 198, 212). Take care, too, not to add aggressive species to a tank of fish they may kill or terrorize.

Aggressive fish Care must be taken when selecting different kinds of fish for inclusion in a mixed aquarium.

Some big or big-mouthed fish are bold and attractive, but if kept with smaller species will kill or bully them.

Aggressive fish that are best kept separately include the freshwater pike (**a**), most big freshwater tropical cichlids (**b**), and, among marine tropicals, the groupers and triggerfish (**c**).

Community fish Different kinds of fish look attractive in the same aquarium but care must be taken to select species that are compatible. Your dealer will help you with this. Examples of compatible groups include:
1 in cold fresh water, the koi, golden orfe, and goldfish;
2 in warm fresh water, toothed carp, catfish, and most of the characins;
3 in warm salt water, wrasses, damselfish, and butterfly fish.

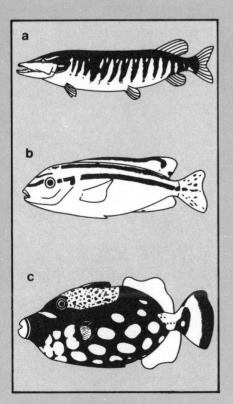

©DIAGRAM

181

Fisn ponds

A pond with fish and water plants is attractive in any garden. Common goldfish, shubunkins, golden orfe, and other hardy fish are likely to grow biggest, to live longest, and to breed if kept in a pond. Mix peaceful species of similar size: at least 2in (5cm). In a pond, tiny water animals, drowned insects, and plants including algae valuably supplement a fish-food diet.

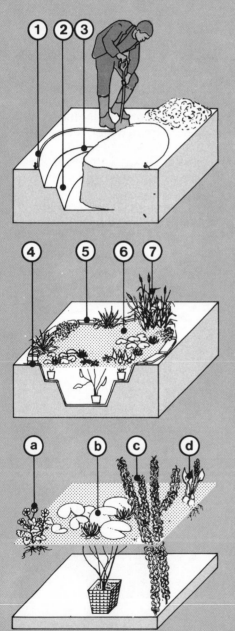

Making a pond Choose a fairly sunny site, not under trees. Choose a formal or informal shape. Mark it out (1), and then dig a hole (2) at least 2ft (60cm) deep, or 3ft (90cm) or more if winter ice is likely to be thick. Add a ledge (3) for shallow-water plants.

The pond is now ready to be waterproofed. Concrete or brick can be used for formal ponds. Pond liners are suitable for any shape of pond. Polythene lasts maybe 2 years; some plastics up to 10; butyl rubber indefinitely. Buy a liner big enough to fit the pond's contours. Lay the liner (4), checking that it rests on soil free from sharp stones. Weight the liner rim with paving stones (5). The next stage is to fill the pond with water (6). If filling pulls the liner rim inward, adjust the paving stones. Add plants (7). The pond should now be left for at least another week before the fish are added.

Pond plants provide fish with food and cover, absorb wastes, and help stop water turning green. Marginal plants, with only their roots submerged, include marsh marigolds (a). Water lilies (b) should be planted in wire or plastic baskets; if the pond is deep, place baskets on the ledge or on a mound of earth. *Elodea crispa* (c) thrives in 2ft (60cm) of water. Water hyacinth (d) is a warm-water floating plant.

Fish bowls

Many people keep fish in bowls, but great care is needed to prevent deaths from lack of oxygen or from foul water. A fish 1in (2.5cm) long, excluding tail, needs 1 US gal (3.8 l) of water. For a good oxygen supply, a broad-rimmed bowl should be full, a spherical one only half full. To keep water sweet, feed only what fish can eat in 5 minutes. Keep bowl away from windows and drafts.

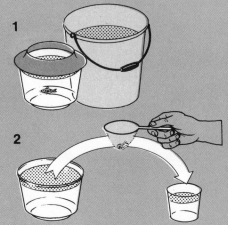

Cleaning out a bowl Body waste (some of it invisible) and any uneaten food soon make fish bowl water foul. Also the oxygen may be depleted. Fish in polluted water stop feeding, gulp air for lack of oxygen, and eventually die. To prevent this, clean out daily as shown, avoiding careless handling or sudden temperature change.

1 Stand a bucket of clean water by the bowl overnight for temperatures to equalize. Avoid buckets that have held cleaning agents or other chemicals.

2 A half hour after feeding, net or ladle the fish into a small jar filled from the bucket.

3 Empty the fish bowl; you may need to wipe the inside with a clean paper towel.

4 Refill the bowl with water from the bucket.

5 Gently return the fish.

©DIAGRAM

183

Fish tanks (1)

Tanks make the best indoor aquariums. The bigger the tank the more fish it holds and the more slowly its temperature varies; fish dislike swift temperature changes. Reckon capacity as length × width × height. If using inches, divide the answer by 1,728 to give cu ft: 1cu ft holds 7.8 US gal (29.5 l). But 1 cu ft of water weighs 62.5lb (28.4kg), so

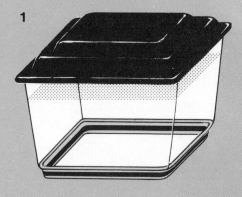

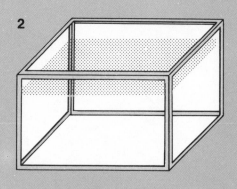

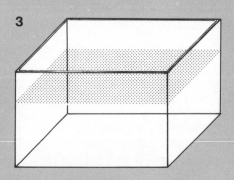

1 Plastic tanks Molded plastic tanks can make attractive small aquariums, some with curved fronts. They lack joints, thus cannot leak unless broken. Also they release no toxic substances in either fresh or salt water. But such tanks are seldom made large enough for use as marine aquariums. Removing algae from the sides presents a problem. Razor blades would scratch the plastic, and plastic scrapers are only partly effective.

2 Angle-iron tanks are made from five sheets of glass fixed by putty in a metal frame. They are strong but tend to rust, and leak if the putty shrinks and hardens. Leaks can be cured by drying the tank and squirting a sealant inside along the joints between the sheets of glass. Using an angle-iron tank for a marine aquarium calls for special treatment. To avoid corrosion, paint joints and metal surfaces with bitumastic paint.

3 All-glass tanks consist of glass sheets glued together by transparent silicone rubber sealant. Cheap, strong, nontoxic, corrosion free, and giving full visibility, they have become immensely popular. Stand them on polystyrene sheets to prevent the glass cracking.

be sure that the floor or shelf can bear a full tank.
Site your tank away from windows: big daily temperature
fluctuations are bad for fish, and daylight lets algae grow
fast and cloak the surfaces inside the tank. Every tank
needs a loose-fitting, nontoxic lid that lets in air but keeps
out dust, stops fish jumping out, and retards evaporation.

Setting up a tank Follow this sequence if including the devices shown on pages 186-187.
1 Clean the tank, thoroughly rinsing with water to remove all traces of any toxic chemicals.
2 Position the tank so the entire base rim is supported.
3 Install (disconnected) biological filter.
4 Wash and install gravel, sloping up to back of tank.
5 Install (disconnected) heater, thermostat, airstone, and mechanical filter.
6 To fill, pour water on a paper or plate laid on the gravel.
7 Add rocks and plants.
8 Connect heater to thermostat, getting expert help if necessary.
9 Similarly link filters and airstone to pump.
10 Add thermometer.
11 Install lighting.
12 Switch on heater, pump, and lights.
13 Add fish one week later.
(Also see pages 190, 198, 212.)

a

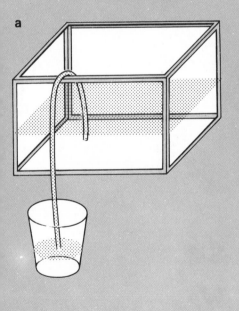

Cleaning a tank Wastes gather in any tank and must be removed. To remove dissolved wastes, many aquarists regularly change up to one-third of the water by siphoning (**a**). To siphon, fill a rubber tube with water. Pinch both ends. Hold one below water in the tank. Hold the other in a bucket at a lower level. Then release the pinched ends. Water flows from tank to bucket. (See also biological filter, p.186.) Solid wastes may be removed from a small tank by a dip tube sediment remover (**b**). Hold the narrow end, pressing one finger over the hole. Lower the funnel over your underwater target. Then lift the finger sealing the narrow tube. Waterborne sediment rushes into the broad tube. Reseal the top and remove the tube. Larger tanks may need a mechanical filter (p.186).

b

©DIAGRAM

Fish tanks (2)

Aeration Many aquarists fit aeration systems to their tanks. In such a system an electric pump (**a**) forces air down through a tube (**b**) that opens under water. The air passes through a porous diffuser stone (**c**) that breaks it into tiny bubbles. Some air from the bubbles dissolves in the water, thus adding to the dissolved oxygen available for fish to breathe. Meanwhile the bubbles cause water in the tank to circulate (**d**), so the oxygen-starved water near the bottom rises to the top, where oxygen can enter from the air above. Because an aerated tank holds more dissolved oxygen than an unaerated tank, you can stock it with more fish without the risk of suffocating them. But avoid overcrowding as this can lead to outbreaks of disease.

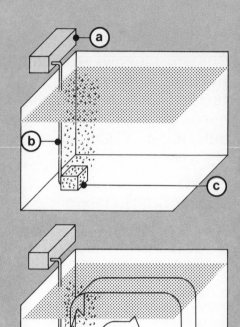

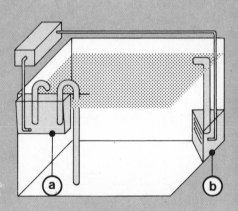

d

Filters do a vital cleaning job in tanks. They come in two main types — mechanical and biological — each powered by an electrically operated pump. Both types are valuable in the same tank.

Mechanical filters chiefly remove solid bits of body waste, uneaten food, and rotting plants. An external filter (**a**) is clipped outside the tank; an internal filter (**b**) sits in one corner of it. In both devices tank water passes through layers of nylon wool and charcoal: the wool traps solid wastes, the charcoal absorbs noxious gases.

Biological filters rid tanks of harmful dissolved salts. A biological filter (**c**) draws water down through gravel where bacteria turn harmful wastes to substances that aquarium plants can use for food.

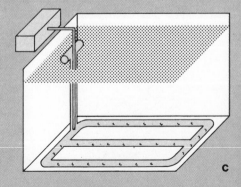

c

Lighting Well-lit tanks show up fish attractively and permit plant growth. A 2ft (61cm) tank needs two 40-watt bulbs (**a**) or better still one 20-watt warm white or Gro-Lux fluorescent tube (**b**). House either system in a metal reflector. Illuminate no more than 12 hours daily.

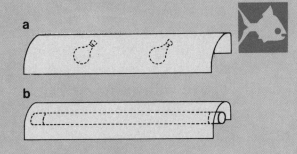

Heaters Tanks for tropical fish must be heated to around 75°F(24°C). Most heaters are wire elements sealed in glass or plastic tubes (**a**) or in flexible rubber (**b**). The first type is laid above the gravel, the other is buried. Use one 100-watt heater for every 24 US gals (90 l) of water in a normally heated room, or a 150-watt heater in a chilly room. You will also need a thermostat and thermometer (see below).

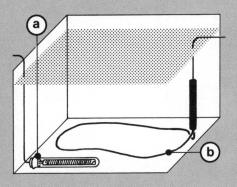

Thermostats control tank temperature. They are wired in series with a heater. A thermostat contains a bimetallic strip. As the strip cools it contracts and bends, completing an electric circuit, and thus switching on the heater. As the strip warms it expands, breaks the circuit, and switches off the heater. Thermostats are adjustable. Some thermostats are housed in a tube (**a**) that is clipped upright in the tank. An external thermostat (**b**) clips to the outside of the tank. It is also possible to buy a heater-thermostat combined in a protective tube casing.

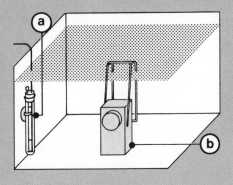

Thermometers allow the tank temperature to be checked. Possible types are a digital thermometer (**c**), one worked by a bimetallic strip (**d**), or a mercury thermometer (**e**).

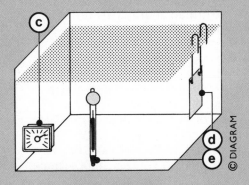

© DIAGRAM

187

Water preparation

A fish's health depends largely on the water that it lives in. Water from a storage tank may be toxic, and fresh tapwater may hold poisonous amounts of chlorine. Let tapwater stand for some days before adding fish. Top up from time to time with boiled, distilled, or demineralized water. Check water hardness, acidity, and, for marine and brackish water fish, salinity.

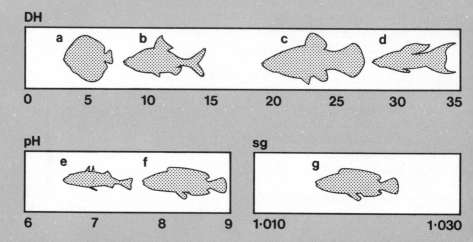

DH
0 5 10 15 20 25 30 35

pH
6 7 8 9

sg
1·010 1·030

Hard or soft? Water rich in dissolved calcium salts is hard. Some tapwater is very hard. Water low in calcium is soft. Distilled, demineralized, and pure rain water are soft. Hardness and softness can be measured in one of several ways, based on the amount of calcium carbonate in water. One method gives grains per gallon in so-called Clark degrees. Another simply gives parts per million. A third gives parts per 100,000 in German degrees of hardness (DH). You can buy kits to help you measure water hardness. Most freshwater fish are not fussy about hardness. The following are examples with a strong preference:
a discus like soft water (0-5DH);
b tiger barb, medium (5-15DH);
c platies, hard (15-30DH);
d mollies, very hard (30DH plus).

Acid or alkaline? Water rich in rotting plants tends to be acid; water rich in calcium carbonate or bicarbonate tends to be alkaline. Kits help you to measure alkalinity or acidity in pH units based on the number of hydrogen ions in water. Below pH7 is acid, above is alkaline. Most freshwater fish (**e**) tolerate 6.4-7.5; marines (**f**) need 8.0-8.3. Sodium bicarbonate will raise pH; potassium dihydrogen orthophosphate will lower it.

Fresh or salt? Most fish are not able to survive in both fresh and salt water. For marines dissolve special salt in tapwater. Measure "saltiness" with a hydrometer, which shows specific gravity (s.g.). A reading of 1.019-1.025 suits most marine species (**g**). (Also see p.212.)

Breeding fish

Marine fish rarely breed in captivity. But freshwater species often do. Goldfish and other coldwater fish will spawn in spring and summer in a well planted pond, where at least some fry should survive and grow. Many tropical freshwater fish will spawn in tanks. For best results put a sexed pair conditioned by live foods into a prepared tank containing no other fish.

Breeding freshwater tropicals
Many livebearers breed quite readily. A plastic mesh breeding trap (**a**) or dense plant cover will help fry to escape their parents' jaws.

To breed egglayers it is a good idea to separate a sexed pair for a week, and then put them in a breeding tank at a degree or two above normal.

Different types of egglayer need different conditions. To stop danios eating their eggs, spawn them over a breeding trap (**a**) or over pebbles or marbles (**b**). Barbs will spawn on weighted nylon mops. Suspend mops (**c**) for egg-hanging toothcarp like *Panchax*. Floating plants such as *Riccia* (**d**) will anchor the bubble nests of anabantid species. With the exception of cichlids and anabantids, both parents should be removed from the breeding tank after spawning.

Feeding young Livebearers can eat powdered dried food soon after birth. Also feed them small live invertebrates. Feed young egglayers infusoria — tiny organisms including *Euglena* and *Paramecium*. These can be obtained by adding tank water and crushed lettuce to jars of water. Keep the jars at 76°F (24°C) for 2 days. Feed fry half a jar of this water twice daily. Larger fry will take brine shrimps and microworms. (Also see pp.228-231.)

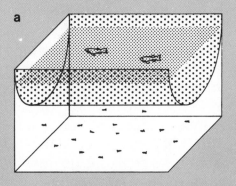

a

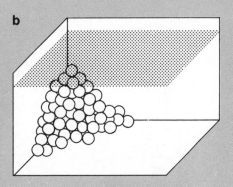

b

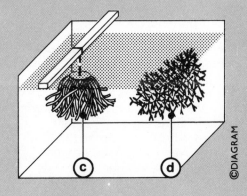

c d

©DIAGRAM

Keeping coldwater fish

Goldfish are the most commonly kept coldwater fish, but some fish caught in the wild are also suitable (p.196). Goldfish are unfussy about pH or hardness (p.188) or temperature. But some coldwater fish need room heat; others need cool conditions. People house coldwater fish in bowls, tanks, or ponds (pp.182-187). A bowl holds only one or two fish, which will never grow to full size. Tanks offer more scope. A tank 2ft x 1ft 3in x 1ft (61cm x 38cm x 30cm) will take four goldfish each 3in (7.6cm) long. Provide a pump to work an airstone and a biological and/or mechanical filter (p.186). Light by indirect daylight, or artificially (p.187). Hardy fish thrive best in a pond; goldfish may live as many as 20 years. If winters are cold the pond must be deep enough for the fish to winter under the ice. Fancy goldfish do not generally make good pond fish as they need about 60°F (16°C). Nor are fish with dark backs suitable since they do not show up well. Netting will stop cats and herons stealing pond fish and also prevent dead leaves from fouling the water.

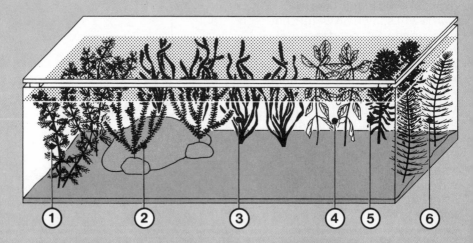

Furnished coldwater aquarium
Plan a natural appearance, grouping rocks and plants to hide tubing etc. Plants help to absorb fishes' body wastes and produce some of the oxygen that fish need to breathe. Spread the roots and cover with gravel, which should have a diameter of ¼ - ³⁄₈in(0.6-1cm). If necessary weigh down with a rock or stone — never with lead. Do not include water snails — they produce waste, and may damage leaves. Suitable plants include:
1 *Myriophylum*; **2** willow moss;
3 *Vallisneria*; **4** *Ludwigia*;
5 *Egeria*; **6** hornwort.

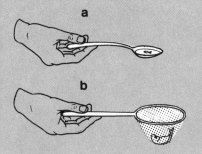

a

b

Handling To transfer from one container to another, use a spoon or ladle for fry (**a**) or a fine-mesh net for fish (**b**). Do not hold a fish in your hand: you may remove the mucus that coats its body, protecting the skin from tiny disease organisms in the water. Transport fish in a leakproof container. On a long trip open the lid from time to time to prevent suffocation. Avoid sudden temperature changes (see p.199 for acclimatization.)

Feeding Provide fish with as much variety as possible. You can buy dried or frozen foods in the form of flakes, pellets, pastes, crumbs, and powder. The finer forms are better suited to small fish. Do not rely too much on starchy biscuit foods. Fish need protein, vitamins, and minerals much as people do. The best source of nourishment is live food such as earthworms, mosquito larvae, and *Daphnia*. Young goldfish can be raised on *Daphnia, Tubifex*, fruit flies, microworms, and brine shrimp — obtainable from dealers. Feed fish three times a day, limiting dried food to what can be eaten in about 2 minutes. Pond fish need little or no feeding in cold winter months. In summer, healthy fish can be left unfed during a 2-week vacation (also see p.199).

Diseases include the following:
1 Skin fluke (fluffy coat and scratching). Daily for 4 days put fish into a US qt (0.9 l) jar of water, adding 10 drops of formaldehyde per minute for 10 minutes.
2 Gill fluke (swollen gills, gasping). Treat as skin fluke.
3 Fish louse (green parasite). Bathe 15 minutes in potassium permanganate solution (weak).
4 Dropsy (bloated body, scale edges jut out roughly). No cure.
5 Anchor worm (pale, projecting

parasite). Remove. Cleanse tank.
6 Ich/white spot (white spots on body and fins). For 1 week bathe in 5 drops of 5% methylene blue per US gal (3.8 l) water.
7 Fungus (cottony patches). Bathe for 1 week in 1 teaspoon salt to 3 US qt (2.8 l) water.
8 Fin rot (eroded fins). Bathe for 5 minutes in solution of 8 potassium permanganate crystals per 3 US qt (2.8 l) water. Cut off rotted fin. Apply 5% methylene blue to remainder.

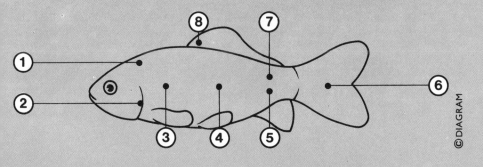

©DIAGRAM

Colored coldwater fish (1)

Red, yellow, and other showy fish of the minnow family (Cyprinidae) have long been popular for indoor bowls and tanks or outdoor pools. All are domesticated, colored varieties of relatively drab wild fish. They include the golden orfe, golden rudd, and golden tench. But easily most popular are the goldfish and the fancy forms derived from it. Goldfish have been prized in China for at least 1,000

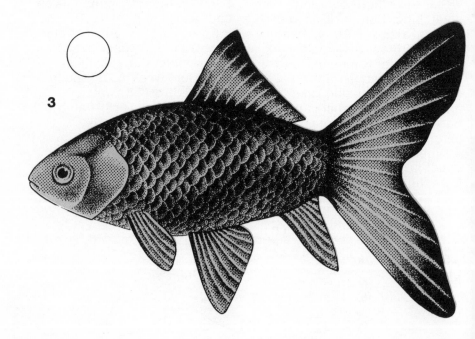

years. Selective breeding from the basic goldfish stock has produced a number of distinctive types, including the comet goldfish and shubunkins pictured on these two pages, also the 10 fancy goldfish illustrated on the next two pages. These last are all in fact deformed, and are thus less hardy and more vulnerable to predators than ordinary goldfish.

1 Golden orfe *(Leuciscus idus)* Europe; 1ft (30.5cm) or more; orange; hardy pond fish; feed fish food, worms, etc.

2 Koi carp *(Cyprinus carpio)* E. Asia; 1ft (30.5cm) or more; white, orange, black, etc; a hardy pond fish preferring soft, slightly acid water at 68°F (20°C); give fish food, worms, etc.

3 Comet USA; a long-finned common goldfish; 1ft (30.5cm) or more; a hardy pond fish.

4 Goldfish *(Carassius auratus)*

E. Asia; up to 1ft (30.5cm); gold, gold and black, gold and white, etc; undemanding; hardy; a good pond fish; feed fish food, worms, etc; pond fish may spawn in weedy, shallow water.

5 Bristol shubunkin E. Asia; a "scaleless," multicolored (calico) form of comet goldfish; less hardy than common goldfish.

6 London shubunkin E. Asia; a "scaleless," multicolored form of common goldfish; hardy.

© DIAGRAM

Colored coldwater fish (2)

1 Ribbontail/fantail E. Asia; double-tailed goldfish with short body and longish fins.

2 Veiltail/twintail E. Asia; double-tailed goldfish with long fins, high dorsal, square-cut tail; rather delicate.

3 Globe-eye/telescope E. Asia; double-tailed, short-bodied goldfish with protruding eyes and long fins.

4 Black Moor E. Asia; a preferably black, globe-eye goldfish; some go gold with age.

5 Pearl scale E. Asia; double-tailed, short-bodied, with short fins and convex scales like hemispherical pearls.

6 Oranda E. Asia; double-tailed, short-bodied, with long fins and a "hood" of puffy skin.

7 Bramblehead/lionhead E. Asia; double-tailed, with short fins and body, a big, warty "hood," and no dorsal fin.

8 Pom-pon E. Asia; double-tailed, shortish fins and body, nasal outgrowths, no dorsal.

9 Celestial E. Asia; double-tailed, with protruding, upturned eyes and no dorsal; delicate.

10 Bubble-eye E. Asia; double-tailed, with short body and fins, no dorsal, and large, fluid-filled sacs below the eyes; a very delicate variety.

Wild coldwater fish

Some of the fish that live in the streams or pools of North America and Europe make fascinating and unusual inmates of a coldwater aquarium. You can catch many by rod and line, or, better, by net to avoid risk of injury. Dealers sell some wild coldwater species, for instance black-banded sunfish, bullheads, medakas, and bitterling. But most species never reach pet stores.

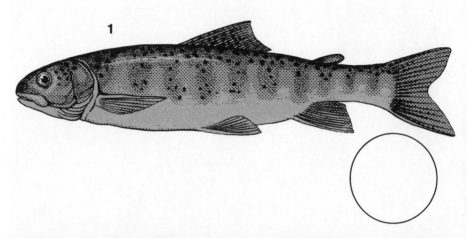

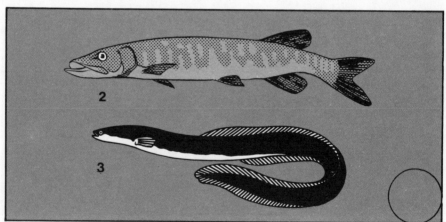

1 Rainbow trout *(Salmo gairdnerii)* N.W. North America; limit to 5in (13cm); darkly marked; aerated water below 70°F (21°C); feed worms, *Daphnia,* etc.

2 Pike *(Esox lucius)* Northern continents; limit to 6in (15cm); green-gray with pale spots; keep alone in aerated tank; feed small fish, worms, chopped raw meat.

3 Eel *(Anguilla* species) N. continents; limit to 8in (20cm); use aerated, closely covered tank; feed worms, small water animals, raw meat, etc.

4 Three-spined stickleback *(Gasterosteus aculeatus)* N. continents; 3in (8cm); green and

The fish on these two pages, or closely similar kinds, occur in all northern continents, and give an idea of the variety available. Keep only young fish of species that grow large as adults. As with tropical fish, beware of mixing other fish with predators unless they are intended as food. Fish from streams may need cool, strongly aerated, and frequently changed water.

silvery, males crimson-throated in spring; feed live *Daphnia*, chopped earthworms.

5 Stone loach *(Noemacheilus barbatulus)* Europe; 4in (10cm); yellowish, brown patches; feed worms, small water animals.

6 Bullhead (*Ameiurus* species) USA; limit to 6in (15cm); brown and yellow; worms, raw meat.

7 Black-banded fish *(Enneacanthus chaetodon)* E. USA; 4in (10cm); pale with dark bars; hardy; give live foods.

8 Perch (*Perca* species) Eurasia and N. America; limit to 5in (13cm); yellowish, dark bars; feed worms, maggots, raw meat.

Keeping tropical freshwater fish

Tropical freshwater fish are comparatively straightforward to keep. Up to 15 of these colorful fish 1¼-2in (3-5cm) long can be kept in a tank 24x15x12in (61x38x30cm). Many pet stores have scores of kinds to choose from, but take care to put only compatible species in a community tank. Any of several types of tank is suitable (p.184). You also need a heater, thermostat, thermometer, and some form of artificial lighting (p.187). Most aquarists use a pump to operate an airstone (bubbler) and mechanical and/or biological filter (p.186). Many freshwater tropicals are unfussy about the hardness and pH of the water (p.188). But let tapwater stand before use. For most species aim at a temperature around 75°F (24°C). A daily fluctuation of 5°F (2.8°C) may be beneficial. A drop to 65°F (15.6°C) or a rise to 90°F (32°C) can kill, especially if prolonged. Constant high temperatures also cause feverish activity and shorten life. (Most tropical fish live several years, but some "annual" toothcarp or killifish — described on p.206 — last only for a year or so.

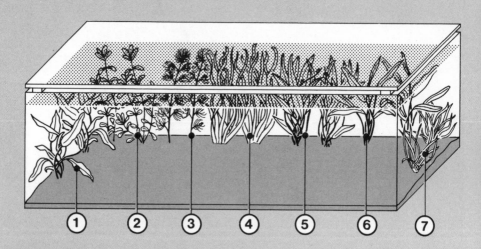

Furnished tropical aquarium
Design is basically like that of a coldwater aquarium (p.190). Include plants, gravel, and rocks. Arrange rather like the wings and backcloth of a stage set. Group all but big specimen plants in clumps or groves. Put thermostat and heater at opposite ends and hide them behind the rocks and plants. The tank illustrated above includes:
1 *Cryptocoryne affinis;*
2 *Hygrophila;* 3 *Cabomba;*
4 *Vallisneria spiralis;*
5 Amazon sword plant;
6 *Cryptocoryne nevilli;*
7 *Echinodorus tenellus.*

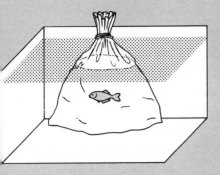

Feeding Feed little and often, varying the diet. Buy dried foods or use dry cat food and flaked baby food. As far as possible provide most fish with live foods. But herbivorous fish such as *Plecostomus* need algae to browse on. *Tubifex* worms, *Daphnia* (water fleas), mosquito larvae, and bloodworms are all valuable foods. Most you can get in ponds or buy from dealers. But such foods may introduce disease. Safer sources of live food include white (enchytraeid) worms, brine shrimps, and fruit flies. (Also see pp.228-231.) If live foods are scarce, try chopped shrimp, flaked, cooked fish, or cod roe, hard-boiled egg yolk, and, for mollies, wheat germ.
For a short vacation leave fish unfed or provide with a long-lasting vacation block or jelly lump.

Handling To prevent chance injury, transfer tropicals by net or spoon as you would for coldwater fish (p.191). When buying new fish take care to prevent chilling on the way home. Pack old woolen clothing or newspaper around the fish's plastic bag and place in a large bag or box. At home, float the sealed plastic bag in your tank for 10 minutes to equalize temperatures. Then slit open the bag to release the fish.

Diseases Freshwater tropicals share some of the diseases also found in other freshwater and marine fish species.
1 Fin rot (fins eroded). Put in weak acriflavin solution.
2 Ich (white spots). Raise temperature to 82°F (28°C) and treat as described on p.191. Leave planted tanks untreated but empty of fish for 10 days.
3 Velvet (gold spots). Treat as ich. Isolate. Sterilize tank.
4 Flukes (slimy fins, gaping gills). Keep 3 days in deep blue methylene blue solution.
5 Fungus (see p.191). Isolate fish. Paint daily with 5% methylene blue until cured.
6 Air bladder troubles (fish cannot rise or sink properly). Place in shallow water.
7 Wasting. May be due to a tumor or old age.
8 Shimmying (swimming without progress). May be due to indigestion or to hard water.
9 Dropsy. (See p.191.)

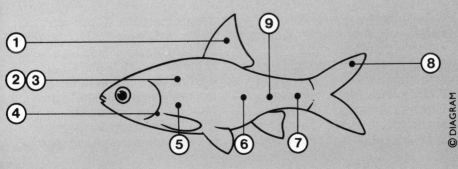

Characins

Many aquarium fish belong to the large Characidae family. Most of its several hundred species come from Central and South America although characins are also found in Africa and southern North America. Characins lack barbels. They have toothed jaws, and most have an adipose fin — a small, rayless fin between the tail and dorsal fin.

They range in size from big, ferocious piranhas to the little

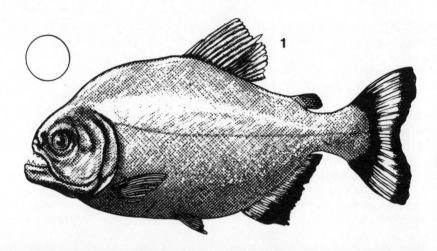

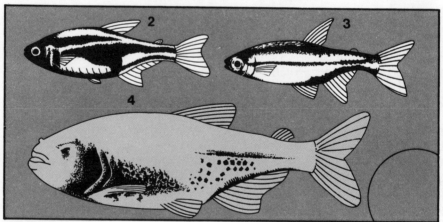

1 Red piranha *(Serrasalmus nattereri)* S. America; 9in (23cm); silvery with red breast; 77°F (25°C); feed live food; can bite top off a finger.
2 Neon tetra *(Paracheirodon innesi)* S. America; 1½in (4cm); red band and "neon" stripe; likes soft water at 71°F (22°C).

3 Cardinal tetra *(Cheirodon axelrodi)* S. America; 1½in (4cm); brilliant blue and red; likes water at pH 6-7 and 79°F (26°C).
4 Blind cave characin *(Astyanax jordani)* Mexico; 3½in (9cm); pinkish; eyes under skin; 70°F (21°C); omnivorous.
5 Serpa tetra *(Hyphessobrycon*

neon tetra. All are predatory and should therefore be given animal food as far as possible. Characins tend to live in running water and swim in shoals.

Many will spawn in subdued light in a tank of soft (eg rain) water, with fine-leaved plants, and floored by coarse sphagnum. Remove parents. Feed fry infusoria five days after hatching. Aerate water gently at eight days.

serpae) S. America; 1¾ in (4.5cm); reddish; soft or hard water at pH 6-7 and 76°F (24°C); feed live and dried foods.

6 Bleeding heart tetra
(Hyphessobrycon rubrostigma) S. America; 2¼ in (6cm); silvery and reddish; keep as serpa.

7 Black-line tetra
(Hyphessobrycon scholzei) S. America; 2in (5cm); greenish and silvery with black stripe; keep as serpa tetra.

8 Glowlight tetra
(Hemigrammus gracilis) S. America; 1½ in (3.8cm) greenish with an iridescent gold stripe; keep as serpa tetra.

Minnows

This family of some 1,500 species of fish is larger than any other. Barbs, carps, and minnows all belong to it. Tropical Africa and southern Asia are its chief centers, but the Cyprinidae includes many well-known North American and European species (see also pp. 192-195). All these fish have teeth in the throat but not in the jaws. Many have barbels. They lack an adipose fin.

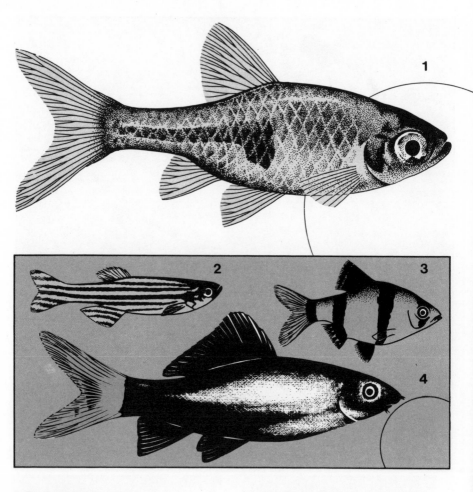

1 Red rasbora *(Rasbora heteromorpha)* S.E. Asia; 1¾ in (4.5cm); silvery gray with dark wedge; care as serpa (p. 200); spawns on *Cryptocorynes*.
2 Zebra danio *(Brachydanio rerio)* E. India; 2in (5cm); blue/gold stripes; keep in hard water at 73°F (23°C); spawns

easily (supply coarse gravel).
3 Tiger barb *(Barbus tetrazona)* S.E. Asia; 2¼ in (6cm); golden with black bands, red on fins; pH 6.9 at 73°F (23°C).
4 Red-tailed black shark *(Labeo bicolor)* Thailand; 4¾ in (12cm); black, tail red; pH 6.7; 76°F (24°C); adults aggressive.

Labyrinth fish

These Southeast Asian and African fish often live in oxygen-starved water. Lung-like labyrinthine structures above the gill cavities help them breathe atmospheric air and thus obtain extra oxygen. Some experts place all in one family, the Anabantidae. Others group them in several families. Most males build surface bubble nests and guard eggs and fry until the fry are free-swimming.

1 Paradise fish (*Macropodus opercularis*) E. Asia; 3½ in (9cm); stands 59°F (15°C); breeds at 75°F (24°C); males aggressive when breeding.

2 Dwarf gourami (*Colisa lalia*) India; 2in (5cm); males striped red and blue-green; 75°F (24°C); undemanding; unaggressive.

3 Siamese fighting fish (*Betta splendens*) S.E. Asia; 2½ in (6cm); red or blue; 77°F (25°C); undemanding; safe with other species; keep males apart.

4 Pearl gourami (*Trichogaster leerii*) S.E. Asia; 4¼ in (11cm); light brown, pale pearly spots; 75°F (24°C); undemanding.

Catfish and loaches

These popular names cover fish of several dozen families, chiefly bottom feeders.

Many catfish have a big head, cat-like "whiskers" to help sense food, a downward-opening mouth, and a naked or armored body without true scales. There are more than 30 families worldwide, but more than half of the total 2,000 species are South American. Strange shapes and unusual

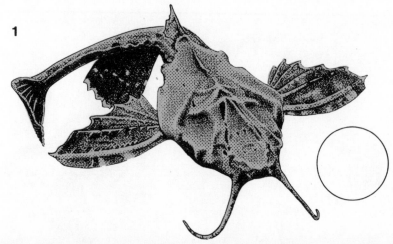

1 Banjo catfish (*Bunocephalus* species) S. America; 6in(15cm); brown; 73°F(23°C); omnivorous; burrows in sand by day.

2 Glass catfish (*Kryptopterus bicirrhis*) S.E. Asia; 4in(10cm); transparent; 73°F(23°C); keep in a shoal; give live food.

3 Leopard corydoras (*Corydoras*

julii) S. America; 3in(8cm); has bony armor; gray-green with bluish squiggles; 75°F(24°C); omnivorous; fine gravel floor.

4 Upside down catfish (*Synodontis nigriventris*) Africa; 2¾in(7cm); brown; swims upside down; 75°F(24°C); algae.

5 Plecostomus (species) S.

habits make catfish intriguing creatures to keep.
Loaches (family Cobitidae) are Old World fish with
generally tiny scales; tiny eyes under transparent skin; a
small head; and three or more pairs of barbels. Most
loaches are easy to keep but seldom breed.
The Chinese algae eater included here is not a true loach: it
is related to the minnow family (Cyprinidae).

America; 10in (25cm); brownish;
sucker mouth; 72°F (22°C);
needs rocks; algae eater.

6 Kuhli loach
(Acanthophthalmus species)
S.E. Asia; 3in (8cm); chocolate
and yellow; soft water, pH 6.9;
77°F (25°C); sandy floor;
omnivorous; nocturnal.

7 Clown loach *(Botia
macracantha)* S.E. Asia; 12in
(30cm); orange and black; 80°F
(27°C); sandy floor; omnivorous.

8 Chinese algae eater
(Gyrinocheilus aymonieri)
Thailand; 12in (30cm); brown,
silvery, with dark marks; 77°F
(25°C); superb algae eater.

Egg-laying toothcarp

Also called killifish, these members of the Cyprindontidae have a wide distribution. Many ("seasonals" or "annuals") are shortlived. Give hard, neutral water floored with boiled sphagnum moss, not sand. When annuals spawn, dry the moss at room heat; store for a month or more at 75°F (24°C); put moss in rainwater at 72°F (22°C) to hatch eggs. Other killifish eggs hatch in water in 2-4 weeks.

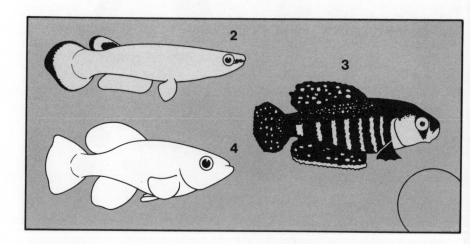

1 Blue gularis (*Aphyosemion coeruleum*) W. Africa; 4in(10cm); brown, green, blue, and yellow; a lyretail; nonseasonal; 72°F (22°C); live and dried food.
2 Blue panchax (*Aplocheilus panchax*) S. and S.E. Asia; 3in (8cm); yellow-gray; nonseasonal; 73°F (23°C); feed live food.

3 Argentine pearl fish (*Cynolebias nigripinnis*); 2¾in (7cm); male blue-black; seasonal; 70°F (21°C); live and dried food.
4 Guenther's notho (*Nothobranchius guentheri*) Africa; 2¾in (7cm); male blue, red, green, yellow; seasonal; 72°F (22°C); live and dried food.

Live-bearing toothcarp

Fish: tropical

Members of the Poeciliidae, live-bearing carp thrive in warm, sunny, weedy pools in the American tropics and subtropics. Most like slightly hard, alkaline water. Many are easy to keep and breed. (Hybridization has produced great variations in color and finnage.) Males have slim, pointed anal fins. Newborn young are larger than egg-layers' newly hatched fry, but some parents eat them.

1 Swordtail (*Xiphophorus helleri*) C. America; 5in (13cm); green, red, albino, etc; 75°F (24°C); omnivorous, eats algae.
2 Platy (*Xiphophorus maculatus*) C. America; female 2¼ in (6cm); black, red, yellow, etc; keep as swordtail.
3 Molly (*Poecilia* hybrid) C. America; 4in (10cm); black; hard, alkaline water at 79°F (26°C); 1tsp salt per gallon (2.6 liters); eats algae, etc.
4 Guppy (*Poecilia reticulata*) C. and S. America; female 2¼ in (6cm), drab; tiny male colorful and long-finned; 72°F (22°C); omnivorous; prolific breeder.

Cichlids

Cichlids comprise some 1,000 species, chiefly from Africa and the Americas. Many strongly defend a chosen area. Some large cichlids are aggressive and unsuitable to put with other fish, but smaller species, known as dwarf cichlids, are generally safe in a community tank. Cichlids are chiefly carnivorous and need live foods, raw roe, or chopped, raw meat. Most species have no special water

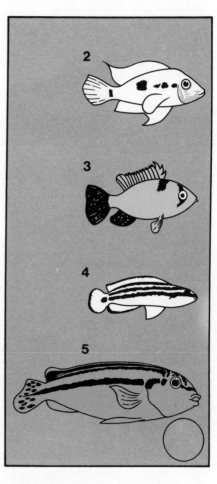

1 Angel fish *(Pterophyllum scalare)* S. America; 5½ in (14cm); silver and black, plus variant strains; 75°F (24°C); likes a well-planted tank; docile.

2 Firemouth cichlid *(Cichlasoma meeki)* C. America; 3in (7.6cm); blue-gray with orange-red belly; 72°F (22°C).

3 Ramirez's dwarf cichlid *(Apistogramma ramirezi)* S. America; 2¾in (7cm); yellow, reddish, and blue; soft water; pH 6.8; 75°F (24°C); docile.

4 Julie *(Julidochromis ornatus)* Africa; 2¾in (7cm); creamy and blackish; hard water at pH 8; 75°F (24°C); mix with similar.

requirements. Those that uproot plants should be given only rocks and gravel.

Breeding many cichlids is easy. Some lay eggs on exposed rocks or leaves, others in crevices. Eggs and young are guarded by one or both parents (but beware cannibalism). Females of the mouth-brooding types lay eggs, then store them in their mouths until they hatch.

5 Golden mbuna
(Melanochromis auratus) Africa; 4¾ in (12cm); medium-hard water at pH 8; an aggressive mouth brooder.
6 Discus *(Symphysodon* species) S. America; brownish or bluish, patterned; very soft water, pH 6.5; 82°F (28°C); keep alone.

7 Blue acara *(Aequidens pulcher)* S. and C. America; 6¾ in (17cm); violet to purple-red; 77°F (25°C); keep with cichlids.
8 Oscar *(Astronotus ocellatus)* S. America; 13in (33cm); chocolate and reddish; 73°F (23°C); keep with firemouths but not plants.

Other tropical freshwater fish

Some tropical freshwater fish of various families have strange shapes, colors, or behavior. Their pecularities make these oddballs attractive to aquarists.

Eight such fish appear on these pages. The leaf fish mimics a dead leaf, and can snap up fish more than half its own size. The hatchet fish can fly by beating its pectoral fins, and glide 20ft (6m). The Indian glassfish is almost

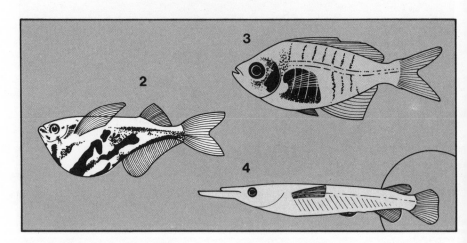

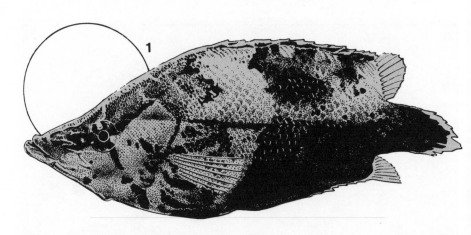

1 Leaf fish *(Monocirrhus polyacanthus)* S. America; 3¼ in (8.3cm); brown; soft water at pH 6.5; 74°F (23°C); live food.

2 Marbled hatchet fish *(Carnegiella strigata)* S. America; 1¾ in (4.5cm); purple and yellow; soft water at pH 6.4; 81°F (27°C); give flies.

3 Indian glassfish *(Chanda ranga)* S. Asia; 2in (5cm); translucent; hard, alkaline water with 1 tsp salt per US gal (4l); 71°F (22°C); live food.

4 Halfbeak *(Dermogenys pusillus)* S.E. Asia; 2¾ in (7cm); silvery; hard water plus sea salt; 68°F (20°C); livebearer; feed flies.

transparent. The halfbeak's long, fixed lower jaw forms part of a living flytrap. The freshwater butterfly fish makes acrobatic leaps to catch insects. A sensitive "trunk" helps the mormyrid probe for its food. The spiny eel's long, slim, sharp-snouted body helps it to burrow and hide. The striped anostomus is a fish with the strange habit of swimming and resting head downward.

5 Butterfly fish *(Pantodon buchholzi)* W. Africa; 6in (15cm); brownish; soft, just acid water; 80°F (27°C); feed insects at surface; somewhat aggressive.

6 Elephant-nosed mormyrid *(Gnathonemus tamandua)* Africa; 5in (13cm); brown and gray; 77°F (25°C); omnivorous.

7 Spiny eel *(Macrognathus aculeatus)* S.E. Asia; 6in (15cm); brown; 75°F (24°C); deep sand, well planted; live food.

8 Striped anostomus *(Anostomus anostomus)* S. America; 6½in (17cm); black, cream, red; softish water; 77°F (25°C); omnivorous.

©DIAGRAM

Keeping marine fish

Gaily colored marine tropicals are immensely attractive but trickier to keep than freshwater species. Beware costly "difficult" species. Allow at least 2 US gallons (7.6 liters) of water per 1 in (2.5 cm) of fish, and use an all-glass tank (p. 184) of at least 20 US gallons (75.6 liters) capacity. Do not allow water to touch metal. Make synthetic sea water by adding prepared sea-salt mixture to tapwater in plastic buckets. Aerate, and leave until any chlorine in the water is lost. You will need a heater-thermostat, thermometer, and a powerful pump to work an airstone and undergravel filter (p. 186). Mechanical filters and costly protein skimmers and ozonizers are not vital. Illuminate with a fluorescent tube (p. 187) to prevent overheating surface water. Keep most marine tropicals at 75°F (24°C); pH 8.0-8.3; and s.g. 1.019-1.025 (see p. 188). Check readings daily. Specific gravity can be adjusted with buffering solutions. Beware cloudy, smelly, frothy water. Change up to one-third of the water monthly. Any changes in conditions must be slow.

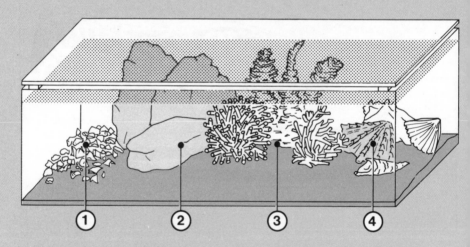

Furnished marine aquarium
Use limestone rock, coral, and shells to decorate, give fish cover, and help keep the water alkaline. First steep shells and dead corals in bleach solution for 3 days; wash under tap for 1 hour; then boil for 2 hours in an enameled saucepan. Soak rocks in salt water and check pH etc before adding to tank. Design the tank as described on p. 190. (See p. 232 if including marine invertebrates.) The tank above includes:
1 crushed shell and coral gravel;
2 limestone rocks; 3 dead coral;
4 sea shells.

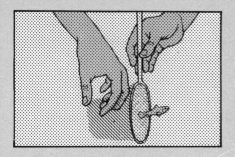

Handling Transfer marine fish by net (never by hand, for the reasons given on p.191). Carry from pet store to home and release in tank as described for freshwater tropicals (p.199). But transport and release marines in dim light or darkness. Disturbance can prostrate and even kill marine fish, so handle as little as possible. If a new fish lies distressed at first, do not prod it or tap the glass. Leave quietly alone to recover.

Feeding Feed little and often especially in a tank less than 3 months old: denitrifying bacteria are too few to transform harmful wastes into harmless nitrates. Quickly remove uneaten food. Feed foods to match mouth size. Many fish take dried food but live or raw food is better. Useful live foods are prawns, shrimps, and sandhoppers; also (non-marine) earthworms, white worms, mosquito larvae, young guppies, *Daphnia,* and *Tubifex.* You can also feed crab, lobster, and mussel flesh, raw fish, and roe. But marine and freshwater live foods both have their snags: marine foods may harbor disease; freshwater live foods soon die when placed in salt water. Also note special food needs, eg tangs like vegetable matter. Some fish never adapt well to a substitute aquarium diet.

Diseases Some of the diseases of marine fish differ from those of freshwater fish (see pp.191 and 199). Certain diseases show up in poor conditions. Check water purity etc frequently.
1 *Oodinium* (grayish cysts cover body; rapid breathing). Treat with commercially available cure such as "Cuprazin."
2 *Lymphocystis* (cysts due to viral infection). Cut off cysts and brush wounds with 1% acriflavin solution.

3 Body rot. Kill responsible bacteria with a solution of acriflavin or mercurochrome.
4 Fin rot. Treat as body rot.
5 Fungus (see p.191). If you have an ozonizer, pump ozonized air through water for a day or so to cure *Saprolegnia* fungus.
6 Ich (white spots). See p.191. Treat with "Cuprazin" or another Oodinium cure.
7 *Benedenia* (triangular parasites on body). Treat with "Cuprazin" or similar.

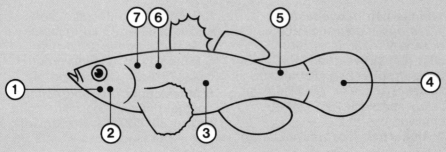

© DIAGRAM

Brackish-water fish

Some fish can live in brackish coastal waters, for at least part of their lives. Those tropical species shown here make good aquarium subjects. The Asian puffer fish and mudskipper like brackish or fresh water. Young scats and fingerfish will thrive in fresh water, but those above 2in (5cm) may need a marine aquarium. Archer fish will live in fresh, brackish, or salt water.

1 Fingerfish *(Monodactylus argenteus)* Indian and Pacific oceans; 9in (23cm); silvery; 80°F (27°C); live/dried food.
2 Asian puffer fish *(Tetraodon fluviatilis)* S.E. Asia; 7¾in(19.7cm); yellow and black; 75°F (24°C); omnivorous.
3 Archer fish *(Toxotes jaculator)*

S.E. Asia; 9½in (24cm); silvery and dark; 80°F (27°C); insects.
4 Scat *(Scatophagus argus)* S.E.Asia; 11½in (30cm), green, black; 75°F (24°C); live food.
5 Mudskipper *(Periophthalmus* species) Indian Ocean; 6in (15cm); brown; 80°F(27°C); 2in(5cm) of water with sand, rocks, worms etc.

Coldwater marine fish

Fish: brackish; marine

Many interesting fish and invertebrates (p.232) live in cool offshore waters. At low tide, a hunt in rock pools may reveal slim-bodied fish squeezed in crannies. A shrimping net thrust through sands of the lower shore may catch a flatfish. Such creatures can be kept in a cool, well-aerated marine aquarium. But any that show signs of discomfort should be quickly freed in the sea.

1 Long-spined sea scorpion *(Cottus bubalis)* E.N. Atlantic; 6in (15cm); browns; feed raw fish, shellfish, prawn etc.

2 Common blenny *(Blennius pholis)* E.N. Atlantic; 5in (13cm); green or yellowish; may climb out on a ledge; feed as above.

3 Plaice *(Pleuronectes platessa)* E.N. Atlantic; young 5in (13cm); upper side brown, lower gray; provide tank with sandy floor; feed raw fish, shellfish etc.

4 Cuckoo wrasse *(Labrus mixtus)* E.N. Atlantic; 10in(25cm); yellow, male blue striped; sleeps on one side; feed crushed shellfish, prawn, raw fish.

Tropical marine fish (1)

Most of the marine fish included in this book live in clear, shallow seas washing coral reefs in the Indian or Pacific oceans or the Caribbean Sea. In general, selections have been made to represent different families.

The curiously shaped sea horse and pipefish belong to the family Syngnathidae, closely related to the shrimpfish's family, Centriscidae. The few marine catfish include this

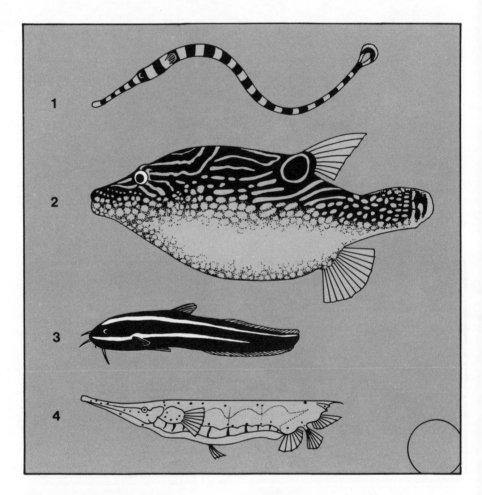

1 Pipefish *(Dunckerocampus* species) W. Pacific; 6¼ in(16cm); mainly black and yellow; keep in water of specific gravity 1.025; 80°F (27°C); feed brine shrimp and other small crustaceans.

2 Diamond flecked pufferfish *(Canthigaster margaritatus)* Indo-Pacific; 6in(15cm); brown flecked with gray; keep as pipefish; omnivorous; hardy.

3 Sea catfish *(Plotosus lineatus)* Indo-Pacific; young 3in(7.6cm); cream and black; keep as pipefish; voracious; adults big and aggressive.

4 Common shrimpfish *(Aeoliscus strigatus)* Indo-

sea catfish, one of the Plotisidae. The common clown anemone fish and three-spot damselfish represent the Pomacentridae. There are other small, attractive anemone fish and damselfish. A number of common clown anemone fish live well together, but most kinds of Pomacentridae fight with others of their species so that only true pairs can be kept.

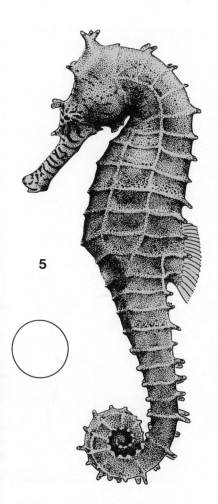

Pacific; 4¾in (12cm); red, yellow, black; keep as pipefish; omnivorous.
5 Sea horse *(Hippocampus hudsonius)* W. Atlantic; 7¾in (19.7cm); brown or gray; specific gravity 1.025; 75°F(24°C); feed small guppies, mosquito larvae; supply corals.

6 Clown anemone fish *(Amphiprion ocellaris)* Indo-Pacific; 4in(10cm); orange and white; keep as pipefish but add anemone for shelter; omnivorous.
7 Three-spot damselfish *(Dascyllus trimaculatus)* Indo-Pacific; 4¾in (12cm); black and white; keep as pipefish; omnivorous.

217

Tropical marine fish (2)

The eight fish on these two pages belong to eight separate families. The prickly leatherjacket is one of the filefish (Monocanthidae), closely related to the triggerfish (shown on p. 222). The pajama cardinal and others belonging to the Apogonidae tend to hang as though suspended in water. Marine butterfly fish of the family Chaetodontidae eat living corals, and are delicate marine aquarium subjects.

1 Prickly leatherjacket *(Chaetoderma penicilligera)* Indo-Pacific; 7in (18cm); golden brown; water of s.g. 1.025; 79°F (26°C); feed live or dried food.

2 Pajama cardinal *(Sphaeramia nematoptera)* Indo-Pacific; 3in (8cm); yellow with red spots; keep as *Chaetoderma*; live food.

3 Sunburst butterfly fish *(Chaetodon kleinii)* Indo-Pacific; 4¾in (12cm); golden with purple-blue spots; as *Chaetoderma*; feed small live foods and roe.

4 Wreckfish *(Anthias squamipinnis)* Indo-Pacific; 3¾in (10cm); orange-yellow; keep in shoal; *Cyclops,* roe, etc.

The wreckfish, in the family Anthiidae, is also not for novice aquarists. The fairy basslet, a member of the Grammidae, swims upside down in caves. Among the wrasses (Labridae), Gaimard's wrasse entirely changes color as it grows. The little striped neon goby and the small but superbly patterned dragonet belong respectively to the families Gobiidae and Callionymidae.

5 Fairy basslet *(Gramma loreto)* Caribbean; 3in (8cm); magenta and yellow; as *Chaetoderma,* with hiding places; live food.

6 Gaimard's wrasse *(Coris gaimardi)* Indo-Pacific; 8in(20cm); red, white, and black when young; keep as *Chaetoderma,* with coral sand; feed worms etc.

7 Dragonet *(Synchiropus splendidus)* Philippines; 2¾in (7cm); green, red, blue, yellow; as *Chaetoderma*; feed *Cyclops* etc.

8 Neon goby *(Gobiosoma oceanops)* Caribbean; 2¼ in (6cm); white, black, yellow; as *Chaetoderma*; brine shrimp, roe.

©DIAGRAM

219

Tropical marine fish (3)

Six families are represented by the fish on these two pages. The turret fish belongs to the Ostraciontidae, whose squarish shapes earn them their popular name of boxfish. The Sciaenidae, to which the jackknife fish belongs, are known as drums for sounds they make by vibrating muscles near the air bladder. The sweetlips is a member of the Pomadasyidae. The spiny puffer, in the

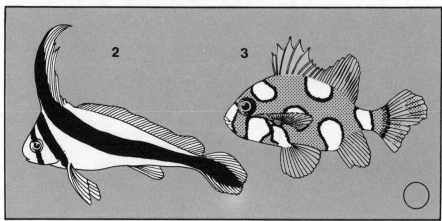

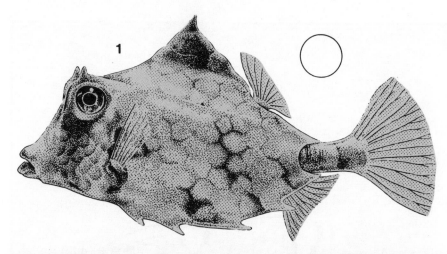

1 Black-blotched turret fish
(Rhinesomus gibbosus) Indo-Pacific; 10in (25cm), golden brown; specific gravity 1.025; 80°F (27°C); omnivorous; docile, easier to keep than most.
2 Jackknife fish *(Equetes lanceolatus)* Caribbean; 8¾in (25cm); black and white;

keep as *Rhinesomus*, but ideally in a shoal and only in a big tank.
3 Harlequin sweetlips
(Plectorhynchus chaetodontoides) Indo-Australian area; 8in (20cm) in captivity; brown and white; keep as *Rhinesomus*; feed mosquito larvae, dead foods.
4 Moorish idol *(Zanclus*

family Diodontidae, deters enemies by inflating its body and thus making its spines stick out. The Zanclidae feature the Moorish idol, whose shape is unmistakable. But arguably the most bizarrely shaped fish of all are the scorpionfish (Scorpaenidae), the family to which the lionfish or dragonfish belongs. Incidentally, this fish's spines are dangerously poisonous.

canescens) Indo-Pacific; 9¾ in (25cm); black, white, yellow; keep as *Rhinesomus* but in tank of at least 260 US gal (1,000 l).

5 Spiny puffer *(Diodon holacanthus)* Indo-Pacific and Atlantic; 16in (40cm); brownish; keep as *Rhinesomus*; docile; inflates when scared, but avoid frightening unnecessarily.

6 Lionfish *(Pterois volitans)* Indo-Pacific; 14in (35cm); reddish and white; keep as *Rhinesomus*; eats live fish and raw fish if moved about; keep only with large fish; poisonous, let no one touch it.

Tropical marine fish (4)

The fish shown here grow large, and most need big marine aquariums. The Balistidae, or triggerfish, are hardy but aggressive. Marine angelfish (Pomacanthidae) are stately and colorful. Like many adult reef fish, those of the snapper family (Lutjanidae) viciously attack fish of their own species. Squirrelfish (Holocentridae) are nocturnal predators unsafe with smaller fish. The nurse shark is a

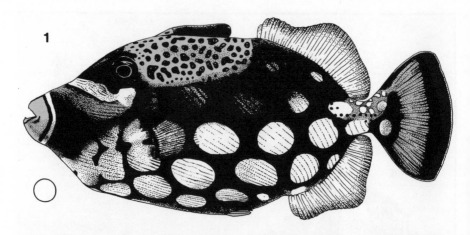

1 Clown triggerfish *(Balistoides · niger)* Indo-Pacific; 20in (50cm); brown or blue and white; specific gravity 1.025; 80°F (27°C); omnivorous; keep alone.
2 Zebra angelfish *(Pomacanthus semicirculatus)* Indo-Pacific; 15¾ in (40cm); adult yellowish, bláck, etc; water as for

Balistoides; eats algae, etc.
3 Blue-striped snapper *(Lutjanus kasmira)* Indo-Pacific; 16in (40cm); yellow and blue; water as for *Balistoides*; omnivorous.
4 Spiny squirrelfish *(Holocentrus spinifer)* Indo-Pacific; 18in (45cm); red and yellow; keep as *Balistoides*; eats crustaceans.

scavenger of the family Orectolobidae. Unlike most fish, sharks have skeletons made of cartilage, not bone. Groupers (Serranidae) are intelligent fish but liable to snap up small companions. Batfish — the family Platacidae — include good species for beginners. Tangs and surgeonfish (the Acanthuridae) have sharp blades in the base of the tail; beware if handling.

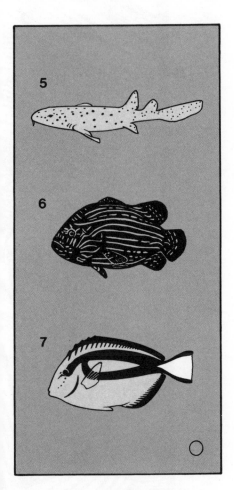

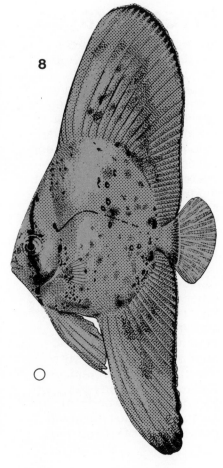

5 Nurse shark *(Ginglymostoma cirratum)* Warm seas; from 13in (33cm); gray; water as for *Balistoides*; feed mussel, squid.
6 Six-line grouper *(Grammistes sexlineatus)* Indo-Pacific; 10in (25cm); dark with yellow stripes; water as *Balistoides*; feed raw fish, beef heart.

7 Regal tang *(Paracanthurus hepatus)* Indo-Pacific; 11¾in (30cm); blue, black, yellow; water as for *Balistoides*; eats algae, spinach, lettuce.
8 Round batfish *(Platax orbicularis)* Indo-Pacific; 20in (50cm); brown: 76°F (24°C); omnivorous; longlived.

3

Invertebrates

Invertebrates are, broadly speaking, all animals without backbones. They comprise 95% of the animal kingdom, and outnumber vertebrates both in species and in individuals. Invertebrates show great variety in form, from the simplest one-celled amoeba to complex insects like bees and ants with highly organized social communities.

Within this large group of living things, are many that have been associated with man for various reasons. Some of the simplest forms are cultivated as food for other captive animals. Aquatic invertebrates are kept with other aquarium creatures. Bees produce honey and help to pollinate crops. Many other insects can be kept temporarily for study. It is even possible to breed butterflies and moths in captivity, and so help in the preservation of rare species.

Right Beekeeper and his bees shown in a woodcut by Sebastian Brand, published in Strasburg in 1502 (Mansell Collection).

224

Invertebrate characteristics

The term invertebrate is used to refer to 95% of all animal species, and means animals without backbones. Within this group, there is immense variety of structure and adaptation. Invertebrates comprise 25 of the 26 phyla; vertebrates form the other (also see page 418). Some of the most primitive species of invertebrates are difficult to distinguish from plants.

Invertebrate characteristics
Invertebrates lack backbones, but many have some other adaptation to give structure and protection to the body. Insects and other arthropods often have a hard outer layer, segmented for flexibility. Mollusks grow chalky shells for protection, while their body is "plastic" or without standard form. Bodily functions also show considerable variety and indicate the animal's environment and sophistication. Breathing may be by gills, through membranes, or by primitive lungs. Food may be ingested, chewed, or, as in spiders, partially digested outside the body by the action of juices. In the lower forms, reproduction is often asexual, eg by simple division. Where sexual reproduction does occur, males are often smaller, and may be eaten by the female after mating.

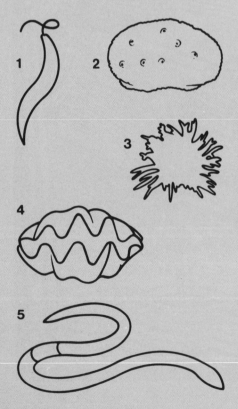

1 Protozoans have one complex, often specialized cell. Some photosynthesize, like plants. Most are microscopic and irregular in shape. Examples are *Euglena, Paramecium,* amoeba.
2 Sponges are multicellular, with a structure consisting of a network of chambers. Most are marine; some live in freshwater.
3 Coelenterates are purely aquatic with symmetrical bodies. They may be slender polyps that attach to objects, or free moving and umbrella-shaped. They include coral and hydra.
4 Mollusks are unsegmented and have no standard shape. They live on land, in freshwater, or in the sea. They often have a chalky shell for protection.
5 Annelids are segmented worms, like earthworms, with bodies divided into similar parts.

6

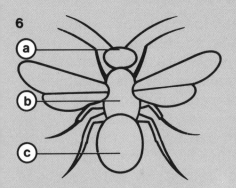

6 Insects are arthropods. The phylum Arthropoda contains the largest number of species in the animal kingdom, and includes spiders (arachnids) and crustaceans, as well as insects. Insects are divided into head (**a**), thorax (**b**), and abdomen (**c**), all encased in a horny layer of cuticle. The head has one pair of antennae and three pairs of mouth parts. On the thorax, there are three pairs of legs and two pairs of wings.

7

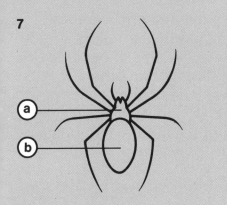

7 Arachnids are land arthropods that breathe through "book-lungs," similar to gills. They have two main parts: a prosoma (**a**), and an abdomen (**b**). Arachnids include, among others, all spiders and scorpions. They prey on smaller arthropods. Spiders build webs to trap small insects. Most arachnids have stings.

8

9

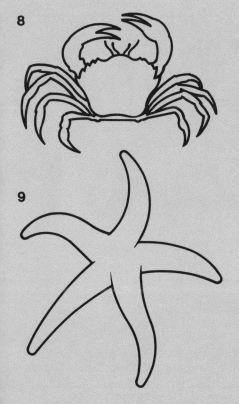

8 Crustaceans are mainly aquatic and breathe through gills. They have two pairs of antennae and three pairs of mouth parts. The body is made up of head, thorax, and abdomen, although the head and thorax are usually fused. Examples include crabs and prawns, and, in freshwater, crayfish and *Daphnia.* The unsegmented larvae of crustaceans is known as nauplius larvae and forms the basic diet for many aquatic animals.

9 Echinoderms (starfish and sea urchins) are the only higher invertebrates with a body cavity which are symmetrically radial in form. They are covered with chalky plates or spines. Movement is slow, and they have no head, and no true brain.

Invertebrates as food

Primitive or small invertebrates form the basic diet of many fish, reptiles, amphibians, and birds. Food invertebrates include microscopic infusoria such as *Paramecium,* planktonic animals, small crustaceans, mollusks, worms, insect larvae, and adult flying insects. Live food is important for many species because it contains necessary trace elements and a high proportion of protein. Live food also enables the animal to catch its own meal — an important requirement for species whose senses are triggered by the movement of prey. Additional care must be taken when feeding live food. Animals collected directly from ponds or streams should be thoroughly rinsed to remove any traces of bacteria or decaying organic material that might harm other aquarium creatures. Any dead and decaying live food must be discarded if uneaten. Hatched larvae may be a nuisance. Live food can be caught in natural habitats, or bought in pet stores, either fully grown or as cultures that can be hatched at a later date.

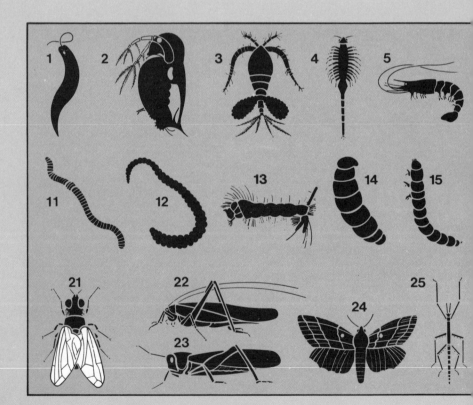

Invertebrates as food Included below are examples of common invertebrates used for feeding other species. (Not drawn to scale.) For feeding fish see pages 189, 191, 199, 213; amphibians 261, 262; reptiles 288, 291, 303, 317; birds 334, 335, 366, 391.

1 *Euglena* are microscopic animals (infusoria). Others include *Paramecium*.
2 *Daphnia* or water fleas are small crustaceans.
3 *Cyclops* is another water flea.
4 Brine shrimps *(Artemia salina)* are often eaten as larvae.
5 Common prawns.
6 Freshwater shrimps.
7 Land slugs are mollusks.
8 Land snails are also mollusks.
9 Microworms are nematode worms only ¼ in(6mm) long.
10 *Tubifex* are a type of freshwater worm.

11 Earthworms.
12 Whiteworms.
13 Mosquito larvae.
14 Maggots are fly larvae.
15 Mealworms are beetle larvae.
16 Bloodworms are midge larvae.
17 Fruitflies.
18 Sandhoppers and other aquatic insects.
19 Aphids.
20 Woodlice — from leaf litter, along with various small insects.
21 Houseflies.
22 Crickets.
23 Locusts.
24 Moths.
25 Stick insects.
26 Small flying insects taken from herbage.
27 Cockroaches.
28 Ants.
29 Spiders, especially wolf and garden spiders.

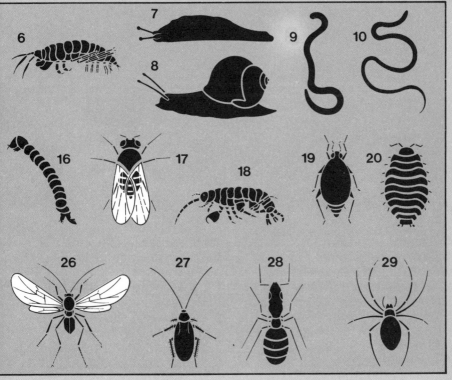

©DIAGRAM

229

Obtaining food invertebrates

Invertebrates to be used as food for other animals in captivity can be obtained in various ways. It is often easiest to buy them from a pet store, either in their adult form, or as eggs which can then be cultured. Many common insects or water creatures can be collected without difficulty from their natural habitats, although this can sometimes prove a time-consuming activity.

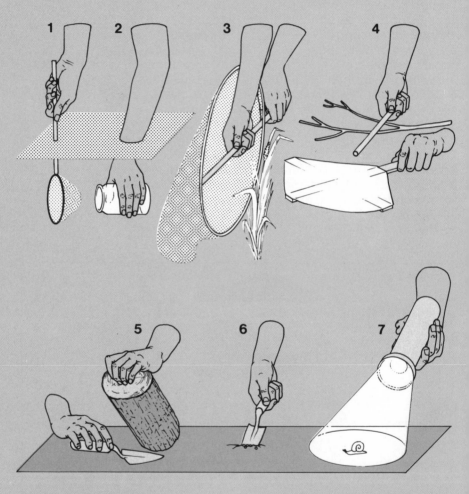

Collecting invertebrates
1 Use a fine mesh net to collect small crustaceans and worms.
2 Use a jar for pondwater containing microscopic animals.
3 Sweep bushes and hedges with a wide net for flying insects and spiders.
4 Collect insects from trees by tapping the branch, and catching the insects underneath as they fall off.
5 Look for grubs and woodlice under logs and stones.
6 Earthworms can be dug from moist ground with a trowel.
7 Slugs and snails are easy to locate at night with a flashlight.

Culturing invertebrates For culturing infusoria see p.189. Brine shrimp eggs from a pet store will hatch in 48 hours in a salt solution at 80°F(27°C). Microworm culture can be spread on a layer of cooled, cooked oatmeal and incubated at 80°F(27°C). The worms can be removed with a small brush. Whiteworms are cultured in a wood box with drainage holes. Baby cereal is placed on top of the culture medium, and covered with glass and a lid. The box is kept in the dark at 55°F(13°C). The worms can be removed from the glass after feeding.

Daphnia, Cyclops, Tubifex, mosquito larvae, bloodworms, and freshwater shrimps are best collected directly from ponds and streams. All should be washed well before feeding.

Trapping insects

a Fly trap Food (sugar solution or meat) is placed in a small dish beneath a funnel on a stand covered with a container. Flies are attracted to the food, fly up through the funnel opening, and are unable to escape.

b Moth or flying insect trap Insects are attracted to the light source and stun themselves on the light bulb, falling through the funnel into a collecting jar.

c Trap for leaf litter insects Collect leaf litter from damp, shady areas and place it in a can with a sieve at the bottom, which fits inside a funnel leading to a collecting jar. These insects dislike light and heat and will move away from the light to the bottom of the can. They then fall through the sieve and funnel into the jar.

Buying invertebrate foods Many pet stores now supply a variety of live invertebrates that can be used as food. Some are also available freeze-dried or preserved. To prevent disease from bacteria, be sure to rinse all invertebrates to be fed to aquatic species.

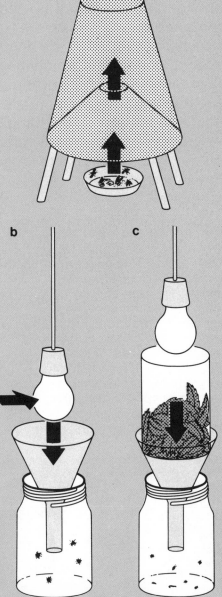

a

b   c

©DIAGRAM

231

Keeping aquatic invertebrates

Invertebrates that live mainly or totally in water can often be kept with success in various types of aquarium. These animals range from microscopic plankton and small crustaceans like *Daphnia* and *Cyclops* that serve as food for fish, amphibians, and larger invertebrates, to complex and more interesting animals like crabs and other shellfish. Many invertebrates are strange and unusual in appearance and make attractive additions to an aquarium. They can also help to make a more balanced environment, as many are scavengers or filter feeders and remove bacteria and waste from the tank.

Not all invertebrates are hardy, however, and many require special conditions which may be difficult for the beginner to provide. Some, like octopuses, grow too large for the average aquarium and must be provided with larger accommodation. Avoid handling aquatic invertebrates wherever possible; many have poisonous secretions or stings which they use to immobolize predators, and some have sharp claws or spines.

Keeping aquatic invertebrates is in many ways similar to keeping fish. See pages 184-188 for types of tank, equipment, and water preparation.
Most of the commonly kept aquatic invertebrates are marine species, needing a pH of 8 and a temperature of 68°F(20°C) or slightly higher. If planning to keep freshwater invertebrates, see pages 184-188, 190, and 198 for aquarium information.
Many aquatic invertebrates are scavengers or filter feeders that eat organic waste which would be removed by a mechanical filter: for this reason it is vital to use only an undergravel filtration system in their tanks.
Most aquatic invertebrate species will not tolerate sudden changes of water.

Aquatic invertebrates in art
a Octopus from a Roman mosaic at Pompeii.
b Crab motif on an ancient Greek coin.

Anemones, corals, sponges

Anemones, corals, and sponges can sometimes be kept in a marine aquarium, and help provide fish with a natural-looking setting. Corals and sponges are filter feeders and must not be kept in an aquarium where there is continual mechanical filtration. An undergravel filtration system may be used. Some species, particularly corals, are delicate and need experienced care.

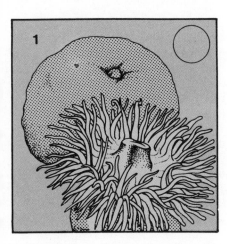

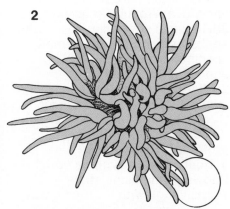

1 Beadlet anemone *(Actina equina)* Worldwide; 1½in-3½in (4cm-8cm); dark red with paler retractable tentacles; hardy in most marine aquaria; feed organic matter, fresh or preserved animal foods.

2 Snake-locks anemone *(Anemonia sulcata)* Mediterranean; 4in(10cm); white, tentacles have purple tips and do not retract; care as beadlet.

3 Bath sponge *(Espongia mollissima)* Mediterranean and Caribbean; 6in(15cm) diameter; white, cream, brown; eats organic matter, bacteria.

4 Red coral *(Corallium rubrum)* Mediterranean; colony size varies with environment and age; soft branching body with red spicules which form rigid core; white polyps retract into cavities; keep below 68°F(20°C); feeds on organic matter.

©DIAGRAM

Aquatic mollusks

Mollusks are an interesting and varied group of animals containing over 80,000 species. There are aquatic and land types (see page 241). All have a basic soft body with a mantle. Many mollusks have a shell, secreted by tissue over the mantle. Other species have lost their shells to increase mobility, and some have some form of internal body protection. Commonly kept aquatic mollusks

1 Giant clam *(Tridacna lamellosa)* Tropical seas; up to 3ft(1m); two strong, curved shells; keep only young, small specimens; needs 77°F(25°C) and light; filter feeder.

2 Pilgrim scallop *(Pecten jacobaeus)* Mediterranean; 5in (12cm); two hinged shells, one flat, one curved; tentacles protrude; filter feeder.

3 Tiger cowrie *(Cypraea tigris)* Red Sea; 4in(10cm); shiny, whitish shell with mottled brown spots; needs 77°F(25°C); feed fresh or dried animal food.

4 Knobbed triton *(Tritonium nodiferum)* Mediterranean; 16in (40cm); long, narrow, white shell, body brown with two stalked eyes; keep in large aquarium at 71°F(22°C); feed large amounts of animal foods; do not keep with starfish.

5 Sea slug *(Doris* family*)* Tropical seas; typically 3in (7.6cm); bright markings; eats vegetable matter.

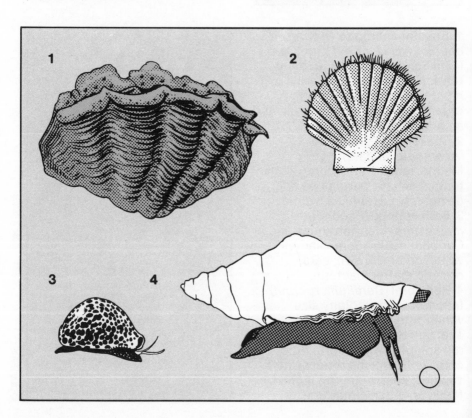

belong to three groups: the bivalves and univalves, including cowries, conches, and clams; snails and other gastropods; and cephalopods, including octopuses and cuttlefish. Cowries and conches are hardy in an established semi-natural aquarium, and graze on algae. They also need some chopped meat. Clams are filter feeders. Snails are scavengers, and destroy plants.

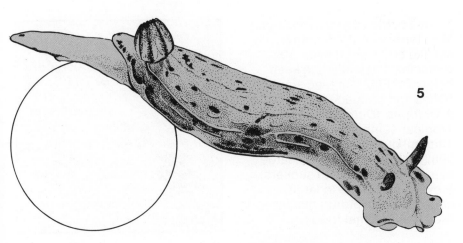

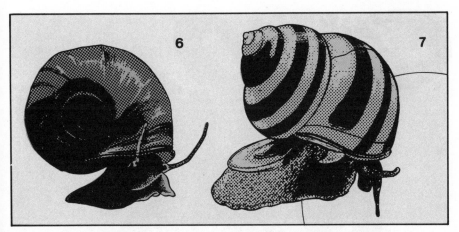

Freshwater snails
6 Great ramshorn snail
(Planorbarius corneus) Europe, Asia; ½in(1cm) shell diameter; brick red with flat coiled shell; keep in freshwater aquarium; feeds on animal and vegetable matter; useful scavenger but may damage vegetation.

7 Viviparus fasciatus *(Viviparus fasciatus)* Southern and Central Europe; ¾in(2cm) average length; short spiral shell, brown or green with dark longitudinal stripes; difficult to keep; needs water temperature below 71°F (22°C); feeds on animal and plant waste material.

© DIAGRAM

235

Cephalopods

Cephalopods, or "head-footed" animals, are the most advanced of the mollusks, possessing a highly-developed nervous system that allows for complex predatory behavior. Most have internal shells or none at all, as in the octopus, and instead of a single foot, have tentacles or arms. All have good vision, and some are among the largest marine creatures.

1 Little cuttle *(Sepiola rondeletii)* Mediterranean; 1½in(4cm); saclike body, large eyes, 10 tentacles; basically red; keep below 71°F(22°C); feed small fishes and crustaceans.

2 Octopus *(Octopus vulgaris)* Tropical, temperate seas; up to 10ft(3m) but keep only up to 30in(76cm); saclike body; large eyes; 8 tentacles with suckers; brown; keep alone in large aquarium with hiding places; feed fresh animal foods.

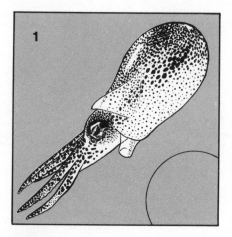

2

Echinoderms

Echinoderms are spined aquatic invertebrates. They are radially symmetrical, having no right or left hand side. All can be divided into five parts around a central axis. Starfish and sea urchins are those most commonly kept. Most echinoderms have an external skeleton of bony plates just under the skin. They are protected by sharp, often poisonous spines, and have remarkable regenerative powers.

1 Cushion star *(Asterina gibbosa)* Mediterranean; 2in (5cm) in diameter; short arms; tube feet at tips of arms; green, yellow; hardy; filter feeder.

2 Brittle star *(Ophiothrix fragilis)* Mediterranean; up to 4in (10cm) in diameter; slender, flexible arms covered with bristles; green, black, or red; lives hidden among rocks in aquarium; keep below 71°F (22°C); feeds on animal matter on aquarium bottom.

3 Echinaster sepositus *(Echinaster sepositus)* Coastal Mediterranean; 8in(20cm) in diameter; arms covered with depressions; tube feet at tips of arms; bright red; temperature below 71°F(22°C); eats animal fragments, small mollusks.

4 Purple-spined sea urchin *(Sphaerechinus granularis)* Mediterranean; 2½in(7cm); bright purple with white-tipped spines; feed organic matter and plants; drop food onto spines.

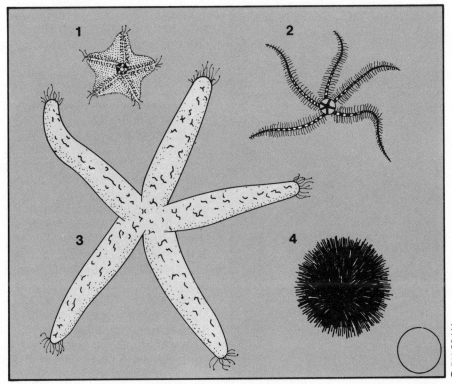

© DIAGRAM

Crustaceans

Crustaceans, like insects and spiders, are members of a large, diverse group of animals called arthropods, which altogether contains over 80% of all animal species. Crustaceans are mainly aquatic, joint-legged animals which breathe through gills, and are covered with a tough, unsegmented skeleton or exoskeleton. They have two pairs of antennae, and three pairs of mouth parts.

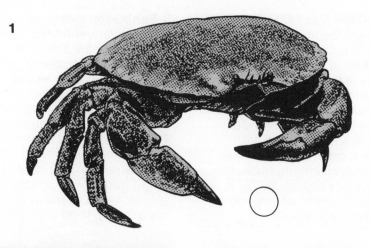

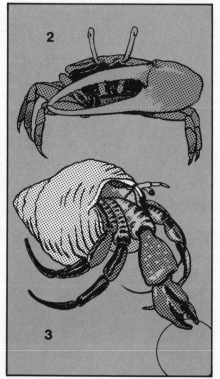

1 Edible crab *(Cancer pagurus)* Mediterranean, Atlantic; 8in (20cm); brown with dark spots on top, greenish yellow underneath; large claws; hairy legs; keep at less than 71°F (22°C); feed any animal food, fresh or preserved.

2 Fiddler crab *(Uca uca)* Tropical Indo-Pacific coasts; body width 1½in(4cm); bright orange; males have one huge claw and one small claw; eyes on tips of long stalks; keep at more than 77°F (25°C); feed fresh or dried animal food.

3 Hermit crab (*Eupagurus* species) Worldwide; 3in(7.5cm) body width; variegated red and brown soft body lacking outer shell; crab protects body with discarded sea shells, often whelk shells; keep in matured aquarium with undergravel filter; eats animal matter; scavenger.

Crustaceans include tiny copepods, which are important as plankton in the diets of many aquatic animals. Brine shrimp, and water fleas like *Daphnia* and *Cyclops,* are also important food sources in both adult and larval forms (nauplius larvae). Crabs, lobsters, shrimps, and prawns are the most familiar larger crustaceans, and some do well in captivity. Many are scavengers.

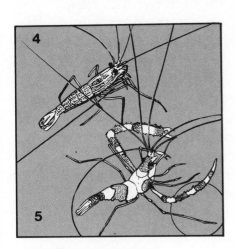

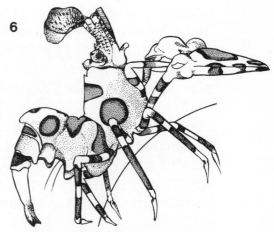

4 Lysmata seticaudata
(Lysmata seticaudata)
Mediterranean; 2in(5cm); bright red horizontal stripes; large black eyes on short stalks; hardy in captivity at less than 71°F (22°C); feeds on any animal matter; scavenger.

5 Banded prawn *(Stenopus hispidus)* Tropical seas; 2in (5cm); white with wide red bands; strong claws; long antennae; bent appearance; popular and hardy in aquaria; needs 77°F(25°C); feed small pieces of meat; keep in matured aquarium; keep only one.

6 Clown shrimp *(Hymenocera picta)* Indo-Pacific coral reefs; 2in(5cm); beautiful coloring, pinkish white with purple-edged pink spots, blue-striped legs; flat, leaf-shaped antennae; keep at 77°F(25°C); pugnacious; eats starfish and other animal food.

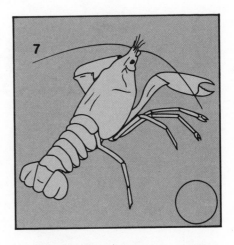

7 Crayfish *(Astacus fluviatilis)*
European freshwater habitats; 4in(10cm); gray, green, brown; large carapace; slender abdomen; two large claws; keep in cold freshwater aquarium at 64°F(18°C); needs hiding places; scavenger, feed animal matter; keep singly.

Keeping land invertebrates

Invertebrates adapted to life on land include a wide
variety of animal species, some of which may begin their
life cycle in water. Most fall within two groups: land
mollusks; and arthropods, including crustaceans,
insects, and arachnids (spiders and scorpions).

Insects make particularly interesting objects of study and
have proved beneficial to man in many ways. They have
been cultivated for centuries for their syrups, wax,
shellac, fine silk fiber, and honey. In the past, some
insects have even been revered, like the Egyptian scarab,
which was a sacred symbol of creative power. Insects
play a crucial role in natural systems as the pollinators of
plants, yet they can also be agricultural pests or carriers
of disease.

Land invertebrates may be collected for temporary study,
or can be bred and raised in captivity. Either way, they
provide an excellent opportunity to observe natural
variety and beauty, and a chance to appreciate the
complexities of life cyles and behavior.

Land invertebrates in art
a Scorpion on a stone from
Babylon, 12th century BC.
b Scarab motif on an Egyptian
breast ornament from the tomb
of Tutankhamun, 14th century BC.
c Children's book illustration
showing Little Miss Muffet
frightened by the spider.

Land mollusks and annelids

Mollusks are essentially aquatic animals, but some species live on land, notably certain types of snail. These can be observed in the garden, or collected for temporary study. Annelids, or segmented worms, include the earthworm which is found in moist garden soil. Its role in aerating plant roots can be demonstrated by building a wormery to show tunnels through soil layers.

1 Edible / Roman snail (Helix pomatia) Continental Europe; 1½in(3.8cm) diameter; brown or reddish brown coiled shell; long antennae which serve as eyes; muscular foot; find in grass near walls, under rocks or logs; keep temporarily in jar covered with cheesecloth, washed out daily; keep away from bright sunlight; feed leafy green vegetables, eg lettuce and spinach; do not allow vegetables to dry out.

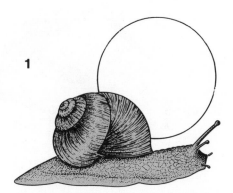

1

2

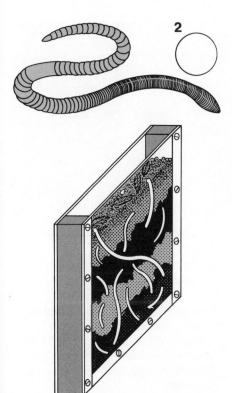

2 Common earthworm (Lumbricus species) Worldwide; length varies with species — up to 10in(25cm); reddish brown; body divided into equal segments with four pairs of bristles on each segment; wide, smooth "saddle" near the front end indicates maturity; find in moist garden earth; nocturnal; house temporarily in wormery; feeds on organic matter ingested with soil.

Wormery Use two 1ft(30cm) squares of rigid transparent plastic, screwed to 1in(2.5cm) wide lengths of wood batten. Fill with layers of different types of soil, and add a dozen worms. Water the wormery, cover with a layer of gravel, and add leaf litter or grass cuttings. Cover the wormery with a light-proof cloth. After a few days, the soil layers will be mixed.

Stick insects and mantids

Stick insects (walking-sticks) and leaf insects belong to the order Phasmida, which includes over 2,000 species from tropical and temperate areas. Most species are large and unusual in appearance, resembling twigs or leaves. All are vegetarians, and can be kept easily in captivity. Mantids (order Mantodea) are large, aggressive insects which must be supplied with living prey.

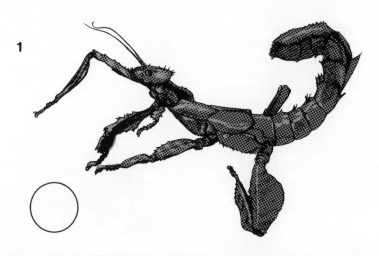

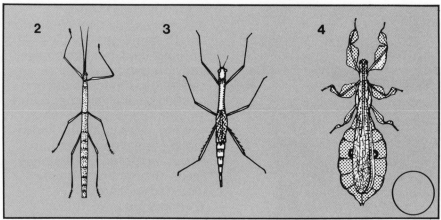

1 Giant spiny stick insect *(Extatasoma tiaratum)* Australia; female 8in(20cm), brown, with undeveloped wings, covered with spikes; male 6in(15cm), paler than female, with fully developed wings.
2 Laboratory stick insect *(Carausius morosus)* Asia; 3in (8cm); resembles a dry twig.
3 Didymuria violescens *(Didymuria violescens)* Australia; 2½in(6cm); greenish brown; slender, winged body.
4 Leaf insect *(Pulchriphyllium* species) Asia; 3½in(9cm); green; flattened body and legs; looks like a leaf.

Care of stick and leaf insects

These insects make hardy pets, and breed easily. It is best to buy them as eggs and rear them. Eggs should be incubated at 75°F(22°C) in moist sand in a plastic box covered with a lid. Hatching may take months. Nymphs shed their skin five times before reaching adult size. They can be kept in an adult cage. Adult container (shown left) is a cylindrical plastic or glass jar covered with a mesh top. It should contain the food plant of the species — often bramble, ash, or ivy — in small flower pots filled with soil or in water. Replace plants twice a week, and spray leaves daily with water to keep a humid atmosphere. Clean out often, removing droppings and eggs. Keep at 70°F(20°C).

5 Praying mantis *(Mantis religiosa)* W. Europe, E. USA; 1½-3in(3.8-7.5cm); illustration shows male (**a**) and female (**b**); sexes are similar, but females are much larger; pale green; front legs in characteristic "praying" position, adapted for seizing prey; sharp spines on legs; well-developed eyes; long antennae; poor fliers; both adults and nymphs feed primarily on other insects; may be aggressive to own species.

Care of mantids These insects are somewhat difficult to keep because they require large quantities of living prey, and may be cannibalistic. Mantids can be kept in a cage similar to that for stick insects, but with the addition of twigs in flower pots for perches. Females are best isolated, although males may be kept together. Mantids eat blow flies, locusts, wasps, bees, moths, and grasshoppers.

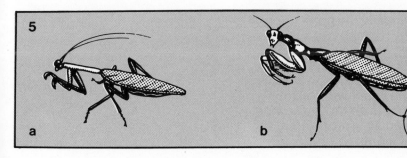

5

a   b

Katydids and crickets

Katydids and crickets are included in the order Ensifera, although they were once classified together with locusts and grasshoppers as Orthoptera. They occur worldwide, and are common in temperate regions of Europe and North America. They make a distinctive chirping sound, and were formerly kept in China to bring good luck. Katydids and crickets make interesting temporary pets.

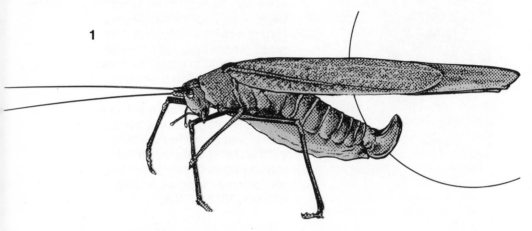

1

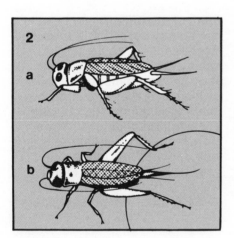

2

a

b

1 Katydid (family *Tettigoniidae*) Temperate areas; up to 1.6in(4cm); green; long antennae; female has ovipositor; male chirps.
2 Cricket (family *Gryllidae*) Temperate areas; up to 1in (2.5cm); male (**a**) and female (**b**); brown; long antennae; female has ovipositor; male chirps.
Care Katydids and crickets can be found in fields on summer evenings. Keep temporarily in a jar covered with cheesecloth. They eat insects and plants.

Stridulation is the production of sound by rubbing two surfaces together. Male crickets and katydids stridulate by rubbing their wings together. A scraper under the upper wing (**a**) rubs against a file on the lower wing (**b**). The noise is most often heard at night.

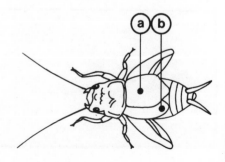

Beetles

Beetles (order Coleoptera) are the largest single group in the animal kingdom. They comprise 140 families — 40% of all insects. They can be distinguished by their front wings, which are hardened into leathery shells and called elytra. Many are vividly colored. Predacious beetles such as the ladybird have been introduced to certain areas to control insect pests.

Beetles range in size from 1/100in(.025cm) to 4in(10cm). They may be black or brown, or brightly colored. The glow worm is able to produce light from chemicals in its body. Beetles are found worldwide. They may be herbivorous, carnivorous, or omnivorous. They are interesting to collect and identify, and may be kept for a short while in a large jar covered with cheesecloth. Try to supply the natural food of the species.

Examples of beetle families
1 Green tiger beetle (family Cicindelidae).
2 Violet ground beetle (family Carabidae).
3 Stag beetle (family Lucanidae).
4 Seven-spot ladybird (family Coccinellidae).
5 Rose chafer (family Scarabaeidae).
6 Glow worm (family Lampyridae).
7 Wasp beetle (family Cerambycidae).
8 Bloody-nosed beetle (family Chrysomelidae).

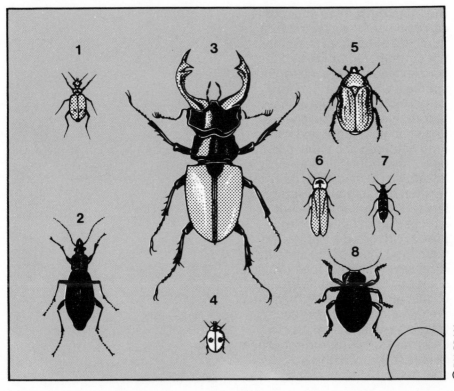

Butterflies and moths

Butterflies and moths belong to the order Lepidoptera, which contains 112,000 species found all over the world. They are noted for their brightly colored wing patterns, which are used for species recognition, concealment, heat absorption, and to signal disagreeable taste to predators. Many species are in current danger of extinction due to the disappearance of their food plants.

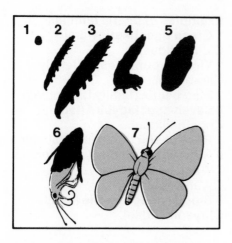

Life cycle Butterflies and moths have complete metamorphosis, like many other higher insects. Development begins with the egg (**1**). Caterpillars (**2**) hatch, and feed on vegetation, shedding their skin several times (**3**). When fully grown (**4**), the caterpillar becomes a pupa with a protective cocoon or chrysalis (**5**), from which the adult later emerges (**6**). At first the wings are wet, but the butterfly soon dries off (**7**).

Breeding butterflies and moths can be a useful way of restoring numbers of species in danger, but certain precautions should be taken. Never release foreign species, which may become pests. Notify local naturalists before releasing local species. Eggs can be bought and kept until hatching in a small plastic box. This should have an airtight lid and be opened once daily to freshen the air inside. Hatched larvae (caterpillars) are kept in a succession of larger plastic boxes with lids (**a**). Supply the main food plant of the species. After several molts, the larvae are ready to pupate and should be placed in a box with branches standing in soil (**b**). Correct temperature and humidity is important when culturing. These details will vary with each species.

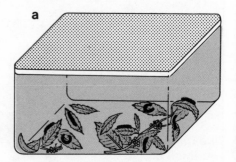

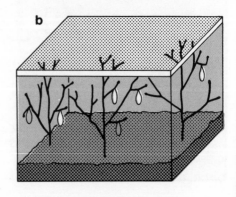

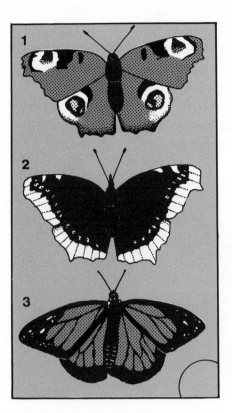

Butterflies, unlike moths, have knobbed antennae.

1 Peacock butterfly *(Inachus io)* Europe; 1.2in(3cm) long; orange and black wings with iridescent violet and yellow spots, like peacock "eyes"; caterpillars black with white dots; food plant nettle.

2 Camberwell beauty *(Nymphalis antiopa)* Europe, N. America; 1.6in(4cm) long; dark wings edged with violet spots and a yellow margin; adults feed on nectar, or sap; food plant of caterpillar is willow; caterpillars spiky, black, with red blotches.

3 Monarch butterfly *(Danaus plexippus)* N. America, Australia; 1.8in(4.7cm) long; orange wings veined in black, black margins with white dots; caterpillars yellow with black stripes; food plant milkweed.

Moths are the most numerous of the Lepidoptera.

4 Emperor moth *(Saturnia pavonia)* Europe; 1¼ in(3cm) long; male orange-brown; female gray; caterpillars large, bright green and black; food plants include hawthorn, heather, bramble, willow.

5 Striped hawk moth *(Celerio lineata)* N. America; 1½ in(4cm); greenish brown with black and white markings on abdomen, pale stripes on wings; mainly eats grapevine leaves.

6 Luna moth (family Saturniidae) N. America, Asia; 4¾ in(12cm) long; 6in(15cm) wingspan; bright green; long tails; each wing has a transparent "window"; feathered antennae; green caterpillars; American species feeds on walnut, oak, beech, birch, and other trees.

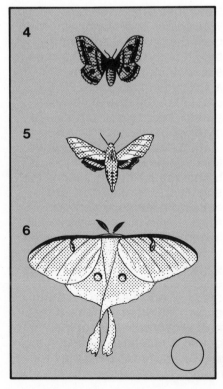

Honeybees

Honeybees are members of the order Hymenoptera, which includes ants and wasps. They are social insects, living in the wild in nests in caves and hollow trees. Bees have been raised for centuries in artificially housed colonies to enable harvesting of the honey they produce. Beginners to beekeeping should arrange for tuition and demonstration of techniques before starting a hive.

Honeybee *(Apis mellifera)*
Worldwide; ¾in(1.8cm) wingspan of worker; two pairs of wings; brown body; sting on abdomen, except in drones; hibernates.

a Drones or male bees are only present in the hive at certain times. Their sole function is to mate with new queens. After mating, the drones die. Drones are large bees with big eyes.

b Queens are highly specialized egg-layers, produced in large cells from larvae fed only on royal jelly. A queen mates once in early life. Queens may live up to 5 years, and may lay 2,000 eggs a day at their peak. No queen will tolerate another in the hive, and will use her sting only to kill other queens. If the hive is overcrowded, or the queen is old, new queen cells will be started to save the hive.

c Worker bees are undeveloped females, and do all the work of the hive including foraging, rearing young (see illustration below), and tending the queen. Foragers usually live 3 weeks. They collect pollen, which sticks to body hairs, and is packed in sacs on the hindlegs. Bees also suck nectar which is turned into honey and stored in the hive for use during winter hibernation. Man harvests the bees' surplus stores in the fall.

Hives The backyard beekeeper should have one or two good hives, sited to face south-east.
Components of modern hive
1 Weathertight roof.
2 Inner cover.
3 Supers — shallow boxes for frames to store honey.
4 Queen excluder — a grill to keep queen and drones below in brood box, where eggs are laid.
5 Brood box — bottomless box for frames for brood cells.
6 Floor with entrance. Hives should be placed on stands to keep out damp.
7 Frames are light wood, filled with wax sheets stamped with a cell pattern. Bees make cells on both sides. Frames must be spaced so they can be removed for inspection. The "bee space" — ¼-⅜in (6-9mm) — is the distance between each frame, and between frames and walls.

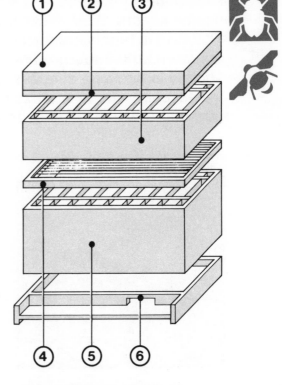

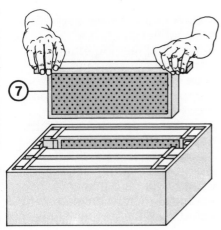

Other equipment Beginners should visit agricultural shows or beekeeping associations to learn about equipment and management of bees. Essential equipment includes protective clothing (hats with veils, cotton suits), hive tools for scraping bee-glue from frames, and a smoker to subdue the bees when examining the hive. Smokers burn charcoal, making the bees gorge with honey and become more docile.

Swarming occurs naturally before the main honey flow, and is a reflection of the colony's increase in size over the summer. A proportion of bees leave the hive with a new queen to start another hive. Keepers aim to control swarming to avoid losing bees.

249

Ants

Ants (family Formicidae) are the most successful of all
social insects. Over 10,000 species are found worldwide.
They live in highly organized communities in nests, which
are often built underground or in plants or trees. Their
society is made up of queens, workers, and at times
males, each with specialized tasks. An ant farm, or
formicarium, can be made to enable closer study.

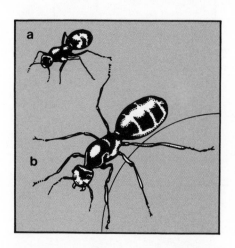

Ant (family *Formicidae*)
Worldwide; up to ½in(1.3cm) in
length; head, thorax, abdomen
clearly divided; long antennae;
glossy black or red; workers (**a**)
are sterile females and may be
divided into soldiers, nurses,
builders, and food gatherers;
queens (**b**) are generally larger
with wings before mating; males
develop from unfertilized eggs
and have wings; males are only
present at some times; all ants
bite or sting.

Collecting ants Colonies can be
found by looking for ant hills,
characteristic ant-built mounds
of earth. Scoop out the nest, and
place it on a cloth, putting
queens, workers, eggs, larvae,
and pupae into separate jars.
Queens are often found at the
bottom of the nest.
Ant farm or formicarium is used
to house and observe ants.
1 Sliding glass lid.
2 Plaster of Paris base molded
into tunnel shapes.

3 Dark cloth to keep out light.
4 Feeding trough.
5 Optional feeding tube
connected to glass jar.
Care Keep the formicarium
damp, covered, and out of direct
sun. Feed the ants small
amounts of dead insects, nuts,
crumbs, and fruit. Provide a
sponge moistened with honey
water. The feeding jar can be
used for larger items of food, or
to contain a stick covered with
aphids, which the ants "milk."

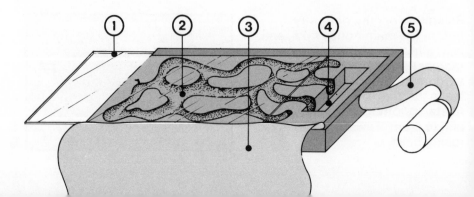

Scorpions

There are many species of scorpion, all found in tropical regions. They are distinguished from other arachnids by their crab-like pincers, which they use for holding prey. Scorpions are famous for their sting, which is carried at the end of a slim tail. The sting of some species is powerful enough to kill humans, but others are weaker. Always handle scorpions with care.

Brown scorpion *(Palamnaeus fulvipes)* Tropical regions; 2½ in (6cm); brown; four pairs of legs; one pair of pincers (pedipalps); long, slim tail with sting at end; nocturnal; carnivorous.

Care House scorpions in a desert environment similar to that for tropical spiders (p.253). To house four scorpions, glass cages should be 1ft x 2ft x 1ft (30in x 60in x 30in). The floor must be covered with a sloping layer of damp sand and rocks arranged to provide hiding places. Keep at 80°F(26°C). Cleanliness is essential. Feed live insects, and provide a small container filled with cotton wool soaked in water for drinking. Move scorpions by coaxing them into boxes with a long-handled paint brush. Do not pick them up.

Breeding The breeding habits of scorpions are notable for the care and attention given by the mother. About 10 fat, white young are born and carried for up to 2 weeks on their mother's back (see above). The female continues to feed her young until about the 60th day.

©DIAGRAM

251

Spiders

Spiders are arachnids, and over 30,000 species are found worldwide. A chief characteristic is the production of silk, spun from spinnerets at the rear of the body. Silk is used to wrap eggs in cocoons, to wrap prey, to build webs, tunnels, or burrows, and to help young spiders migrate in the wind. Not all spiders have webs to trap prey. Wolf spiders, giant bird-eating spiders (or

1 Wolf spiders (family Lycosidae and Pisauridae) Worldwide; up to ½in(1.3cm) body length; brown.
2 Red-legged tarantula (*Brachyrelma smithi colima*) Mexico; 7in(18cm) leg span; black with red bands on legs.
3 Jumping spiders (family Salticidae) Worldwide; less than 7/10in(1.7cm); often highly colored.
4 Orb-weavers (family Araneidae) Worldwide; ½in(1.3cm); acute sense of touch.
5 House spiders (*Tegenaria* species) up to 6/10in(1.5cm); long legs; weaves sheet webs.

tarantulas), and jumping spiders are ground hunters relying on good eyesight and agility to leap on their victims. Orb-weavers make the classic web common in gardens, and house spiders build sheet webs indoors or in sheltered areas. Spiders have been the subject of many myths and fears, but they are chiefly harmless and benefit man by controlling insect populations.

Care Large tropical tarantulas or bird-eating spiders can be kept in a frequently cleaned aquarium tank (see below).
1 Screen top.
2 Rock shelter.
3 Floor covering of gravel.
4 Light bulbs to provide heat.
5 Cactus or tropical plant.
6 Sponge in water dish — spiders do not drink directly, but brush their mouth parts with moisture. Feed live insects, especially locusts and crickets. Spiders molt regularly, and during this period may change color and remain inactive.
Smaller spiders, including web-makers can be caught and kept for a few days in plastic or glass jars with perforated lids. Supply live insects, sticks to attach webs to, and plant leaves covered in moisture. Some spiders may be "tamed" by offering them mealworms.

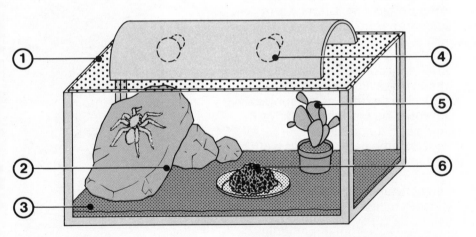

Webs The classic spider's web is built by the orb-weavers, and is often found in gardens. Each strand is no more than 0.003mm in diameter; the outer spiral is covered with sticky gum. Vibrations enable the spider to locate its prey, which it kills by biting with venomous fangs.

© DIAGRAM

4

Amphibians

Amphibians are cold-blooded vertebrates with damp, smooth, scaleless skins through which they absorb moisture. Since they do not drink, a damp atmosphere or water to soak in is essential if they are not to die of dehydration. Most breed in water, laying eggs encased in jelly. Young breathe through gills, but most gain lungs and live on land as adults. On land, they eat only moving prey. Amphibians come from warm and temperate lands.

Frogs, toads, and salamanders make attractive pets. Some are strikingly colored — especially those frogs and salamanders with skin secretions poisonous to would-be predators. Many frogs and toads have entertaining calls. Successful keeping of amphibians depends on the right combination of temperature, humidity, light, cleanliness, and food.

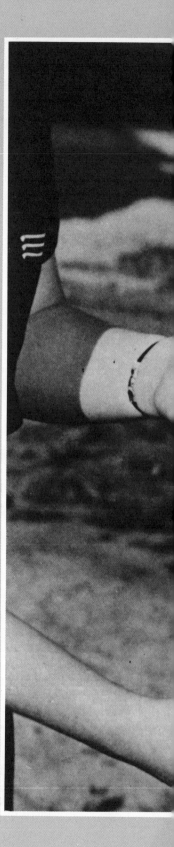

Right A handsome frog photographed at a farm in California (Popperfoto).

254

Amphibian characteristics

The most common amphibian pets are frogs, toads, and salamanders (including newts). Frogs are tailless, slimmer than toads, and tend to have longer hind legs. Many live in or by water. Toads are short, squat, and tailless. Many live in fairly dry conditions but breed in water. Salamanders are long bodied and long tailed. Some are entirely aquatic; others land based but breeding in water.

a Frogs Features of true frogs of the family Ranidae are given here. (Other families of frogs and froglike amphibians, such as tree frogs of the family Hylidae, are anatomically more like toads.)
1 Head rather long and narrow.
2 Eardrum usually visible.
3 Pulls eyes into head to close.
4 Skin is smooth, damp, and shed regularly. It absorbs water and oxygen from air or water.
5 Some frogs' skins secrete poison to deter predators.
6 Tailless.
7 Fairly slim, waisted body.
8 Hind legs usually long; frogs leap rather than hop or walk.
9 Hind feet are usually webbed, but tree frogs tend to have well-separated toes ending in flat disks for gripping branches.
10 Carnivorous; eats moving prey but ignores all other food.
11 Adult male frogs tend to be smaller than adult females.
12 Males croak in breeding season.

b Toads True toads belong to the family Bufonidae; they have no teeth in the upper jaw. But some other amphibians of broadly similar build are also known as toads. The features shown here occur in bufonid toads.
1 Head short and broad.
2 Skin is dryish, warty, and shed regularly. It absorbs water and oxygen.
3 Skin may cover eardrum.
4 Pulls eyes into head to close.
5 Parotid and other glands secrete poison as a defense against would-be predators.
6 Body short and squat.
7 Tailless.
8 Hind legs short; toads hop, walk, or run.
9 Hind feet usually webbed for swimming.
10 Carnivorous; toads eat only moving prey.
11 Adult male toads tend to be smaller than adult females.
12 Males croak in breeding season.

c Salamanders and newts
1 Keen sense of smell.
2 No movable eyelids.
3 No ears.
4 Toes lack claws.
5 Skin is smooth or warty, shed regularly, and absorbs water and oxygen.
6 Skin secretes poison.
7 Long, often thin body.
8 Long, often flattened tail.
9 Limbs short (sirens lack hind limbs); lost limbs regrow.
10 Males tend to bulge here.
11 Carnivorous.
12 Some squeak if handled.
13 Many male newts have crests in spring.

257 ©DIAGRAM

Housing amphibians

Most frogs, toads, and salamanders need a damp home with some water. Illustrated here are a tall tank with plants and branches ideal for tree frogs, and a woodland setting suitable for many amphibians. Make sure that plants are suited to required heat, humidity, and light levels. Perforated lids must fit closely; amphibians that escape indoors dry up and die. Replace soil when it smells

Tree frog vivarium
1 Glass tank.
2 Hinged and perforated lid, securely fastened.
3 Moss, kept watered.
4 Water dish.
5 Branch.
6 Tall pot plant.
Woodland setting
7 Glass tank.
8 Perforated zinc lid on wood frame.
9 Moss, kept watered.
10 Bark hideaway.
11 Acid-free peat (treated by soaking in water) 2in (5cm) deep.
12 Charcoal and coarse gravel 1in (2.5cm) deep.
13 Water dish.
14 Pebble surround.
15 Pot plants (pots sunk in peat).
16 Drainage holes.

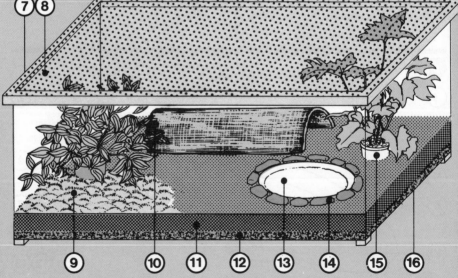

unpleasant. Provide daylight. For tropical species active at night a tinted bulb may double as a heater. For others, a dimmed neon tube will give light without too much heat. Some amphibians need a semiaquatic setting (see p.282, but include more land) or water only (pp.184,190). Hardy toads and frogs thrive in an outdoor reptiliary (p.280), but beware escapes. (Hibernate as aquatic turtles, see p.285.)

Vivarium needs Table showing the vivarium needs of different amphibians.

Legend:
- ○ Some species or at some times
- ◐ Most species
- ● All species

	Frogs	Tree frogs	Toads	Aquatic salamanders	Land salamanders	Newts
Woodland setting	●	◐	●		○	○
Semiaquatic setting	○				○	○
Water-filled aquarium				●		○
Outdoor reptiliary	○		○	○	○	○
Damp atmosphere	●	●			●	●
Over 70°F (21°C)	○	○	○			
Some sun	●	●	●			
Live food	●	●	●	●	●	●
Branches		●				
Water dish	●	●	●		●	
Soil to burrow in	○		●		●	
Hiding places	●		●		●	●

©DIAGRAM

Handling amphibians

Sensitive, slippery skins and violent wriggling make some amphibians very difficult to hold. Amphiumas (p.271) also bite severely. If possible, amphibians should be picked up in a damp muslin net. Otherwise use your hands, but first moisten them with cool or tepid water. After handling, wash your hands thoroughly to remove poison secreted by the skins of some species of frogs, toads, and salamanders.

Handling Some slippery frogs and salamanders pose special problems. Shut small ones in one or two cupped hands (**a**), leaving no gaps but taking care not to cause injury. For larger frogs, grip around waist with finger and thumb (**b**), or use a damp muslin net. Hold a large land-dwelling salamander in your hand, with its head projecting between your first two fingers and its tail emerging between your palm and little finger (**c**).

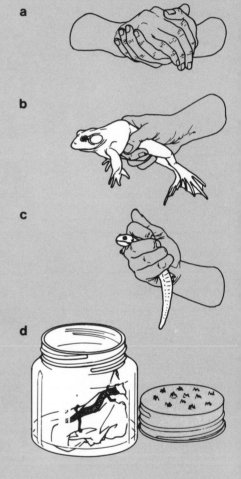

a

b

c

d

Transporting Any container must contain wet moss, paper towels, or plastic foam. Small amphibians can be carried in plastic jars with tight-fitting lids in which air holes have been drilled (**d**). For short journeys a plastic bag sealed to enclose air may be used. Large amphibians may be transported in muslin bags (see p. 287) inside a ventilated polystyrene box. Beware of crushing. Never put a container where it may fall. (Note that sturdy animals may move a bag bodily.) Keep out of the sun.

Dispatching For road, rail, or air journeys of short duration, a few small specimens may be sent, together with wet moss, paper towels, or plastic foam, in a strong plastic bag sealed to enclose air, or, better still, in a rigid plastic jar or box with air holes. Place larger specimens in a muslin bag containing damp moss, paper towels, or plastic foam. Put in a strong, rigid, ventilated box, amid a cushion of crumpled paper. Label "perishable," and give the animal's scientific and common names. Never dispatch in bitter winter weather.

Feeding amphibians

Amphibians are carnivorous. On land, adults eat moving prey only. In water some eat motionless bits of meat or fish. Some eat only at night. Feed separately if a greedy individual steals the others' rations. Amphibians may take raw meat or fish from forceps waved to and fro nearby. Vary the diet. Separate large and small animals to avoid cannibalism. For feeding young, see p. 262.

Foods For details of obtaining foods see p. 230. Always avoid creatures that have been exposed to pesticides. The diagram (right) shows foods for different types of amphibian.
1 Many frogs eat worms, slugs, maggots, flies, beetles, crickets and locusts, and stick insects.
2 Small frogs eat small worms, fruit flies, aphids, flies, crickets and locusts, and small insects from leaf litter.
3 Toads eat worms, slugs, mealworms, beetles, flies, crickets and locusts, baby mice, and stick insects.
4 Giant frogs and toads eat slugs, flies, crickets and locusts, baby mice, and stick insects.
5 Tree frogs eat fruit flies, aphids, flies, crickets and locusts, moths, stick insects, and insects from leaf litter.
6 Salamanders and newts eat worms, slugs, meat or fish, flies, crickets and locusts. On land, they may take food from forceps (see below).

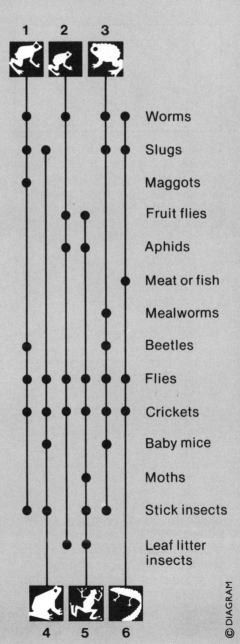

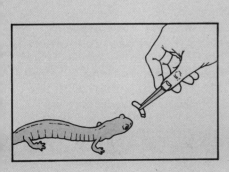

© DIAGRAM

Raising young amphibians

Watching the hatching and development of tadpoles or salamander larvae is a fascinating experience. But all too often people fail to provide them with their basic needs — including food. Avoid overcrowding. If the water smells, change it. Make sure you provide a shore for when the creatures are ready to leave the water — when frogs and toads gain legs, and when salamanders gain lungs.

Development The drawings show stages in the development of a frog (**a**) and a newt (**b**). The larvae hatch from jelly-like eggs and undergo metamorphosis (major change) to become adults.

Aquarium An untilted tank with deeper water is suitable for young larvae, but metamorphosing frogs risk drowning unless precautions are taken (see below).
1 Lid. On corks for ventilation.
2 Glass tank. Tilted during metamorphosis period to give different depths of water.
3 Shallow water (at room temperature for most species).
4 Sphagnum moss (or paper towels or plastic foam) to climb on during metamorphosis period.

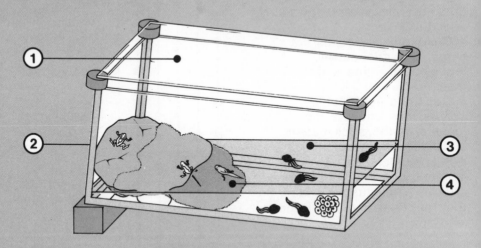

Feeding larvae Most tadpoles like green pond scum (algae), boiled lettuce, grass powder mixed to a paste, and tiny bits of worm, scraped meat, and egg yolk. Feed salamander larvae and spadefoot tadpoles on water fleas, white worms, and bits of raw liver and earthworm. Do not foul the water by overfeeding. Hungry young newts bite off each other's limbs; keep singly.
Feeding young on land Give chopped earthworms, white worms, or, for tree frogs, fruit flies. Also feed tiny insects from leaf litter. Young may take meat from a moving twig.

Health and disease

Some healthy amphibians live 20 or more years. But infection, injury, and wrong conditions can cause hunger strikes, lethargy, and early death. Skin troubles and those due to poor conditions may be treatable, internal diseases may not. Quarantine new arrivals for two weeks, and isolate sick individuals. Forced feeding can injure and is not worth trying. If necessary, kill humanely.

Conditions causing poor health
1 No direct sunlight. Let some in through a mesh screen lid, not tank or window glass. Or give very limited ultraviolet light.
2 Poor ventilation. Prop glass lid on card, cork, or paper strips — or replace by muslin, nylon, or perforated zinc or plastic.
3 Light inhibits feeding at night. Switch off, or shade, or use a blue-tinted bulb.
4 Too hot or cold. Adjust heater, shading, or location in room.
5 Overcrowding. Keep fewer animals together in one tank.
6 Fouled floor. Clean often.
7 Air too dry or damp. Adjust water content or tank covering.
8 Poisoned by fly spray. Do not spray in a room with amphibians.
9 Wrong food. Check food needs.
10 One species poisoned by skin secretions of another. Separate incompatible species.

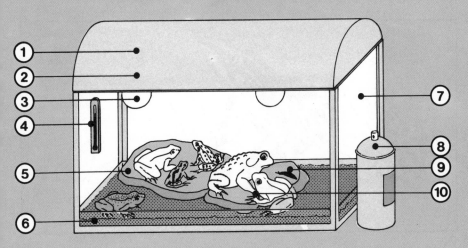

Injury and disease
Infected skin abrasions should be painted with mercurochrome. Amphibians kept in overheated, polluted tanks may suffer fungal skin infections. Isolate, lower temperature, and treat with a petfish fungicide.
Frogs may contract red leg — a contagious and often fatal disease of bacterial origin. The frog is bloated and lethargic, with reddening on the undersides of the hind legs. Isolate the infected animal and add salt (up to 0.06%) to water. Antibiotic treatment may succeed (see a veterinarian). Disinfect the tank.

©DIAGRAM

Frogs (ranids)

True frogs of the family Ranidae are powerful swimmers
and some can jump 8ft (2.4m). Found worldwide, some
species are under 1in (2.5cm) and others up to 11in (28cm)
long. Ranids breed in water, males clasping females to
fertilize the eggs as they are laid. Many make good pets.
Provide generous space. Hardy kinds thrive in a predator-
free reptiliary (see p. 280) with 3ft (1m) walls.

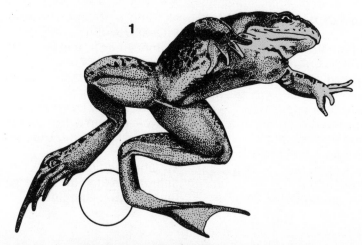

1 Common frog *(Rana
temporaria)* Eurasia; 3½ in (9cm);
yellow, brown, gray, or dark; feed
live earthworms, insects, grubs,
etc; likes damp and shade.
2 Leopard frog *(Rana pipiens)*
Canada and N. United States,
3½ in (9cm); brown or green with
spots; keep as common frog.

3 Edible frog *(Rana esculenta)*
Eurasia; 4½ in (12cm); green or
brown with black blotches; feed
worms, etc, treat as bullfrog.
4 American bullfrog *(Rana
catesbeiana)* N. America; 6in
(15cm); green or greenish brown;
in wild eats live fish, mice, worms,
etc; needs large terrarium.

Leptodactylids and pipids

Barking and horned frogs belong to the Leptodactylidae, a big family of New World and Australian frogs, of varied shape and size. Some breed on land, laying eggs from which fully developed hatchling frogs emerge.
The clawed frog and Surinam toad represent the Pipidae. The so-called "tongueless toads" form a primitive aquatic group found only in Africa and South America.

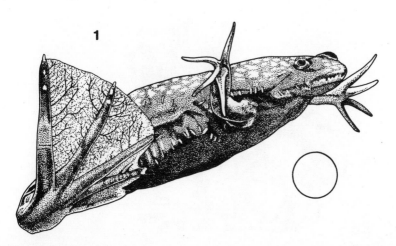

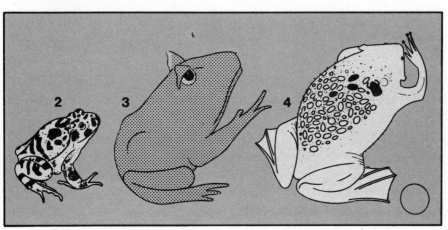

1 Clawed frog *(Xenopus laevis)* Africa; 6in (15cm); grayish with pale belly; feed worms, raw meat/fish, fishmeal pellets; needs water at 70°F (21°C).
2 Barking frog *(Hylactophryne augusti)* S.W. North America; 3in (7.6cm); toadlike; gray, brown, or greenish; feed spiders, insects; needs sandy floor and rock cave.
3 Horned frog *(Ceratophrys cornuta)* Amazon Basin; 6in (15cm); black, tan, pink; mice, lizards, insects, worms, frogs; needs heat, sandy soil, dead leaves, moss.
4 Surinam toad *(Pipa pipa)* South America; 6in (15cm); brown/gray; keep as *Xenopus*, at 75°F (24°C).

©DIAGRAM

265

Tree frogs

Tree frogs come in great variety, and many make attractive pets. Tall plants, water, and live insects and spiders are basic requirements. Tropical species need heat. There are over 450 species belonging to the family Hylidae, with worldwide distribution. Some are minute, others about 5in (13cm) long. Most have slim waists, long limbs, and toe pads. They are agile climbers. Some can change color.

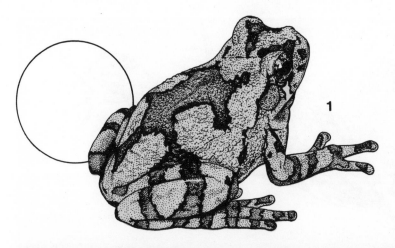

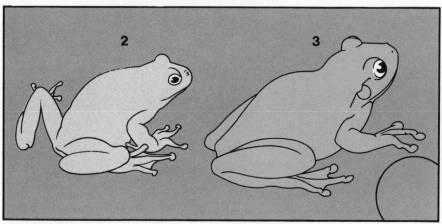

1 Gray tree frog *(Hyla versicolor)* E. North America; 2in (5cm); gray or green but variable; males trill; feed flies, moths, etc; provide a tall terrarium with pot plants, and a pool for breeding.
2 European tree frog *(Hyla arborea)* S. and C. Europe; 2in (5cm); green but variable; treat as gray tree frog.
3 Cuban tree frog *(Hyla septentrionalis)* W. Indies, S.E. United States; 3½in (9cm); green to bronze warty skin; hides somewhere moist by day; eats insects, small frogs.
4 Western chorus frog *(Pseudacris triseriata triseriata)*

Some call noisily at night or after rain. They include marsupial frogs whose females have a back pouch for carrying eggs. Two other families of tree frogs are also represented here. Tiny arum frogs belong to the Rhacophoridae of Asia and Africa. The poison arrow frogs of South America are in the Dendrobatidae, a family of brightly colored frogs with very poisonous skins.

C. North America; 1½ in (3.8cm); striped brown; timid climbers.

5 Marsupial frog *(Gastrotheca marsupiata)* South America; 2in (5cm); greenish-gray with dark markings; treat as gray tree frog but needs 70-75°F (21-24°C).

6 Arum frog *(Hyperolius horstockii)* Southern Africa; 1in (2.5cm); tones of brown; feed tiny insects; provide humid, mossy terrarium at 70-75°F (21-24°C).

7 Poison arrow frog (Dendrobatidae) S. America; 1½in(3.8cm); black and white with red head and back; treat as arum frog.

Toads

Toads of the family Bufonidae are among the best amphibians to keep. There are hundreds of different kinds, found almost worldwide. They are the common garden toads, with dryish, "warty" skins, heavy bodies, and short limbs. The largest measure 9in (23cm) in length. Poisonous skin secretions deter many predators (wash your hands after handling). Many kinds feed at night and enter water

1 Giant toad *(Bufo marinus)*
Tropical Americas; 9in(23cm); brownish; eats mealworms, live mice, etc; needs heated cage with a pool or dish of water.

2 Common toad *(Bufo bufo)*
Eurasia, N. Africa; 4½ in (12cm); brownish; eats insects, worms; tames easily; longlived.

3 American toad *(Bufo americanus)* E. North America; 3½ in (9cm); brown with dark spots; feed live insects; give soil for burrowing.

4 Green toad *(Bufo viridis)*
Eurasia; 3in(8cm); gray-green with black-edged green patches, some have red warts; eats

only to breed. Most like a coolish tank, drier than for frogs. Examples are also included here of several other species of toads and toadlike amphibians that are sometimes kept as pets. Spadefoot toads (Pelobatidae) burrow with "spades" on their hind feet. Midwife toads and the more aquatic fire-bellied toads belong to the Discoglossidae ("rounded tongue") group of amphibians.

invertebrates; likes to burrow.
5 Eastern spadefoot toad *(Scaphiopus holbrooki holbrooki)* E. and S.E. United States; 2¼ in (5.7cm); brown; feed maggots, earthworms; provide soft soil for burrowing.
6 Midwife toad *(Alytes obstetricans)* W. Europe; 2in (5cm); gray-brown; male carries eggs on back until they hatch in shallow water; feed insects, worms; needs land and water.
7 Fire-bellied toad *(Bombina bombina)* E. Europe; 2in (5cm); dark back, orange-red on belly; feed insects and worms; needs land and water.

Aquatic salamanders

Some salamanders spend all their lives in water. Many but not all of them keep their gills as adults. All-aquatic salamanders are chiefly found in North America, Europe, and East Asia. They include the largest amphibians alive today. Six families of aquatic salamanders are represented on these pages. Hellbenders, like giant salamanders, belong to the Cryptobranchidae. The olm, amphiumas,

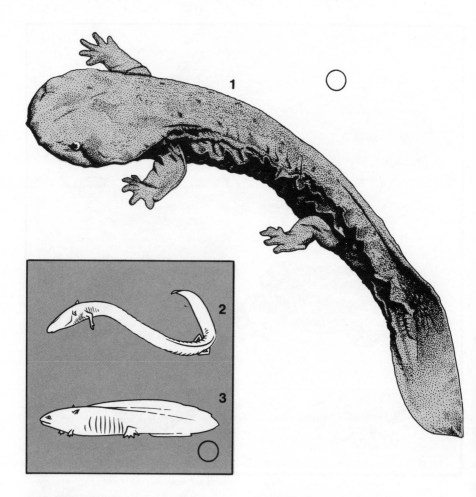

1 Hellbender *(Cyrptobranchus alleganiensis)* E. USA; 30in (76cm); gray; eats meat, fish, dogfood; needs water 12-18in (30-46cm) deep.

2 Olm *(Proteus anguinus)* S. Europe; 12in (30cm); white; eats *Tubifex* and other worms; needs dim light and under 50°F (10°C).

3 Axolotl *(Ambystoma mexicanum)* Mexico; 9in(22.5cm); brown or white with big, feathery gills (it loses these if given thyroid extract, and then lives on land like other ambystomids); both forms can breed; may live 20 years; feed worms, slugs, etc.

mudpuppies, and sirens have their own respective families. The axolotl is an unusual member of the typically land-based Ambystomidae.

All-aquatic salamanders should be kept in water below 70°F (21°C), with plants or rocks to hide beneath, and a weighted screen lid to prevent escapes. They need frequent cleaning out, with chlorine-free water.

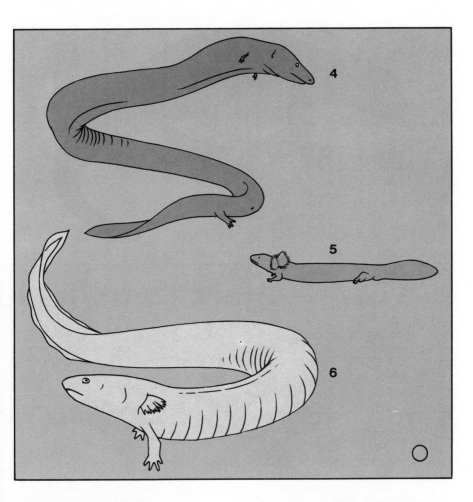

4 Two-toed amphiuma
(Amphiuma means) S.E. USA; 30in (76cm); brownish-black; dislikes bright light; bites; feed worms, fish, shellfish, etc.
5 Mudpuppy *(Necturus maculosus)* E. North America; 13in (33cm); brown, with gills; longlived; feed worms, beef, fish; water needs an air pump.
6 Greater siren *(Siren lacertina)* S.E. USA; 30in (76cm); eel-like, with gills and forelimbs only; olive/gray; feed worms, raw beef.

Land salamanders

Robust land salamanders are among the most decorative, popular, and easily kept of all amphibians. Included here are examples from the Salamandridae (also including the newts, p.274) and from the Ambystomidae, or mole salamanders. Fire and alpine salamanders bear live young — the first in water 1in (2.5cm) deep, the second on damp land. Mole salamanders, more typically, lay eggs in water.

1

1 Alpine salamander
(*Salamandra atra*) Europe; 6¼ in (16cm); bears young on land; slugs, worms; keep cool; hibernate.
2 Fire salamander (*Salamandra salamandra*) Europe, S.W. Asia, N. Africa; 9½ in (24cm); black and yellow; bears live young; feed slugs, worms; damp, mossy,

shady tank with dish of water.
3 Tiger salamander (*Ambystoma tigrinum tigrinum*) USA; 7in (18cm); dark with pale brownish spots; keep as fire salamander.
4 Marbled salamander
(*Ambystoma opacum*) E. USA; 4¼ in (11cm); black and whitish; keep as fire salamander.

Lungless salamanders

Salamanders of the family Plethodontidae fail to develop lungs as adults but "breathe" instead through their skins and mouths. Confined almost exclusively to the New World, this large family of usually slender, frail-looking creatures contains both aquatic and land-based forms. The latter require damp, cool conditions, and worms and insects to eat. Small ones need live white worms and *Tubifex*.

1 Slimy salamander(*Plethodon glutinosus*) E. USA; 6¾ in (17cm); black, spotted, and sticky; feed *Tubifex* worms, slugs, etc; keep in cool, moist conditions.
2 Northern red salamander (*Pseudotriton ruber ruber*) E. USA; 6in (15cm); reddish with black spots; keep cool; damp moss, bark, and shallow water.
3 Northern dusky salamander (*Desmognathus fuscus fuscus*) E. USA; 4½ in (11cm); brown or gray; lives by mountain streams.
4 Oregon salamander(*Ensatina eschscholtzi oregonensis*) W. USA; 5½ in (14cm); brown, pale belly; damp, woodland setting.

Newts

These members of the Salamandridae have flatter tails than others (p. 272), and on land their skin is rougher and less slippery. Most live in Europe, Asia, and North America. Breeding occurs in water, and adults of some species are wholly aquatic. Many males have crests and bright colors in the breeding season. The male produces a gelatinous capsule containing eggs, which the female takes into her

1 Crested newt *(Triturus cristatus)* Eurasia; 6¼ in (16cm); "warty," black and orange, male has white dots and tail band and saw-edged crest in spring; feed worms, etc; keep cool and moist.
2 Smooth newt *(Triturus vulgaris)* Eurasia; 3½ in (9cm); brownish, but males black, blue,

orange, and crested in spring; hardy; treat as crested newt.
3 Marbled newt *(Triturus marmoratus)* S.W. Europe; 6¼ in (16cm); green and black, male strikingly crested in spring; hardy; treat as crested newt.
4 Alpine newt *(Triturus alpestris)* Europe; 4in (10cm); black,

body. To see newts swim, court, and lay eggs, put them in early spring into an all-water aquarium stocked with fine-leaved water plants. Then remove the adults to a suitable aquarium or woodland setting (p. 258); otherwise they eat the eggs or larvae. (For raising young see p. 262). In water newts will take raw meat, insects, and earthworms. On land they ignore all food that does not move.

orange, blue, male is crested in spring; hardy.

5 California newt (*Taricha torosa*) California; 6½ in (16.5cm); dark with orange belly; hardy.

6 Ribbed newt (*Pleurodeles waltl*) S.W. Europe, N.W. Africa; 8¾ in (22cm); largest newt; gray-brown, with orange "warts"; rarely leaves water; feed worms.

7 Red spotted newt (*Notophthalmus viridescens viridescens*) E. North America; 4 in (10cm); post-larval young (red efts) are terrestrial, eat insects; adults are olive and yellow with red spots, aquatic, and will take canned dog food.

© DIAGRAM

5

Reptiles

Reptiles — lizards, snakes, crocodilians, and turtles — are cold-blooded vertebrates with dry, scaly skins. Some species bear living young while others lay leathery or hard-shelled eggs, all on land.

Some reptiles tame readily and respond to handling. Many make intriguing pets for people prepared to give them proper care. Any endangered, very big, poisonous, or pernickety reptile must, however, be considered unsuitable for anyone but the most dedicated keeper with specialized facilities; even so, legal restrictions often apply. Most reptiles come from warm climates, and many are active only when warmed by basking. Overheating or chilling can kill. Reptiles are mainly carnivorous. To stay healthy, many need food rich in calcium and vitamin D as well as plenty of direct sun. Clean conditions are vital.

Right Undeterred by their observers, these African chameleons are out to enjoy the sun (Mansell Collection).

Choosing a reptile

Select only healthy specimens kept in clean conditions. Price will reflect your tastes, but bear in mind the following practical considerations. Some reptiles are shortlived. Some need foods that are difficult to obtain. Lizards feed more frequently than snakes. Aquatic turtles need cleaning out more often than dry-land reptiles. Crocodilians and pythons may grow unmanageably large. Some reptiles inflict painful — even lethal — injuries. Legal restrictions apply to the keeping of rare and dangerous species.

a Snakes
1 Choose shy, lively specimens.
2 Eyes should be bright and clear except when sloughing (p. 303).
3 Avoid slow-moving, "trusting" individuals.
4 Beware mouth injury.
5 Beware gaping mouth and labored breathing.
6 Beware colds with coughing.
7 Avoid specimens with poor skin condition.
8 Avoid snakes with blisters.
9 Beware mite infestation.
10 Avoid animals that will not eat.
11 Do not buy snakes in cold weather unless chilling can be avoided.

b Lizards
c Crocodilians
1 Select shy, lively animals.
2 Eyes should be bright and clear.
3 Avoid specimens that are "trusting" and slow-moving.
4 Beware mouth or snout injury or rot.
5 Beware gaping mouth and labored breathing.
6 Beware colds with coughing.
7 Beware jaw deformity.
8 Beware spine deformity.
9 Avoid animals with poor skin condition.
10 Beware mite infestation.
11 Beware hind limb paralysis.
12 Avoid animals that will not eat.
13 Do not buy in cold weather unless chilling can be avoided.

d Turtles
1 Turtles should be shy, with lively movements.
2 Eyes should be bright and clear.
3 Head, limbs, and neck should be free of sores, lumps, or white fungal spots.
4 Nostrils should be free of any discharge.
5 Mouth should be free of yellow fungus.
6 Shell should be free from erosion.
7 Shell weight should seem great for size.
8 In young (except soft-shelled and pancake turtles) shell should be hard.
9 Growth rings on shell and worn nails denote old individuals.
10 Turtles in same pet store cage should seem healthy.
11 Aquatic turtles should soon dive and swim well if placed in water.

©DIAGRAM

Keeping reptiles outdoors

Hardy lizards, snakes, and aquatic turtles can be kept out of doors for part or all of the year in an unclimbable outdoor reptiliary similar to that shown below. But remember the possibility of bullying and cannibalism when keeping some reptiles together. Land turtles require a special pen like that shown on the next page. (For details on the hibernation of different types of reptile see p. 285.)

Outdoor reptiliary
1 Enclosure in an open, sunny location.
2 Wall made from asbestos or pvc sheeting nailed to support posts: 3ft (90cm) above ground and 1ft (30cm) below.
3 Overlap of sheets.
4 Big stones and creeping, shrubby, or other plants. (Keep well clear of reptiliary wall.)
5 Shrubs for cover and shade.
6 Sandy, rocky hillock (with core of stones or broken bricks) at

least 1ft 6in (46cm) high—more where subzero temperatures occur. (Keep well clear of wall.)
7 Low level sides for drainage.
8 Basking beach.
9 Pool made from plastic liner or concrete—must be more than 2ft (60cm) for hibernation of aquatic turtles.
10 Shallow, shelving end of pool.
11 Tethered log, and water plants.
12 Dead branches and logs as basking places.

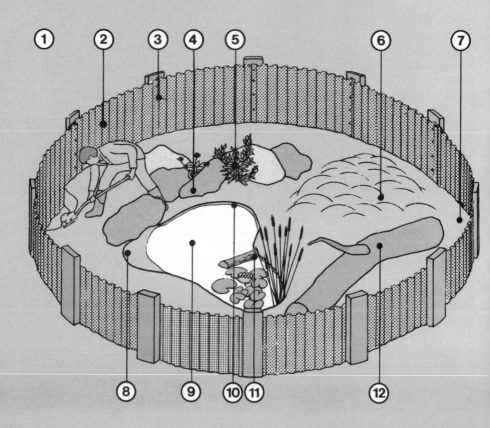

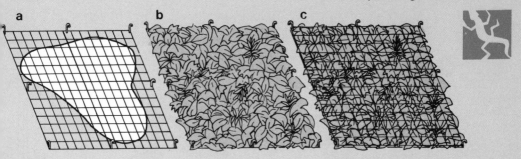

a b c

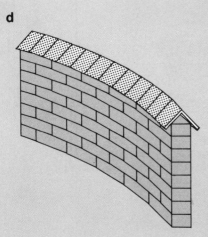

d

Preparing the pool for winter

Clean the pool in the fall. At winter's onset, cover it with netting (**a**), add leaves (**b**), and pin with more netting (**c**). Keep leaves out of the water.

Alternative reptiliary wall

A pvc wall is cheap and easy to make, but pvc becomes brittle and may tear in a gale. For a more durable structure build a brick or stone wall with tiled double overhang (**d**) to stop escapes or entry by rodents.

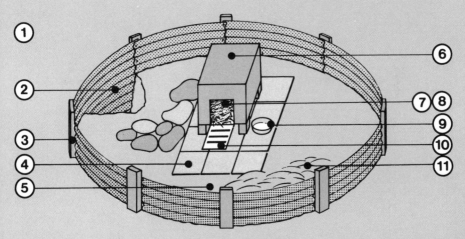

Land turtle pen

1 Open, sunny enclosure.
2 Pvc sheeting 1ft (30cm) high. Must be sunk deeply in ground if burrowing species are kept.
3 Support posts.
4 Easily cleaned tiles.
5 Grass, sand, and stones.
6 Rainproof hut on low legs,
facing southeast.
7 Shady interior.
8 Clean straw or hay.
9 Low, untippable dish for drinking water (which needs frequent changing).
10 Broad, gently sloping ramp.
11 Undulating area for exercise.

© DIAGRAM

Keeping reptiles indoors

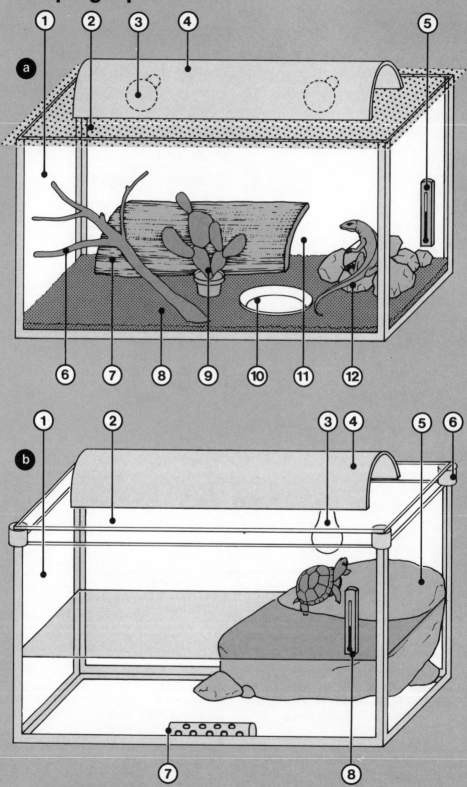

Snakes, lizards, and land turtles need a dry, ventilated glass tank, or a glass-fronted wood or metal cage. Any climbing species must have a tall terrarium to accommodate branches and rocks. The cages of venomous snakes or lizards must always be padlocked. A table of vivarium ingredients is given on p.284. Heating may be by a light bulb or a tubular heater — but protect animals from the heat source. Sun-basking reptiles in particular need hot and cooler areas within the terrarium. Avoid rough surfaces if snakes are kept. Fine sand, stones, and cacti suit desert species. Hothouse plants and loam or peat on charcoal above gravel suit iguanas — but avoid too much dampness. Paper floors are easiest to clean.
For crocodilians and aquatic turtles use stone, brick, or wood to make land and water areas in an aquarium. Add a ramp if necessary. A combined heater-thermostat in a protective casing is recommended. Frequent cleaning is essential with these animals. Most filters are not particularly effective. A gravel floor makes matters worse.

a Terrarium suitable for lizards, snakes, or land turtles
1 Glass tank.
2 Perforated zinc cover.
3 Light bulb for heating.
4 Reflector.
5 Thermometer.
6 Branch.
7 Cork bark.
8 Gravel floor.
9 Cactus.
10 Water dish.
11 Shady hiding place.
12 Stones resting on cage floor.

b Aquaterrarium suitable for crocodilians or aquatic turtles
1 Glass tank.
2 Sheet of glass.
3 Light bulb heater in use only during daytime.
4 Reflector.
5 Stone out of water for basking.
6 Cork or wood slices to raise top for ventilation.
7 Heater-thermostat and wiring, housed in perforated plastic or metal cylinder for protection.
8 Thermometer.

Temperature gradient A terrarium should have areas at different temperatures, allowing the animal to select where it feels most comfortable. A rock or branch raised under a heater provides a hot spot (**a**) and a range of temperatures down to a cooler area (**b**).

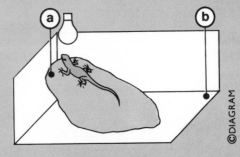

©DIAGRAM

283

Vivarium ingredients

Included below is a table showing the various vivarium contents and conditions recommended for the keeping of different types of reptile.

Contents	Lizards	Snakes	Crocodilians	Land turtles	Aquatic turtles
Paper floor	●	●			
Sand floor	●	●			
Gravel floor	●	●		●	
Pebble floor	●	●	●	●	
Dry earth with peat or sand	●	●			
Potted plants	●	●	●	●	●
Branches	●	●			
Cardboard house	●	●			
Dark hiding place	●	●		●	
Water dish	●	●		●	

Conditions	Lizards	Snakes	Crocodilians	Land turtles	Aquatic turtles
Heat source	●	●	●	●	●
Dry atmosphere	●	●	●	●	●
Ventilation	●	●	●	●	●
Water area			●		●
Sunshine or ultraviolet light	●	●	●	●	●

Hibernation

In nature, hardy reptiles stop eating in the fall, burrow (or submerge), and grow torpid. In captivity, they stay active if kept warm but may lose appetite. Except for indoor aquatic turtles, most reptiles live longer if allowed to hibernate somewhere cold but frost free. Wake them in early spring. Mild weather makes hibernators wakeful and liable to starve unless cooled or fully warmed and fed.

Land turtles (outdoors) If climate is not too cold or damp, allow turtles to burrow in soft soil or supply a pile of dead leaves held by pegged netting.

Land turtles (indoors) Place turtle in a box (**a**) containing straw (**b**), hay, dry leaves, or screwed up newspaper, and covered loosely with a lid (**c**). Put in a draft-free, frost-free shed or in a cold room and cover with a blanket. (To keep out rats use a metal box and a tight-fitting lid with air holes.)

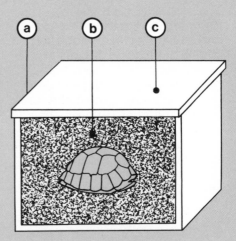

Aquatic turtles (outdoors) Well-grown, hardy specimens can hibernate in a pond deep enough never to freeze solid. Dead leaves sandwiched between nets just above it insulate the pool (see p. 281).

Aquatic turtles (indoors) May be best kept awake. Otherwise, place in a large water-filled aquarium floored with sand. Keep somewhere cold but frost free. Feed if temperature exceeds 50°F (10°C), then change water.

Lizards and snakes (outdoors) Hardy species will burrow in a rubble hillock. Or supply a rubble and earth mound (**d**) containing a rock or brick cave (**e**) that is stuffed with dead leaves (**f**) and entered by a narrow drainpipe (**g**) sloped to keep out the rain. Site hibernaculum in a well-drained position below frost level.

Lizards and snakes (indoors) Fill cages with leaves and dry moss. Position somewhere cold, frost free, and draft free.

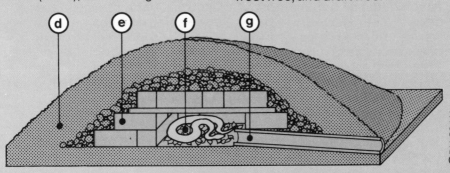

©DIAGRAM

Breeding reptiles

Some reptiles produce liveborn young, but most lay eggs in soft soil or mud. To hatch, these need warm, rather humid conditions. (Too much moisture may encourage fungus, too little causes drying up.) Eggs should hatch in 10-12 weeks or less. Babies should be raised away from adults big enough to harm them. Some babies need special food and higher temperatures than adults. Most need sun.

Hatching in a bag Reptile eggs may be hatched in a plastic bag (a) with damp sand (b), soil, or peat moss in the bottom. Place the eggs (not turning them) in individual dents made in the sand or other material. Bulge the bag's sides out and tightly seal the top with a rubber band (c). Place the bag in an airing cupboard, or over a radiator, or float it in a tropical aquarium—anywhere with a temperature of about 80°F (27°C). If no moisture (d) forms in the bag, add a few water droplets. After some weeks, the eggs should be inspected daily for signs of hatching.

Hatching in a box Alternatively, reptile eggs may be hatched in a large wood box (e) heated by a light bulb (f). With this method, care must be taken to keep the sand (g) or other material moist.

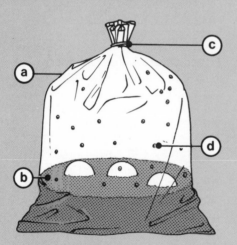
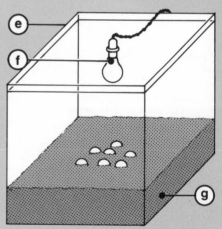

Feeding young Lizards will eat small insects, spiders, white worms, and meat scraps. Young chameleons need fruit flies.
Try feeding baby snakes worms and newly born mice.
Give baby crocodilians small fish (chopped or whole), tadpoles, insects, and mealworms.
Aquatic turtles eat chopped fish, worms, mealworms, pond snails, and meat with bonemeal and powdered vitamins.
Baby land turtles eat crushed vegetables and fruit with bonemeal, vitamins, and a little animal protein (canned cat or dog food).
Baby box turtles like worms, mealworms, and raw meat, with bonemeal, vitamins, and a little fruit and vegetables.

Transporting reptiles

Great care must always be taken to avoid risk of injury to any transported animal, yourself, or others. Described here are a number of containers suitable for transporting different types of reptile. Always remember the dangers of overheating or chilling when reptiles are transported. Also take care not to lose your animal on arrival—containers should always be opened in a secure room.

Jars or cans A transparent plastic jar (**a**) is recommended for transporting small, easily crushed reptiles. The jar should have a screw-top lid with holes punched in it. (Holes should be punched so that the jagged edges face outward, and a file used to remove roughness.) Alternatively, a can with a punched clip-on lid may be used. Always keep containers out of sun.

Bags A bag made of fabric (**b**) is suitable for transporting snakes and some other reptiles. Use a sound pillow case, or make a bag from unbleached muslin, closely stitching the edges with a sewing machine. When the reptile is inside, the bag top should be tied with an overhead knot. With biting snakes, grasp the bag above the knot and hold it away from your body. Take care not to crush reptiles that may be climbing inside a bag. With small, easily crushed animals it is advisable to place the bag inside a ventilated box even for only a short journey.

Dispatching reptiles First check legal restrictions and carrying companies' regulations. Generally, reptiles can be carried in a jar, can, or bag (see above) wedged into a nest of rumpled newspaper in a sturdy, ventilated box (**c**). Label "livestock" plus common and scientific names. Also give a telephone number for emergencies.

a

b

c

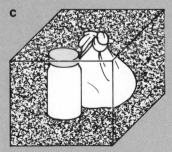

©DIAGRAM

Reptile diseases

The most common diseases and disorders of reptiles are described below, together with actions to be taken. In the

Lizards
1 Snout abrasion. See a vet.
2 Mouth rot. Isolate. Needs antibiotics. See a vet.
3 Rickets (jaw and tooth deformity or weakness, or hind limb paralysis). Multivitamins and sunlight. See a vet.
4 Hunger strike. Force feed, if necessary by syringe.
5 Mite infestation. Hang pest strip in cage, out of reach.

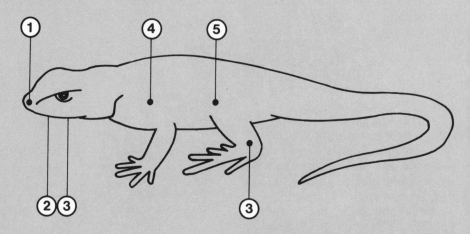

Snakes
1 Snout abrasion. See a vet.
2 Mouth rot. Isolate. Needs antibiotics. See a vet.
3 Hunger strike. Tempt with food on forceps and place in mouth. If this fails, force feed (if necessary by syringe).
4 Colds with coughing. Isolate at 86°F(30°C).
5 Pneumonia. Isolate at 86°F (30°C). Needs antibiotics. See a vet.
6 Mite infestation. Hang pest strip in cage, out of animal's reach.
7 Ticks. Suffocate ticks with liquid paraffin or kerosene. Use tweezers to remove dead ticks entirely.
8 Blisters. See a vet.
9 Failure to slough. Leave for 24 hours in a damp linen bag. Tweezers may help to start the process (from the snout).

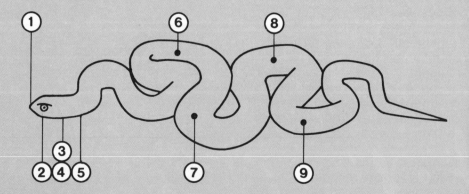

majority of cases prompt veterinary treatment is required. Antibiotics are recommended for many infections.

Crocodilians

1 Snout abrasion. See a vet.
2 Mouth rot. Isolate. Needs antibiotics. See a vet.
3 Hunger strike. Force feed.

4 Rickets (jaw and tooth deformity or weakness, or hind limb paralysis). Give multivitamins in food, and sunlight. Also see a vet.

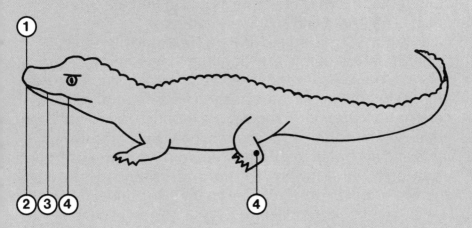

Turtles

1 Canker (yellow fungus in mouth). Isolate. See a vet.
2 Eyelids stuck after hibernation. Bathe with tepid water.
3 Eye infection. Needs antibiotic ointment. See a vet.
4 Colds and pneumonia. Keep warm. See a vet.
5 Fungal spots on skin (aquatic turtles). Keep warm. Bathe with brine for 15 minutes daily. See a vet unless it clears quickly.
6 Plastron sores. See a vet.
7 Soft shell (young). Add powdered calcium and fish-liver oil to food. Give direct sunlight.
8 Shell rot (shields flake off). See a vet as rot can be checked.
9 Ticks (land turtles). Treat as for lizards.
10 Cuts and sores. Needs antibiotic ointment. See a vet.

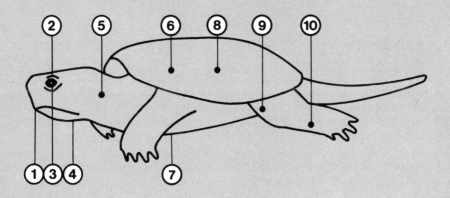

Keeping lizards

People occasionally confuse these agile animals with salamanders (p.256). But a lizard's skin is dry and scaly, a salamander's damp and smooth. Certain lizards are more colorful or curiously shaped than others. Some live on the ground, some climb on rocks or trees, some burrow. There are more lizards than any other kind of reptile, and outside the polar regions their distribution is worldwide. Lizards are generally sun-lovers. Most kinds eat insects and spiders. Big lizards prey on birds and mammals. A few species eat fruits and salad vegetables.

Lizards make lively pets. They are clean and odorless. Cages must be roomy, with constant heat for tropical species. Hardy lizards need heat only by day, but frost-free night or winter quarters are needed for sleeping or hibernation. Sunshine and natural foods or foods with added vitamins help to keep most healthy. Some never tame and are quick to wriggle free from the hand or through a gap left by an ill-fitting cage lid. Lizards tend to have shorter lives than other reptiles, many living under five years.

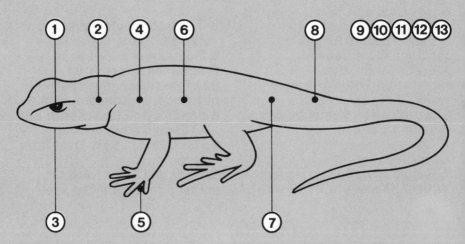

Characteristics

1 Most lizards have eyelids.
2 Most have external ears.
3 Tongue used as sensor.
4 Sheds skin in pieces.
5 Most have 5-toed legs, but some are limbless.
6 Long body.
7 Males of some species have thicker tails than the females.

8 Long tail that may snap if seized, but regrows.
9 Mostly carnivorous.
10 Some sip drops from leaves but will not drink from a dish.
11 Most need direct sunlight.
12 Tropical species need constant heat.
13 Most lay eggs, but some bear live young.

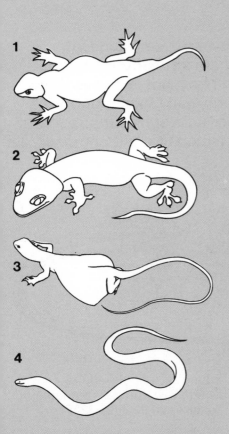

Types Most lizards are built for running on the ground. But some have bodies designed for a more specialized mode of life.

1 Typical ground-dwellers have a long, low body, short legs, and a long tail.

2 Geckos have toe pads with fine "hairs" that grip the smoothest surface, enabling them to run up walls and across ceilings as they hunt night-flying insects.

3 Asiatic flying lizards glide from tree to tree with the help of skin flaps stretched over long ribs that jut from the flanks.

4 Some burrowing lizards have a shiny, limbless body that helps them burrow in sand or soil.

Handling Illustrated below are methods of handling a small lizard (**a**) and a larger one (**b**). Grip the animal firmly by the body, using fingers to imprison two legs if possible. Beware sudden wriggling, and never grasp a lizard's tail — it may come off.

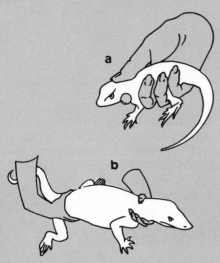

Feeding Tiny lizards take live fruit flies, or insects swept from herbage with a fine net.

Most small and medium lizards eat live spiders and insects such as flies, mealworms, crickets, locusts, cockroaches. Some lizards enjoy earthworms. Slowworms relish slugs.

Big lizards and some skinks take canned dog food or raw ground beef with beaten raw egg in addition to fruit.

Iguanas and chuckwallas need some animal protein, but mainly eat fruit or salad vegetables.

Add powdered cuttlebone and multivitamins to lizards' foods.

Feed individually if bullying means that some lizards run the risk of starving.

Reptiliary See page 280.
Hibernating See page 285.
Breeding See page 286.
Diseases See page 288.

©DIAGRAM

Iguanid lizards

A mainly New World family, iguanid lizards range from southwest Canada to the southern tip of South America — from prairies to tropical forests, from hot deserts to cool mountainsides. Iguanids come in many shapes and sizes, some with similar but unrelated Old World counterparts. In addition to iguanas, the family includes anoles, horned, spiny, and various other lizards.

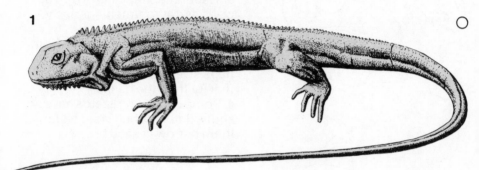

1 Common iguana *(Iguana iguana)* Tropical Americas; 6ft 6in (2m); green; tree-dweller; young eat insects, adults chiefly raw fruit and vegetables; requires 80-90°F (27-32°F).

2 Coast horned lizard *(Phrynosoma coronatum)* S.W. USA; 6in (15cm); brown and black; eats insects, chiefly ants; needs 85°F (29°C).

3 Chuckwalla *(Sauromalus obesus)* S.W. North America; 17in(43cm); brown/black; eats fruit, flowers, leaves; dry heat.

4 Common anole *(Anolis carolinensis)* S. USA; 7in (18cm); mainly green, can change color; needs 64/82°F (18/28°C) night/day; drinks sprinkled water.

5 Western fence lizard *(Sceloporus occidentalis)* W. USA; dark markings; needs 80-85°F (27-29°C); stones and bark.

Agamid lizards

These are Old World counterparts of the New World iguanid lizards. Their chief homes are Africa, southern Asia, and Australia. In common with most lizards, these active, sturdy beasts like heat and sunshine. The majority require a varied diet of insects, but a few species eat plants. Some agamids have elaborate courtship and threat displays, with colors that intensify during excitement.

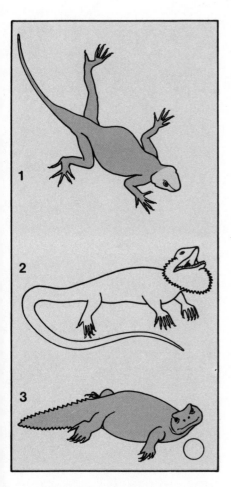

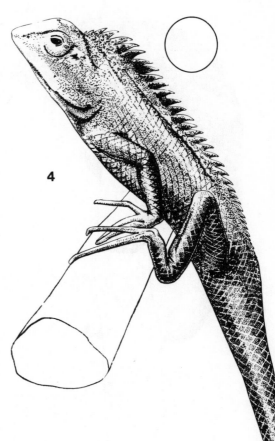

1 Common agama *(Agama agama)* Africa; 1ft (30cm); brown, blue-black, head orange; insects.
2 Bearded lizard *(Amphibolurus barbatus)* Australian deserts; 2ft (61cm); grayish; inflates throat; eats insects, lizards, mice, plants.
3 Black spiny-tailed agama *(Uromastix acanthinurus)*

Deserts of N. Africa; 13½ in (34cm); gray-brown to black; feed insects, raw vegetables; 82-90°F (28-32°C) by day; deep sandy soil for burrowing.
4 Tree lizard *(Calotes calotes)* Tropical Asia; 16in (41cm); green, head red if excited; eats insects, small lizards; needs branches.

© DIAGRAM

293

Chameleons

Chameleons are sluggish lizards with deep, narrow bodies, opposable toes, prehensile tails, and an ability to change color. Each bulging eye works independently. Chameleons shoot out their long, sticky tongues to trap insects. Most come from Africa and southern Asia. They need a vivarium temperature of 75-85°F(24-29°C), and foliage sprayed with water for them to sip. Chameleons tend to be shortlived.

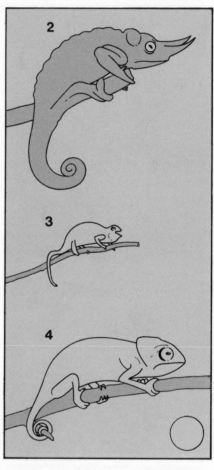

1 Flap-necked chameleon
(Chamaeleo dilepis) Africa; 13in (33cm); handsomer and less delicate than the Mediterranean species; varied diet with flies.
2 Jackson's chameleon
(Chamaeleo jacksoni) E. Africa; 12in(30cm); basic color greenish; males lock horns in combat.

3 Kenya dwarf chameleon
(Chamaeleo bitaeniata) Kenyan Highlands; 5-6½in(13-16cm); brownish; bears living young.
4 Mediterranean chameleon
(Chamaeleo chamaeleon) S.W. Europe, E. Mediterranean, N. Africa; 10in (25cm); varied diet with flies.

Geckos and cordylids

Geckos are chiefly tropical, nocturnal lizards with toe pads enabling them to run on ceilings. Some call loudly. Some bite. They need 70-80°F (21-27°C), bark to climb and hide behind, and water to sip from leaves.

Cordylids are African desert dwellers. Most are 1-2ft (30-60cm) long. Some species have reduced limbs, and some have inflatable or heavily armored bodies.

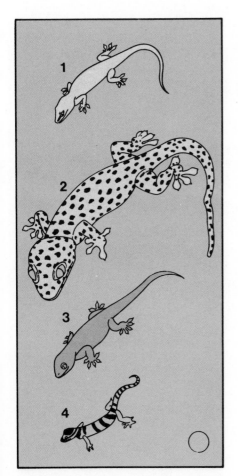

1 Madagascar day gecko
(Phelsuma madagascariensis)
Madagascar; 7in (18cm); green marked with scarlet; diurnal.
2 Tokay gecko *(Gekko gecko)*
S.E. Asia; 1ft 2in (35cm); gray with red dots; eats insects, mice, small lizards.
3 Moorish gecko *(Tarentola mauritanica)* Mediterranean area; 7in (18cm); gray-brown; partly diurnal; eats insects, spiders.
4 Banded gecko *(Coelonyx variegatus)* Desert areas of S.W. United States; 5in (13cm); yellowish with dark transverse bands.

5 Girdle-tailed lizard *(Cordylus cordylus)* S. Africa; 1ft (30cm); brownish; characteristic spiny tail; stands with fore part raised; eats insects, mice; needs a warm, dry cage.

Lacertid lizards

These Old World lizards are mainly under 1ft (30cm) long and resemble North America's slim, agile racerunners and whiptails. Lacertids range from the Arctic south to deserts in Africa. They are Europe's dominant lizards. Kept well-fed, smaller kinds live amicably in a spacious outdoor reptiliary with drinking water and plant cover. Hardy European species will hibernate outdoors.

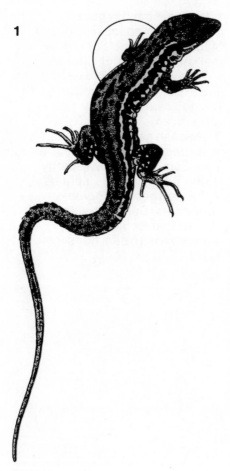

1 Wall lizard *(Lacerta muralis/Podarcis muralis)* C. and S. Europe; 8in (20cm); brown, variable; hardy; insectivorous.
2 Viviparous lizard *(Lacerta vivipara)* N. and C. Europe; 6in (15cm); brown, patterned; hardy, dislikes strong heat; eats worms, insects, etc.

3 Green lizard *(Lacerta viridis)* C. and S. Europe; 1ft 3in (38cm); green; hardy; worms, mealworms, raw egg with raw ground beef.
4 Eyed lizard *(Lacerta lepida)* S.W. Europe, N.W. Africa; 2ft 6in (76cm); green with blue blotches; insects, mice, fruit, raw egg and beef; needs roomy enclosure.

Teiid lizards

Teiids are a large New World family of mainly tropical lizards. Most are slim, long-tailed, and lively, moving jerkily with side-to-side head movements. Some are burrowers with small stumps for limbs. They include the chiefly South American tegus and ameivas, and North America's racerunners and whiptails. Teiids may have given rise to lacertids, which they closely resemble.

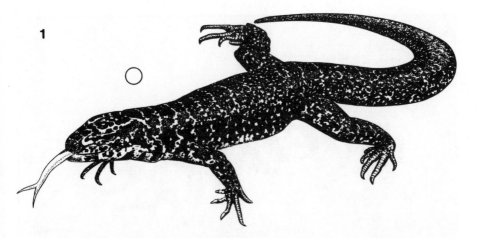

1

2

3

1 Banded tegu *(Tupinambis teguixin)* Tropical S. America; 4ft (1·2m); shiny black with white markings; bites powerfully until tame; will take small rodents, and raw egg with raw ground beef; needs 85°F (29°C).

2 Six-lined racerunner *(Cnemidophorus sexlineatus)* E. United States; 9in (23cm); brown and black with pale stripes; feed insects; keep dry and warm.

3 Giant ameiva *(Ameiva ameiva)* C. and S. America; 2ft 1in (62cm); dark with spotted sides; eats insects, mice, lizards; needs heat.

©DIAGRAM

297

Skinks

Smooth shiny skins and tiny or no legs are features often found among these lizards. There are more than 600 skink species, with a worldwide, chiefly tropical, distribution. Many are secretive and like to burrow in loose soil or sand. Heat is essential. Skinks are longer lived and more adaptable than most lizards, and many kinds will eat prepared foods and drink water from a dish.

1 Sand skink *(Chalcides chalcides)* S.W. Europe, N.W. Africa; 15in (38cm); gray, green, or brown; burrows; eats insects, slugs.

2 Blue-tongued skink *(Tiliqua scinoides)* Australia; 20in(51cm); dark bands, blue tongue; bears live young; eats insects, fruits, also raw egg and ground beef.

3 Stump-tailed skink *(Trachydosaurus rugosus)* Australia; 18in(46cm); brown or gray; live young; unfussy feeder.

4 Five-lined skink *(Eumeces fasciatus)* S.E. USA; 7in(18cm); brownish, young more colorful; eats insects, raw egg and ground beef; needs about 80°F(27°C).

Gerrhosaurids and anguids

Gerrhosaurids comprise some two dozen long-bodied, short-limbed species of lizard from Africa and Madagascar. Some African species lack front limbs. Anguids are Old and New World lizards with short or no limbs. They include North America's alligator lizards, and glass "snakes." Some anguids lay eggs, others bear live young. Most adjust well to captivity.

1 Yellow-throated plated lizard
(Gerrhosaurus flavigularis) S. Africa, Madagascar; 18in (46cm); brown with colored throat; needs hot, dry conditions.

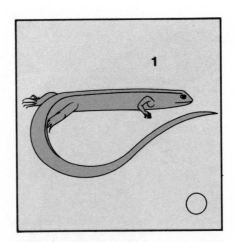

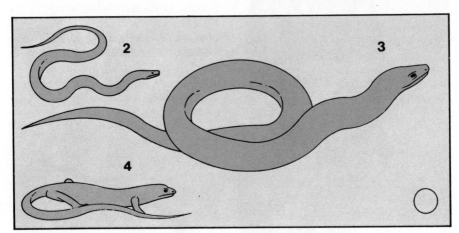

2 Slowworm *(Anguis fragilis)* Europe, N.W. Africa; 15in (38cm); limbless, shiny brown; eats slugs, earthworms; hardy, dislikes great heat; likes burrowing; can be hibernated.
3 European glass snake
(Ophisaurus apodus) S.E. Europe to C. Asia; up to 4ft (1.2m); limbless, like a big slowworm; eats snails, eggs, chopped beef.
4 Southern alligator lizard
(Gerrhonotus multicarinatus) W. and S.W. USA, N.W. Mexico; 17in (43cm); side folds; eats insects, small lizards, etc; drinks from sprinkled leaves; needs dry cage with sand, rocks, bark.

Monitors and poisonous lizards

Monitors are big, strong lizards from tropical Africa, Asia, and Australasia. They include the Komodo dragon, the world's largest lizard (now protected), and various smaller species adapted to very different habitats.
Monitors need 80-90°F (27-32°C), and a large, easily cleaned cage. Untamed monitors bite, scratch, and lash painfully with their whiplike tails.

1 Sand monitor *(Varanus gouldi)* Australia, New Guinea; 5ft 6in (1.7m); pinkish-brown, with spots; eats lizards in the wild.
2 Nile monitor *(Varanus niloticus)* Africa; 6ft (1.8m); black and yellow; carnivorous; likes to soak, but change water often.
3 Lace monitor *(Varanus varius)* Australia; 6ft 6in(2m); black, banded with stripes and spots.
4 Mexican beaded lizard *(Heloderma horridum)* Mexico; 2ft 6in(76cm); cream on dark background; poisonous.
5 Gila monster *(Heloderma suspectum)* S.W. USA, N. Mexico; 2ft (61cm); beadlike scales, patterned with yellow or orange and black; poisonous; will eat raw egg with raw ground beef; needs dry cage, 75-80°F (24-27°C).

Two heavy-bodied helodermatid lizards from North America's southwestern deserts are the world's only known poisonous lizards. There is no serum treatment for their sometimes fatal bite. Tame ones are docile — but take no risks. Captives thrive without direct sunlight. They need a dry, heated cage with a dish of water to soak in. Well-fed specimens have plump tails that store fat.

©DIAGRAM

Keeping snakes

Snakes evolved from monitor-like lizards more than 65 million years ago. Their legless bodies, sinuous crawl, and gaping jaws (some armed with poisoned fangs) fill many people with dislike. But most snakes are harmless, and many are beautifully marked or colored. Moreover, their skins are dry and glossy, not slimy as people often think.

Some snakes are shorter than an earthworm, others longer than a bus. There are over 2,000 species including kinds that climb, burrow, swim, and even glide from trees.

Many of the harmless species make fascinating pets. Most settle down well in captivity, becoming tame enough to be handled. Snakes make relatively few demands, but skilled care is required. Cages need not be particularly large, but they must be warm and dry. Adult snakes need feeding only once a week or so, but few will take substitute foods in place of a natural diet. Drinking water must be provided. Given these conditions, snakes should live healthily in captivity for many years.

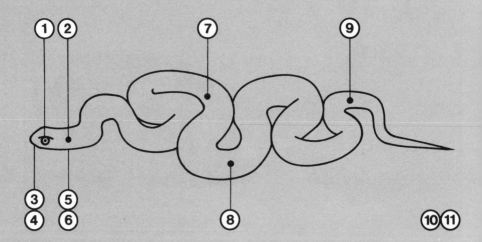

Characteristics

1 Lacks movable eyelids.
2 Lacks external ears.
3 Tongue used as sensor.
4 Venomous snakes have grooved fangs.
5 Dislocates jaw to swallow large prey (feeds once weekly).
6 Most drink often.

7 Long, limbless body. Moves by pushing back on uneven ground.
8 Healthy snakes periodically shed (slough) their skins.
9 Tails longer in males.
10 Basking species benefit from sun. Most like 80-85°F(27-30°C).
11 Most kinds lay eggs, others bear live young.

Fangs In venomous snakes fangs transmit poison from poison sacs (**a**) in the upper jaw. In the back-fanged Colubrid snakes (**1**), the fangs are grooved and at the back of the jaw (**b**). In Elapidae and Viperidae (**2**), the fangs are hollow and at the front (**c**). Viperidae have long, hinged fangs.

Sloughing or shedding the outer layer of skin occurs every 1-3 months in healthy snakes. The eyes become opaque. Then the skin comes off, in one piece, inside out. If bits stick to the snake, wrap it in a damp cloth bag for some hours, then use tweezers to peel off the skin.

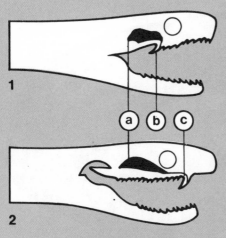

d New skin.
e Old skin doubled back.
f Old skin.

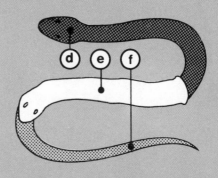

Handling Pin down the snake with a snake stick (**a**); then grasp the animal behind the jaws, positioning your thumb and fingers as shown (**b**). As an alternative, pick up the snake with special spring-action tongs 3-4ft (90-120cm) long.
Reptiliary See pages 280 -284.
Hibernating See page 285.
Breeding See page 286.
Diseases See page 288.

Feeding Adult snakes need food only once a week or less. Most snakes eat only whole (often freshly dead) animals. Refusal to eat substitute foods keeps snakes relatively free from deficiency diseases.
Some small snakes will eat invertebrates. North American brown snakes eat worms and slugs. Green snakes eat stick insects.
Garter and ribbon snakes eat frogs, newts, and fish. *Natrix* water snakes eat fish.
Rat snakes and baby giant constrictors take freshly killed or defrozen mice and chicks. Large constrictors swallow fowls and rabbits whole. Kingsnakes and milksnakes may be cannibalistic so should be kept alone.

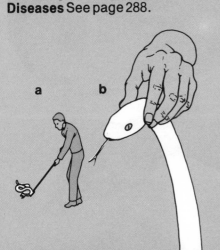

© DIAGRAM

Giant snakes (boids)

Pythons and boas are giant snakes of the family Boidae.
Tropical boids include the world's largest snakes; sand or
ground boas are much smaller. Many big constrictors are
beautifully patterned. Prey is squeezed until it suffocates.
A tamed, big, moving constrictor can be held as if paying
out rope; gripping may provoke constriction. Untamed
specimens must be grasped behind the head (see p.303).

1

Always have someone nearby to unwind the snake by its tail in an emergency. Boids grow fast and live 20-30 years. They need heat, and should be fed once weekly or less with whole animals injected with multivitamins. Provide a plain, clean cage with a branch and dry atmosphere. Sand boas need sand. Allow snakes to soak in tepid water before sloughing (shedding their skins).

1 Anaconda *(Eunectes murinus)* S. America; 25ft (7.6m), largest New World snake; olive-brown; longlived but morose; bears live young; feed dead rats, rabbits, fowls; needs 80°F (27°C); tepid water to soak in (change often).

2 Boa constrictor *(Boa constrictor)* Tropical Americas; 12ft (3.7m); often tan with reddish crossbands (red-tailed Amazonian form is handsome and easily tamed); live young; heat and feed as anaconda.

3 Ball python *(Python regius)* W. Africa; 5ft (1.5m); yellowish with dark patterns; rolls into a ball-like coil when scared; heat and feed as anaconda.

4 Asiatic ground boa *(Eryx conicus)* India; 4ft (1.2m); brown and white; buries in sand; eats mice and small birds.

5 Reticulated python *(Python reticulatus)* S.E. Asia; 28ft (8.5m), may be the world's largest snake; brown, gold, black; tames well; care as for anaconda.

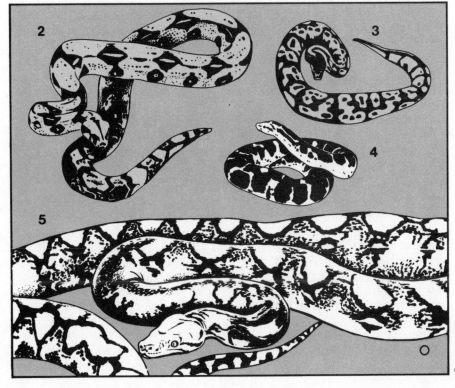

© DIAGRAM

Colubrid snakes (1)

More than three-fourths of all snakes belong to this family, found in all continents but Antarctica.
Colubrid snakes are harmless or back-fanged. Types vary from bulky bull snakes to pencil-thin vine snakes. Many eat mice or birds; others live on a special diet of slugs, snails, eggs, fish, or lizards. Harmless colubrids simply swallow prey or kill by constriction; freshly caught specimens may

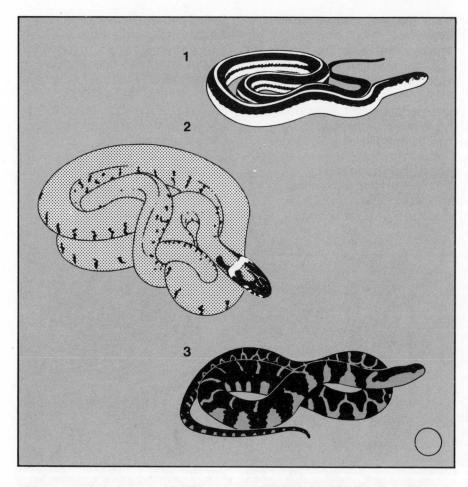

1 Garter snake *(Thamnophis sirtalis sirtalis)* North America; 2ft 2in (66cm); various colors; hardy; eats frogs, fish, earthworms; needs water and sunlight.
2 Grass snake *(Natrix natrix)* Europe; 5ft (1.5m); olive-gray with yellow patches behind head;

harmless, does not bite; hardy; eats fish, frogs, newts; needs water and sunlight.
3 Northern water snake *(Natrix sipedon sipedon)* North America; 3ft 6in (1.1m); gray-brown or blackish; swims freely; hardy; harmless; eats fresh or canned fish; cage needs cleaning often.

inflict a painful but not poisonous bite. Back-fanged snakes seldom bite man and the thorn-like fangs at the back of the jaws can generally only puncture a finger. In most the venom is weak, but twig snakes and boomslangs are certainly dangerous. All back-fanged snakes should in any case be handled with care, like the venomous snakes described on pages 310-311.

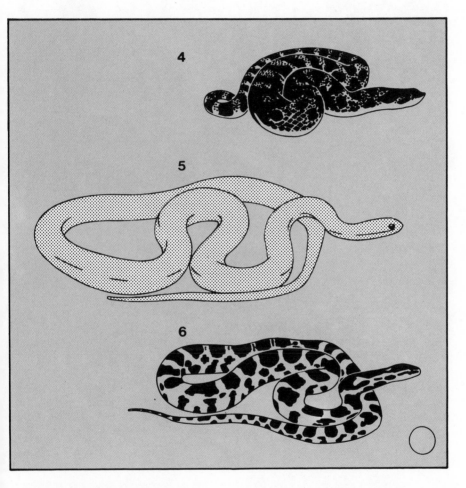

4 Eastern hognose snake *(Heterodon platyrhinos)* E. USA; 2ft 9in (84cm); mainly yellow, red, gray, or black; hardy; harmless; if scared spreads head, hisses, shams dead; feed toads and frogs.
5 Blue racer *(Constrictor constrictor foxi)* North America; 5ft (1.5m); blue-black; dislikes handling; feed mice; needs hiding place in clean, dry cage with water.
6 Corn snake *(Elaphe guttata guttata)* S.E. North America; 4ft (1.2m); yellowish with black-edged reddish blotches; active day and night; climbs; feed mice or rats.

Colubrid snakes (2)

7 California kingsnake
(*Lampropeltis getulus
californiae*) W. United States;
4ft (1.2m); ringed with dark and
pale bands; harmless; eats mice,
small birds, and other snakes.
8 Mangrove snake (*Boiga
dendrophila*) S.E. Asia; 8ft (2.4m);
black with yellow bands;
venomous; feed dead birds, rats,
fish; house alone; constant heat.
9 Northern pine snake (*Pituophis
melanoleucus melanoleucus*)
S.E. United States, 5ft 6in (1.7m);
black and white; eats mice; needs
water once weekly; keep singly.
10 Eastern milk snake
(*Lampropeltis triangulum*

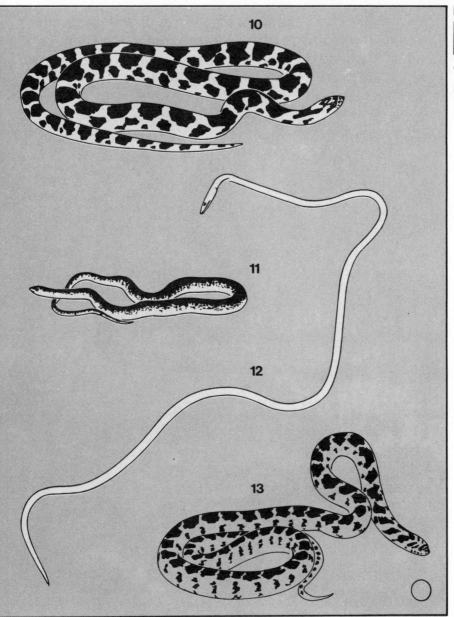

triangulum) E. North America; 3ft (91cm); gray with reddish saddles; mainly nocturnal; may bite; eats mice, snakes; needs hiding places, perches, water.
11 Smooth green snake (Opheodrys vernalis) C. and E. North America; 1ft 8in (51cm); green; hardy; spiders, insects.

12 Green vine snake (Oxybelis fulgidus) Tropical S. America; 4ft (1.2m); green; venomous; eats mice, lizards; needs 80°F (27°C).
13 Blotched egg-eating snake (Dasypeltis scabra) Africa; 2ft 6in (76cm); gray-brown with chocolate blotches; feed small hens' eggs whole; constant heat.

©DIAGRAM

Venomous snakes

These snakes kill by puncturing skin with hollow fangs through which poison from sacs located in the snake's head is injected into the victim's bloodstream. Some venoms kill body tissue, others paralyze.

There are two main families of highly venomous snakes. Cobras, coral snakes, and mambas belong to the Elapidae. Vipers belong to the Viperidae; its subfamily Crotalinae

1 Indian cobra *(Naja naja)* S. and S.E. Asia; 7ft 6in (2.3m); brown, black, or yellowish with "spectacles" on neck; eats mice, birds, frogs; needs heat.
2 Common viper *(Vipera berus)* Temperate Eurasia; 1ft 11in (58cm); gray or brown with black zig-zag line; bears living young;

feed fledglings, lizards, mice; needs heat in captivity.
3 Eastern coral snake *Micrurus fulvius)* S.E. United States; 2ft 6in (76cm); ringed black, red, yellow; nocturnal; eats small lizards, other snakes; needs 75-80°F (24-27°C); will burrow in moss or wood pulp.

takes in the rattlesnakes, cottonmouths, and tropical pit vipers. We here describe only a few of the many snakes that fall within these groups.

Serious study should alone justify keeping these animals — and then only experienced, adult snake collectors should consider it, where laws permit. Correct, viable antivenom and human help when handling are essential.

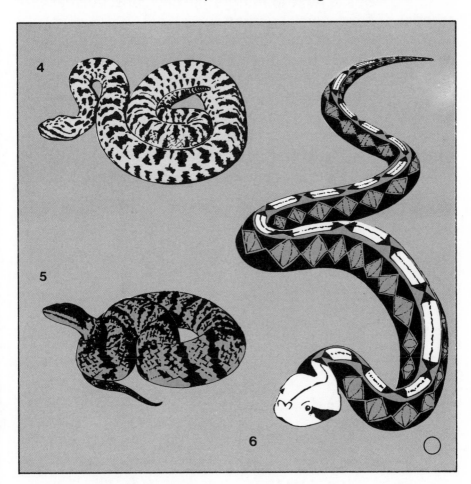

4 Prairie rattlesnake *(Crotalus viridis)* N.W. America; 3ft 9in (1·1m); greenish-gray with dark brown blotches; bears living young; eats mice; the hardiest and most easily kept rattlesnake.

5 Eastern cottonmouth *(Agkistrodon piscivorus)* S.E. United States; 4ft (1.2m); brown or black; bears living young; semiaquatic; eats mice, frogs, fish.

6 Gaboon viper *(Bitis gabonica)* Equatorial Africa; 6ft (1·8m); browns and grays; bears living young; eats mice, rats; keep singly in dry cage; needs 78-85°F (26-29°C).

© DIAGRAM

Keeping crocodilians

Apart from poisonous snakes, no other reptiles are so widely feared as crocodilians. Some of these big, lizardlike amphibious beasts are lethally designed to seize large prey and then drown it under water or tear it up by spinning over and over. Crocodiles have a worse reputation than alligators as maneaters, but both should be respected. Even hatchlings can inflict savage bites. Frequent handling helps to tame alligators and caymans, but many crocodiles are never to be trusted.

Keeping a young cayman or alligator housed, fed, and heated is feasible. But as hatchlings grow they need larger tanks with filter systems to avoid the need for frequent cleaning out by hand. Within five years or less, many are too large to house and handle safely in the home. Getting rid of unwanted crocodilian pets is not easy. Owners have supposedly flushed them down their lavatories, giving rise to tales of alligators living in the New York City sewers. A half-grown crocodilian is far too bulky for even this inhumane method of disposal.

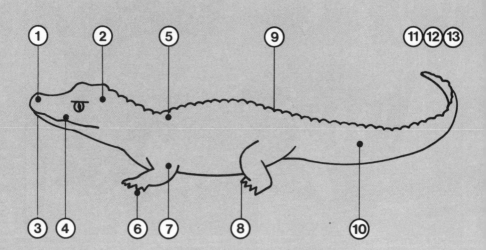

Characteristics

1 Valved nostrils keep water out of respiratory system.
2 Valved ears.
3 Powerful jaws.
4 Mouth can be closed off from respiratory system — allowing it to be kept open under water.
5 Heavy cylindrical body.
6 Runs well for short distances.
7 Front legs shorter than hind.
8 Webbed toes.
9 Scaly hide.
10 Swims and lashes with flattened, muscular tail.
11 Direct sunlight beneficial.
12 Needs constant heat.
13 All crocodilians lay eggs.

Types There are three families of crocodilians. The best way to tell which family a specimen belongs to is by examining the shape of its head and snout.
1 Crocodiles (the Crocodylidae) have a tapering snout and a notch in the upper jaw into which the fourth lower tooth fits. This tooth is visible when the crocodile's mouth is shut.
2 Alligators and caymans (the Alligatoridae) have much broader snouts than crocodiles. When the animal's mouth is shut the lower fourth tooth fits into a socket and is invisible.
3 Gharials (the Gavialidae) have a long, extremely narrow snout. In males, the top of the snout tip has a balloon-like flap.
Choosing See page 278.
Housing See page 282.
Breeding See page 286.
Diseases See page 289.

1

2

3

Handling Always take great care to avoid bites. The best way to hold a small crocodilian is illustrated (right). Grasp the animal just behind its head, with your thumb at the opposite side of its head to your fingers. Use your other hand to support the crocodilian's body and to restrain its hind legs. Always use leather gloves if handling a crocodilian that is 3ft (1m) or longer. Two people will be needed for large animals.

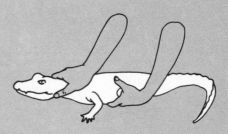

Feeding Crocodilians are carnivorous, and need plenty of calcium and vitamin D if they are to remain free from deformed bones and teeth. Gharials should only be fed fish. Others take dead mice, rats, and other backboned animals including fish and fowls. Give whole animals small enough to be swallowed without being torn in pieces. This helps keep the water clean. Inject food animals with multivitamins. Once every few months put pebbles in the water. In the wild, crocodilians swallow pebbles for hydrostatic purposes.

© DIAGRAM

Crocodilians

Any person considering keeping a crocodilian must look into questions of practicality, safety, and legality. A young crocodilian may look appealing but it will grow quickly and cause a lot of trouble and expense. A semiaquatic cage with air and water temperatures of 80-90°F (27-32°C) is needed. Direct sun or rationed ultraviolet light is beneficial. Crocodilians may fight if kept together.

1 Spectacled cayman *(Caiman crocodilus)* South America; 6ft (1.8m); grayish, young with brown crossbands; ridge across head in front of eyes; feed fish, mice, rats, fowls, etc.
2 American alligator *(Alligator mississippiensis)* S.E. USA; 16ft (4.9m); adults blackish, young black and yellow; diet as cayman.
3 Dwarf crocodile *(Osteolaemus tetraspis)* W. Africa; 6ft (1.8m); gray-black; short snout, upturned in some; diet as cayman.
4 Gharial *(Gavialis gangeticus)* India; 18ft (4.6m); dark gray; long slim snout; eats only fish.

The most commonly available crocodilian is the South American cayman, a smaller relative of the alligator. The American alligator is tamed more easily, but it grows to 16ft and is now a protected species after being made scarce by hunting. It is no longer available to the petkeeper. Other protected crocodilians include the West African dwarf crocodile and the Indian gharial.

© DIAGRAM

Keeping turtles

Turtles are an extremely ancient form of reptile. The armored ancestors of today's turtles are known to have stomped around on land 200 million years ago. Later, some took to water and gave rise to streamlined swimmers. Today, land turtles (tortoises) and freshwater turtles (terrapins) are among the most popular of all reptile pets. This is not surprising. Land turtles are generally easy to feed and handle. Many young aquatic turtles are extremely attractive with their beautifully marked shells. Most species are longlived — some turtles living over 100 years in captivity. As with all animals, however, turtles must be properly looked after. Many brought from warm to cool lands die soon after arrival — victims of poor shipment or cold weather. Others starve to death or suffer from malnutrition — especially young aquatic turtles fed dried foods instead of live water insects or vitamin- and mineral-enriched fresh fish or meat. Other turtle fatalities are caused by failure to provide proper conditions for winter hibernation (see p. 285).

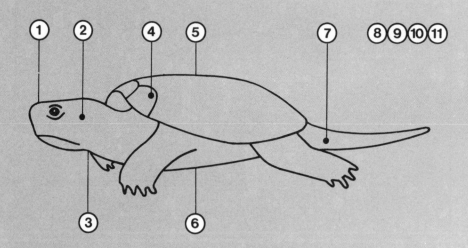

Characteristics
1 Horny beak instead of teeth.
2 Lacks external ears.
3 Pumps throat to breathe.
4 Most species have horny plates sheathing a bony shell fused to rib cage and backbone.
5 Carapace (upper shell).
6 Plastron (lower shell) — concave in male turtles.
7 Males have longer tails with thicker bases than females.
8 Land turtles mainly herbivorous, aquatics mainly carnivorous.
9 Most benefit from direct sun.
10 Tropical species need heat.
11 All turtles lay eggs.

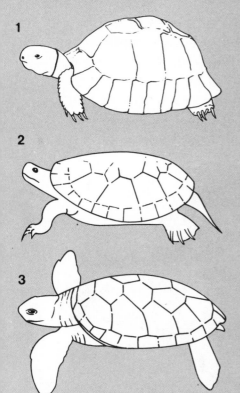

Types There are three major groups of turtles.
1 Land turtles (tortoises) belonging to the family **Testudinidae**. These tend to have a domed carapace and stumpy legs with blunt claws.
2 Freshwater turtles (called terrapins in Britain). Most of these belong to the family **Emydidae**. Its members tend to have flatter shells than tortoises and their feet are webbed and bear sharp claws. Box turtles, however, are emydids that look and live more like land tortoises.
3 Marine turtles are big, streamlined aquatic turtles with limbs evolved as flippers. Hunting has made them scarce and in need of protection. Adults in captivity need huge marine aquariums. They should not be kept as pets.

Handling Snapping and softshell turtles bite painfully. Hold a small snapper by the tail, supporting its body, and keeping its head away from your body (**a**). Hold a softshell at the back of the shell as shown (**b**), keeping its head away from you to prevent biting. Also beware sharp claws. Large biting animals are best moved in a container.

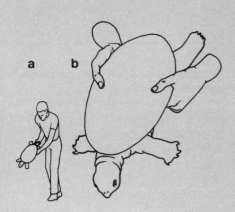

Feeding land turtles Most land turtles are chiefly herbivorous. Many eat dandelion, buttercup, plantain, and clover leaves. They are attracted by yellow flowers. Most enjoy lettuce, cabbage, cucumber, tomato, apple, peach, blackberry, and other vegetables and fruits. Vary the diet. Note individual food fads and tastes that alter with the seasons. Give cuttlebone to gnaw, and smear vitamin D on food twice weekly.
Feeding freshwater aquatic turtles Most are chiefly carnivorous. Feed worms, mealworms, small dead fish, or chopped fish, minced meat, or dog food with cuttlebone and vitamin D. Bear in mind that aquatic turtles tend to eat only under water.
Housing See pages 280-284.
Breeding See page 286.
Diseases See page 289.

©DIAGRAM

317

Tortoises/land turtles

Tortoises are land turtles with domed shells, stumpy legs, and unwebbed feet. They range from creatures as small as a man's hand to great island giants large enough to give a person a ride. There are more than five dozen species in all, found in Africa, Eurasia, and the Americas. Most need sunny, dry, warm places with shade; clean drinking water; and fresh fruit and vegetables, with

1

2

3

1 Spur-thighed tortoise *(Testudo graeca)* S.W. and S.E. Europe, N. Africa, S.W. Asia; shell length 1ft (30cm); yellow or brown and black; horny "spurs" on rear thighs; longlived; can be hibernated in winter.
2 Margined tortoise *(Testudo marginata)* S.E. Europe; shell 1ft

(30cm); dark with yellow patches on marginal shields; rear marginal shields serrated and spread out to form a flange.
3 Desert tortoise *(Gopherus Agassizi)* S.W. North America; shell 1ft 2in (36cm); brown shields with yellow centers; burrows; needs a sandy pen.

bonemeal, multivitamins, and occasional animal protein. In warm regions, tortoises make ideal reptile pets for young children. They are harmless, slow moving, easy to handle, and soon become trusting. Food can be found in gardens or easily bought. But beware of escapes: a tortoise that has been left on a lawn or burrows out of its pen can leave an unwalled garden in a matter of minutes.

4 Starred tortoise (Geochelone elegans) India; shell length 8in (20cm); black stripes on yellow shields; needs temperature of at least 70°F (21°C) all year.
5 Forest tortoise (Geochelone denticulata) South America; shell length 1ft (30cm); dark reddish brown; needs 75-80°F (24-27°C); dislikes strong sunlight.
6 Leopard tortoise (Geochelone pardalis) Africa; 2ft 6in (76cm); pale brown with darker spots; eats grasses, fruits; needs at least 70°F (21°C) all year.

Freshwater turtles (1)

Freshwater turtles are found in all continents but
Antarctica. Most have flatter shells than tortoises, and
largely live in water. Many of those kept as pets belong to
the Emydidae family, which also includes the land-
dwelling box turtles. Other families represented here are
the snapper (Chelydridae), big-head (Platysternidae),
stinkpot and mud (Kinosternidae), softshell (Trionychidae),

1 Red-eared turtle *(Chrysemys
scripta elegans)* C. and S. United
States; shell length 8in (20cm);
green, with red stripe behind eye;
adults hardy, young delicate;
needs basking place.
2 Snapping turtle *(Chelydra
serpentina)* E. North America;
shell 1ft (30cm); black-brown;

vicious; rarely leaves water;
needs no sunlight if fed meat and
fish with vitamins and calcium;
likes 65-70°F (18-21°C).
3 Big-headed turtle
(Platysternon megacephalum)
Northern S.E. Asia; shell length
9in (23cm); similar to snapping
turtle in appearance and needs.

and two side-necked families (Pelomedusidae and Chelidae).
Freshwater turtles make good pets, but some bite.
Feeding underwater, most eat meat or fish (enriched with
vitamins and bonemeal). Provide land and water, sunlight,
and heat for tropical species. Tanks need cleaning often,
but large, well-planted ponds do not. Wash your hands
after handling: infected creatures can cause food poisoning.

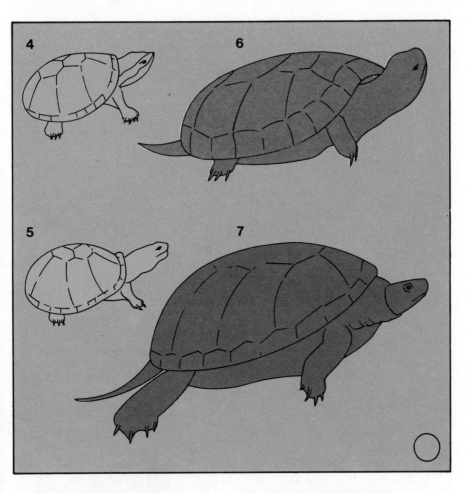

4 Stinkpot *(Sternotherus
odoratus)* E. North America; shell
4½in (11cm); brown; musky
odor when first caught; hardy;
needs no sun if fed properly.
5 Eastern mud turtle
*(Kinosternum subrubrum
subrubrum)* S.E. USA; shell 4in
(10cm); brown; bites at first;

thrives in shallow aquarium.
6 Spanish terrapin *(Mauremys
caspica leprosa)* S.W. Europe,
Africa; shell 8in (20cm); brown
or olive; needs basking place.
7 European pond turtle *(Emys
orbicularis)* S. Europe, W. Asia,
N.W. Africa; shell 10in (25cm);
brown; hardy; basking place.

©DIAGRAM

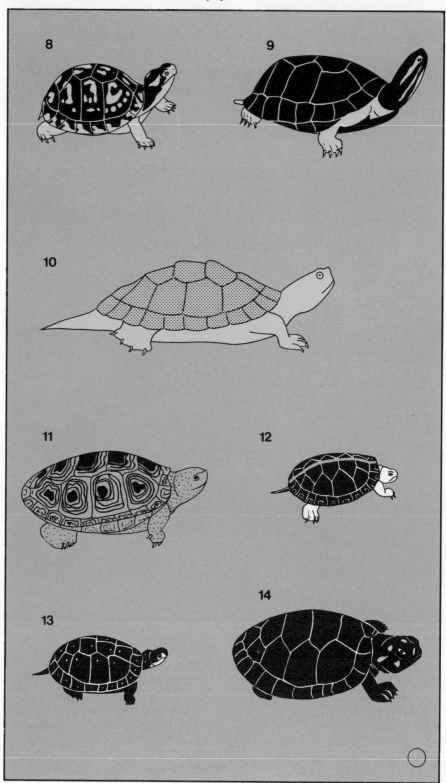

8 Eastern box turtle *(Terrapene carolina carolina)* E. USA; shell 6in (15cm); black or brown with yellow; can close hinged plastron; a land turtle that soaks in shallow water; omnivorous.

9 Three-lined box turtle *(Cuora trifasciata)* N. Indochina, S. China; 8in (20cm); similar to US species but with striped head and 3-ridged carapace; needs land/water; 75-80°F (24-27°C).

10 Mississippi map turtle *(Graptemys kohni)* S. USA; shell 10in (25cm); brownish with yellow head stripes; chiefly carnivorous; basking place.

11 Northern diamondback terrapin *(Malaclemys terrapin terrapin)* E. USA; shell 9in (23cm); mainly black, brown, or gray; needs brackish water; feed mollusks from time to time.

12 Southern painted turtle *(Chrysemys picta dorsalis)* S.

USA; shell 5in (13cm); black shell with broad red stripe; eats plant and animal food; basking place.

13 Spotted turtle *(Clemmys guttata)* E. USA; shell 4½in (11cm); dark with yellow spots; hardy; basks but not in summer heat; likes shallow water.

14 River Terekay *(Podocnemis unifilis)* Tropical S. America; shell 8in (20cm); grayish olive, yellow spots on head; side-necked; mainly aquatic; omnivorous; needs 75°F (24°C) and basking place.

15 Snake-necked turtle *(Chelodina longicollis)* Australia; 4½in (11cm); side-necked; "snorkels"; eats fishes, snails.

16 Eastern spiny softshell *(Trionyx spiniferus spiniferus)* E.C. USA; shell 17in (43cm); gray or brown; bites, scratches; keep alone; give shallow water floored with fine sand; no land needed.

323

6

Birds

Birds are warm-blooded, air-breathing vertebrates with a unique body covering of feathers. Most species can fly, and some live mainly on water. Adaptations for life in a variety of habitats have resulted in great differences in appearance. Throughout the centuries many species have been kept for their attractive appearance, in cages, in aviaries, or on water. Other species have proved of great value as comparatively easily kept domestic farm animals. Today, many birds are in danger as man encroaches upon their natural habitat. Irresponsible transportation of birds for the pet trade results in numerous fatalities. Legal restrictions now govern the taking of many bird species from the wild. In general, aviculturists should keep only aviary-bred birds and should make every effort to encourage their birds to breed.

Right Detail from "The Sermon of St Francis to the Birds" by Giotto, c.1266-1337 (Louvre, Paris: Photo Giraudon).

Bird characteristics

Birds are distinguished from all other animals by their unique body covering. Insects and bats can fly, but only birds have feathers. Other principal characteristics are forelimbs modified into wings, and toothless beaks. Birds are thought to have evolved from reptiles, and scales on their feet and legs provide evidence for this view.
Birds are classified in 28 orders, comprising over 9,000

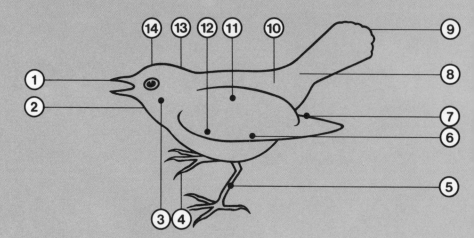

Anatomy A bird's wings are modified forelimbs. They are one of the distinctive features of the class as a whole.

Parts of a bird
1 Bill.
2 Throat.
3 Ear coverts.
4 Claws.
5 Tarsus.
6 Secondaries.
7 Primaries.
8 Tail coverts.
9 Tail feathers.
10 Rump.
11 Scapulars.
12 Alula.
13 Nape.
14 Crown.

Feathers There are four types.
a Coverts — most feathers.
b Quills or flight feathers.
c Down feathers.
d Filoplumes.

Flight Adaptations for flight include a light skeleton, feathers, and acute vision for judging distances. Wings are streamlined to reduce friction and designed to produce lift. The four basic types of flight are gliding, soaring, flapping, and hovering.

species so far identified. Distribution is worldwide, and adaptations to different environments have produced very considerable differences in structure and appearance. More than one half of all living bird species are included in a single order — the Passeriformes, or perching birds. Members of this order have proved better able than most to adapt to major environmental changes.

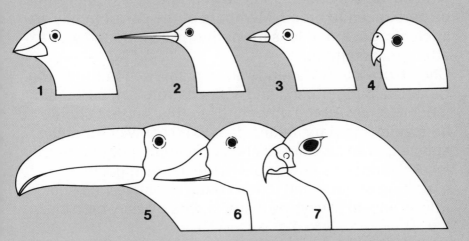

Bills Birds use their bills as tools for feeding, preening, nest-building, and other activities. Bill shape often gives an indication of diet.
1 Seed-eater's bill.
2 Nectar-eater's bill.
3 Insect-eater's bill.
4 Parrot's bill — double-hinged, used as a climbing aid.
5 Fruit-eater's bill — no typical shape in this group.
6 Waterfowl's bill.
7 Bird of prey's bill.

Feet Birds' feet are adapted to different ways of life.
a Perching birds have three toes in the front, and a hind toe that is not reversible.
b The two fore toes and two hind toes of members of the parrot family are useful for holding food.
c Waterfowl have extensive webbing between the toes to aid propulsion through water.
d Birds of prey have strong talons for tearing flesh.

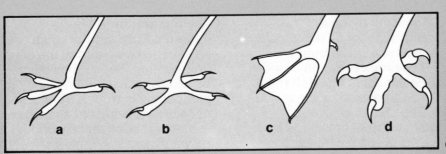

©DIAGRAM

327

Keeping cage and aviary birds

Throughout the centuries, many species of birds have been kept in cages and aviaries, as amusing pets, or as interesting and colorful animals for study. Most cage and aviary birds belong to one of two orders — the Passeriformes (perching birds), and the Psittaciformes (parrots and parakeets). Passerines encompass a number of different, interrelated families. Their complex patterns of behavior are best displayed in aviaries, where they may be persuaded to breed. Members of the parrot family are sociable, governed less by instinct, and respond well to attempts at taming.

Choice obviously depends on available accommodation. Canaries, budgerigars, and some parrots can be kept in indoor cages. All the other birds in this section should be housed in an aviary, taking care to mix only compatible species. In an attempt to check declining populations, legal restrictions now apply to the importing and exporting of birds and to the taking of native wild species. Efforts should always be made to obtain aviary-bred birds.

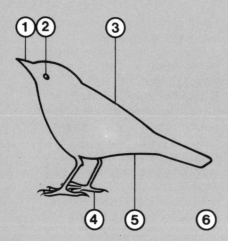

Obtaining Common cage birds like canaries and budgerigars can be easily obtained from pet stores. Along with more unusual aviary birds they can also be obtained direct from breeders or by answering advertisements in specialist papers. Thousands of exotic birds die in transit every year. Obtain aviary-bred birds whenever possible. Aviary-bred birds can be identified by a leg band giving the date of hatching.

Chooosing for health
1 Bill must not be overgrown.
2 Eyes should be bright.
3 Appearance should be sleek.
4 Feet must not be deformed.
5 Tail area must be clean.
6 Bird should be lively.
Quarantine all new birds for 2 weeks in case of illness.

Acclimatization All birds imported from warmer countries need expert care during the first few months. Precautions must be taken against chilling, particularly in winter. Birds also need time to adjust to changes in diet; use open dishes until they are used to hoppers.

Basic types There are two basic types of cage and aviary bird: passerines, represented here by the canary (**a**), and psittacines, represented by the budgerigar (**b**). Canaries and budgerigars can be kept in cages or aviaries. Most other birds require aviary accommodation.

a b

Aviary selection Obtain expert advice before putting any birds in the same aviary. Birds that are similar in size can often be kept together, but some large birds are gentle while some small ones are aggressive. Also requiring consideration are the food and temperature needs of different species, and whether aviary vegetation is needed or likely to be destroyed. Many birds will breed only if each pair has its own aviary.

Special care Examples of birds with special housing needs are:
1 lovebirds, best housed in pairs in their own aviary;
2 red-rumped parakeet, typically aggressive with other species;
3 Sunbird, needs sheltered housing with nectar-eaters only.
Mixed collections Examples:
4 black-headed mannikin, zebra finch, orange-cheeked waxbill;
5 cut-throat finch, Pekin robin, Fischer's whydah.
6 jay thrush, cockatiel, toucanet.

©DIAGRAM

Bird cages

Caging is needed for indoor pet birds, such as canaries, budgerigars, and parrots, for acclimatizing foreign aviary birds, and for housing indoor collections. All cages should be as large as possible. Commonly available all-wire cages are suitable for canaries and budgerigars. It may be difficult to find a commercial cage large enough for a parrot, but a secure home-made cage is very often

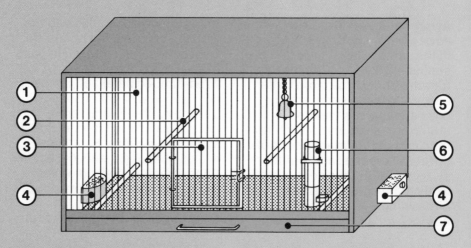

Box cage A typical box cage is illustrated above. A pair of birds the size of a budgerigar can be housed in a cage 36×18×15in (90×45×38cm). Site cages in a secluded corner, away from drafts and bright sun but facing natural light.

1 Wire front with ½in(1.25cm) mesh — ³/₈in(0.9cm) mesh for small waxbills.

2 Perches — two set apart halfway up the cage, allowing clearance for head and tail, and two lower down near food and water supplies.

3 Door with secure fastening.

4 Pull-out drawer dishes for food and grit at each side of the cage (or use movable dishes to encourage exercise).

5 Bell — useful for amusing budgerigars. Avoid cluttering cages with too many toys.

6 Gravity-flow water bottle.

7 Removable floor tray covered with sand, sawdust, sandpaper, or, for softbills, newspaper.

Perches All perches should be small enough to allow the bird to get a good grip. Oval-shaped, softwood doweling perches (**a**) are ideal for cage birds. Some aviary birds prefer natural twigs (**b**) of varying thicknesses. All perches should be cleaned often, and replaced if chewed.

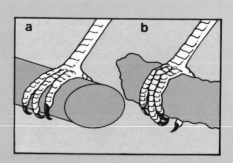

preferable. Simple box cages with three wood sides and a wire front can be stacked in a "bird room" to house a collection of small birds. All cages must be placed in a draft-free area with plenty of natural light. At night, cages can be covered with a cloth to give protection against drafts and disturbance. Many cages are raised on stands. Sudden temperature changes must be avoided.

Parrot cages Commercial cages are usually only 36 x 24 x 24in (90 x 60 x 60cm). The cage illustrated is made of stout wire, with a wire floor over a removable tray, and a solid side for seclusion. Home-made cages can be made for larger parrots, but cover any wood surfaces with metal. Parrots destroy wood, and perches must be replaced often. A tame bird will be happiest on a high perch outside its cage.

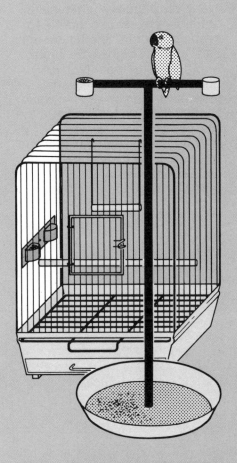

Cleaning Cages should be cleaned every day for softbills or fruit-eaters; cleaning every 2-3 days is sufficient for most other cage birds. Replace soiled sand, sawdust, or newspaper, and clean all food and water dishes. Any uneaten food should be removed each evening. Perches must be scraped often and washed in good disinfectant. About once every 3 months, the entire cage needs cleaning with warm water and disinfectant.

Exercise Cages are rarely big enough to allow sufficient exercise even for small birds. Easily tamed birds such as canaries and budgerigars benefit from regular exercise periods outside their cages. Close supervision is vital. Before release, cover all windows and mirrors, close doors, and screen off fires. Keep other pets out of the room. Release the bird before feeding, using food as a lure to return it to its cage. Parrots should have one wing clipped if they are to be allowed extensive periods of liberty outside their cages.

Aviaries

Aviary accommodation is recommended for most bird species commonly kept in captivity. Many passerines have complex behavior patterns displayed only if there is enough space for individuals to claim their own territory. Aviaries allow flying exercise, crucial to the health of many species, and provide sufficiently natural conditions to encourage some birds to breed.

Outdoor aviary

1 Dry, draft-proof shelter made of timber but set in concrete to keep out vermin. Shelter should be at least as high as the flight — birds like to roost high up. Shelter size determines how many birds can be kept — allow 1sq.ft(0.09sq.m) for each bird the size of a budgerigar.
2 Windows to let in daylight and fresh air — with mesh inside to prevent escapes.
3 Pop-hole with sliding door, giving birds access to the flight.
4 Door into the shelter, which contains perches, feeding dishes, water dishes or bottles.
5 Wire-netting flight built on wood or metal frame. Mesh ½in(1.25cm); finer for small birds.
6 Dead branches or twigs for perching on — provide plenty of perches to prevent fighting.
7 Planted shrubs attract insects into an aviary for softbills.
8 Exit door 4ft(1.2m) high — or a two-door porch to stop escapes.

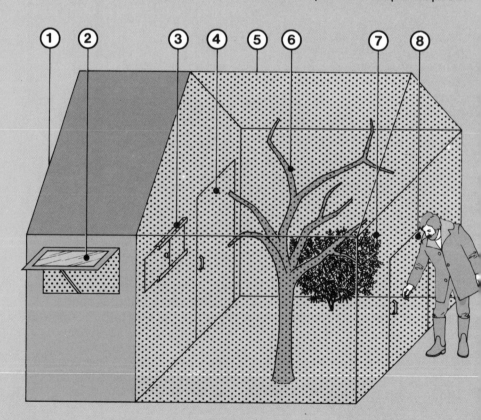

Aviaries must be as large as possible and should be securely fitted against escapes or intrusions. Mix only compatible species, and avoid overcrowding. Once acclimatized, many foreign birds can be kept all year in an outdoor aviary. Some species may need extra protection and heating in winter. Delicate species are usually best housed in a conservatory or indoor aviary.

Aviary designs Various types of accommodation are designed to meet the particular needs of different bird collections. Two examples are illustrated below.
a A greenhouse is ideal for birds needing extra heat — a mesh-covered open window provides ventilation. Plants attract livefood for insect-eaters.
b A series of individual flights and shelters is suitable for breeding pairs or other birds best housed separately.

Cleaning Remove all uneaten food at the end of each day. Seed, water, and grit dishes should be thoroughly washed each week, and all husks and droppings removed from the aviary. Perches should be cleaned regularly, and replaced as necessary. At the end of each breeding season, birds should be placed in temporary accommodation while the entire aviary is thoroughly cleaned and redecorated.

a b

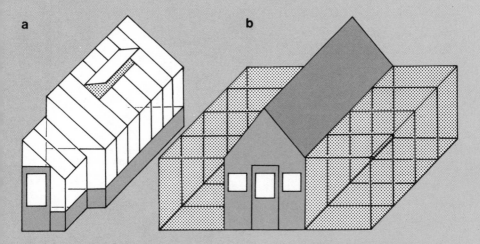

Protection from vermin Aviary birds must be protected from predators and from animals that steal and spoil food. Burrowing animals are deterred by extending the wire netting about 1ft(30cm) along the ground and securing it with heavy wire staples as shown (right).

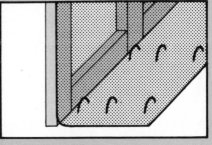

© DIAGRAM

Feeding cage and aviary birds

Birds have higher body temperatures and faster metabolic rates than most mammals. They must never be allowed to run short of food and water. Be sure to blow away seed husks from open dishes and to check levels in hoppers. All dishes for food and water must be placed well clear of perches to prevent fouling by droppings. Cage and aviary birds can be divided into three basic

Dietary requirements

○ Some species or at some times

● All species

	Hardbills	Softbills	Fruit-eaters	Nectar-eaters	Parakeets	Parrots
Seed mixture	●				●	○
Oily seeds	○				●	●
Spray millet	○					
Fresh twigs					●	●
Greenfood	●	○			●	●
Fruit	○	●				○
Cake with honey		○		●		
Nectar mixture				●		
Boiled egg/raw meat	●	○	●			
Insectile mixture		●	●			
Live insects	●	●	●	●		
Cuttlebone	●				●	
Grit	●				●	○
Vitamins/minerals	○				●	

types according to diet. Seedeaters are simple to feed, thriving on various seed mixtures, greenfood, grit, and cuttlebone. Softbills range from birds that are mainly insectivorous to others that thrive on a varied diet of insects, fruit, and seed. Nectar-eaters do well on commercial nectar substitutes and live insects. All birds need extra nourishment while breeding and rearing young.

Methods of feeding A variety of different containers suitable for feeding cage and aviary birds is illustrated below. Some are designed for hanging on bars or netting; others can safely be placed on the ground.
1 Seed dish for attaching to cage bars. Can also be used to feed grit or water.
2 Seed hopper — an excellent container for feeding a mixture of seeds.
3 Wire rack for greenfood. Can be attached to bars or netting.
4 Plastic jar with perforated lid. Used to store insects, etc for later release in the aviary.
5 Headless nails on a perch can be used to spike pieces of fresh fruit.
6 Cuttlebone can be securely wedged between cage bars.
7 Nectar mixture is best fed from a special gravity-flow bottle with a curved tip.
8 Gravity-flow water fountains keep water clean.

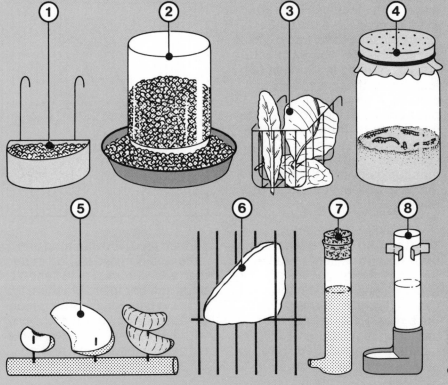

©DIAGRAM

Handling cage and aviary birds

All birds kept in aviaries and most caged birds should be handled as little as possible. Birds are timid and frighten easily, so it is best to avoid disturbing them more than is necessary. Domesticated pet birds and many parrots, however, tame easily and often become responsive pets. Canaries, budgerigars and parrots tame well if they are acquired when young. Many species of the parrot family

Catching Birds in an aviary can be caught with a butterfly net (a). Wave something like a handkerchief to distract the bird and then place the net over it when it is in a convenient position — usually when hanging onto the wire. Take care not to frighten any other birds. Cage birds can be caught by reaching inside the cage and grasping the bird firmly but gently around the body (b). Hold the bird's head between your index finger and thumb, applying gentle pressure on either side of the bill. With your other fingers, keep the bird's wings clasped to its body. Never put pressure on a bird's chest, and never grasp the wing or tail feathers as these are likely to pull out. Alternatively, cage birds can be trained to perch on your finger for lifting out of the cage (c). When training, place your hand inside the cage for 15 minutes daily until the bird learns to accept your finger as a perch.

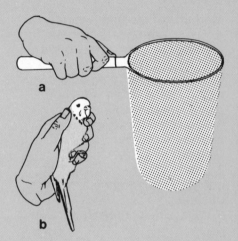

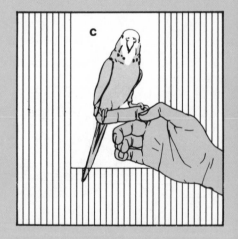

Transporting birds Occasionally birds have to be sent by rail or air. Transporting causes trauma in many species, and improper caging during a journey adds to the stress. First find out the particular regulations of all handlers involved. Send birds in sturdy, ventilated boxes with padded tops. Provide food and water for journeys lasting more than a few hours. Try to send birds at night to enable them to arrive in time for a morning feed. Do not overcrowd. Label the box with full details, including name of the species and instructions in case of emergency.

are naturally sociable, and in the absence of their own kind, seek human company and affection. Do not wear heavy gloves when handling pet parrots, as they are likely to cause fear. Gloves can be useful for avoiding a bite from some species of aviary bird, but they do not allow the type of gentle treatment that is essential if a bird is to be completely tamed.

Taming parrots Large, vicious parrots can be dangerous pets because of their strong bills. All parrots need exercise outside their cages, so taming is essential for your safety and the parrot's well-being.

Begin by opening the door of the cage and offering treats of food (**a**). Carrots are useful at the start if the parrot shows signs of aggression. Continue offering food each day until the parrot becomes curious enough to leave its cage. When it is used to being outside the cage, get a stick and place it near the parrot. At first the parrot is likely to be suspicious of the stick. Continue offering food until the parrot loses its fear. Finally, slowly pick up the stick and rest it against the bird's chest, above its legs. Lift the stick to encourage the parrot to climb onto it (**b**). Make sure that the stick is pointing up, so the parrot will not be tempted to climb onto your arm.

Training to talk Members of the parrot family are noted for their ability to imitate speech. It is never possible to ensure that a bird from a "talking" species will become a good mimic unless it has proved this ability with a previous owner. Otherwise, the best way to get a talker is to acquire a young bird and keep it as a single pet. Begin short daily training sessions with a simple word. Repeat the same lesson until the bird has learned to say the word before going on to a new lesson. Some parrots talk only when their owner is out of sight!

©DIAGRAM

337

Bathing and clipping

Birds require little in the way of grooming but nearly all species must be allowed to bathe. Bathing stimulates the bird to preen — to cover its feathers with an oily secretion that keeps them in flying condition. Care must also be taken to ensure that bills and claws do not grow too long; clipping may be necessary. Wing clipping is needed only for big parrots given extensive liberty.

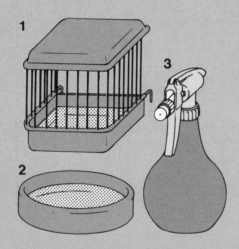

Bathing Different species have their own bathing requirements.
1 An enclosed bathing cage that attaches to the bird cage door is suitable for canaries and other indoor birds.
2 Shallow earthenware dishes are ideal for small aviary birds since the rough clay surface allows a good grip.
3 Parrots like to bathe by spreading their wings in a shower of rain. Use a plant or bird spray as an alternative.

Wing clipping aims to restrict the flight of birds allowed to fly at liberty. There are two methods. Either clip all the flight feathers on one wing (**a**), or clip every other flight feather on both wings (**b**). Cut straight across the feathers, and repeat the process after molting when new feathers grow.
Bill and claw clipping is necessary when bills and claws become overgrown. Use nail scissors if the bird is small and tame, or get a vet to help. Prevention is best — provide roughage in the diet and make sure perches are the right size.
Molting is a natural process which may occur in regular annual periods, or throughout the year. It can be a strain on the bird's health, so provide food supplements of egg or insects, and keep temperatures constant.

Diseases

The provision of healthy living conditions is the best safeguard against disease. Bird diseases often develop rapidly and some are transmissible to humans (p.418-419). Learn to recognize signs of trouble and isolate affected birds at the first opportunity. Heat is often the most effective remedy. Drugs should only be given under veterinary supervision; correct dosage is vital.

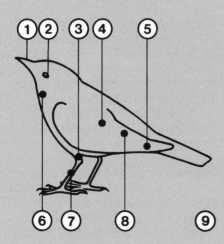

Signs of illness
1 Nasal discharge; crust on bill.
2 Change in eye color.
3 Swellings; swollen joints.
4 Ruffled feathers, shivering indicate fever; outstretched wings are a sign of overheating.
5 Soiled vent (diarrhea); protruding vent (egg-binding).
6 Noises when breathing.
7 Scales on legs.
8 Poor feather condition; excessive preening.
9 Weakness; refusal to eat.

Ailments Always consult a vet at the first sign of illness. Isolate sick birds at once to prevent the spread of infection.
a) Avian pox is a viral disease that is difficult to diagnose.
b) Enterobacterial diseases are common in nestlings and cause diarrhea and weakness.
c) Aspergillosis is a fungal disease causing lung growths.
d) Chills, colds, and other respiratory troubles commonly arise in damp conditions.
d) Canker is a mouth infection, carried in the water supply.
f) Birds are prone to various parasites. External ones include lice, and red mites causing scaly leg. Internal parasites can result in debilitating conditions such as coccidiosis.
g) Diarrhea and constipaton may indicate incorrect diet.
h) Parrots indulge in feather-plucking if bored. This can sometimes lead to cannibalism.
i) Bumblefoot (swellings on the feet) is caused by too much fat in the diet.

Hospital cage Heat is often the best cure for sick birds. Isolate the bird in a "hospital cage" heated by a light bulb to 85°F (29°C). The cage should have a glass sliding front to retain heat, and a side door for feeding and cleaning. Do not overheat.

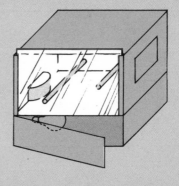

©DIAGRAM

Breeding cage and aviary birds

Breeding birds in captivity is always preferable to taking species from the wild. Many wild birds are in any case no longer available to the aviculturist, following the introduction of much-needed legal controls to check declining populations. The successful breeding and raising of young birds in captivity is a worthwhile aim for anyone interested in keeping an aviary collection.

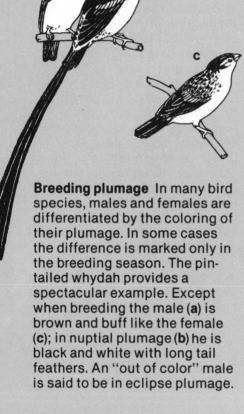

Breeding plumage In many bird species, males and females are differentiated by the coloring of their plumage. In some cases the difference is marked only in the breeding season. The pin-tailed whydah provides a spectacular example. Except when breeding the male (**a**) is brown and buff like the female (**c**); in nuptial plumage (**b**) he is black and white with long tail feathers. An "out of color" male is said to be in eclipse plumage.

Care of breeding birds The behavior patterns and needs of different species vary a great deal. Novice owners should seek expert advice before breeding is attempted. Some birds breed freely in colonies, but the majority are most likely to breed successfully if each pair is housed in its own aviary. A few species are what are known as parasitic breeders; they lay their eggs in the nests of birds belonging to a different species. To bring them into breeding condition, most birds should be fed "condition food" — oily seed, hard-boiled egg yolk, and plenty of live insects.

Both during breeding and after the eggs are laid, birds must be disturbed as little as possible. Particularly in winter, a hen bird will occasionally become egg-bound. The bird typically lies helpless on the ground, and examination shows her vent to be protruding. Heat treatment is usually effective (see p.368).

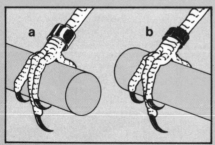

Banding All aviary-bred birds are banded with the date of hatching. Bands can be bought from a pet store. Metal bands (**a**) are fitted on baby birds. Plastic bands (**b**) can be opened and put on birds of any age. Plastic bands come in many colors for easy identification.

The willingness of birds to breed in captivity is very largely dependent on their surroundings, which need to conform as closely as possible to a natural environment. Many birds are most likely to breed if each pair is given its own aviary, but other species will breed only if other birds are present. With some species there is the even more basic problem of finding a correctly sexed pair.

Nest boxes Most birds must be provided with a nest box if they are to breed in captivity. Requirements vary a great deal, depending on the size of the bird and on the type of nest that would be built in the wild. Examples of different types of nesting accommodation are illustrated below.
1 Wicker basket suitable for small seedeaters and tanagers.
2 Wood nest box suitable for finches. A 6in (15cm) cube, it has a slot opening at the front and is fitted with a perch.
3 Tall wood nest box for parakeets The bottom has a depression for holding the eggs.
4 Canary breeding cage with separate compartments for the male and female. A wood and a wire partition separate the two compartments. The wood one is removed first; if the birds appear compatible, then the wire partition is also removed. A nest pan will also be needed.

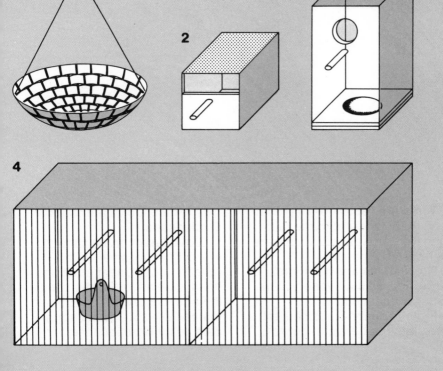

© DIAGRAM

Canaries

The canary *(Serinus canarius)* is a type of finch native to the Canary Islands. Well-known for its singing ability, this popular bird has been domesticated for centuries. The wild canary is drably colored, but numerous fancy varieties have been developed in captivity. Colors include yellow, green, blue, white, red, and cinnamon. Type varieties differ in shape and structure. They include

1 Border canary 5½in(13.5cm); small, neat appearance, sleek plumage; feed basic diet of canary seed, rapeseed, greenfood, cuttlefish bone, sea sand as grit; if kept outdoors increase ration of rapeseed, add hemp and linseed; provide baths.

2 Yorkshire canary 6¾in(16cm); long body tapering to the tail, long legs, upright carriage; care as for Border canary.
3 Norwich canary 6in(15cm); large, heavily built variety; care as for Border canary.
4 Frilled canary 8in(20cm); tall and slim, feathers curl out to give ruffled look; care as for Border canary.
5 Gloucester corona canary 4¾in(12.7cm); small with rounded chest, neat crest on head; care as for Border canary.
6 Roller canary 5½in(13.5cm); males have soft, sweet song; care as for Border canary.

Border, Norwich, Yorkshire, and Gloucester canaries.
Roller canaries are bred for their particular singing ability.
Only male canaries of any variety can sing.
Canaries are hardy and simple to care for. They are often
kept as single pets in indoor cages, but they also do well
in an outdoor aviary. Canaries breed freely in specially
designed breeding cages (see p. 341).

©DIAGRAM

343

Hardbills (1)

Finches and finch-like birds belong to a group of birds known as hardbills or seedeaters, since their most characteristic feature is a short, conical bill adapted for splitting seeds. All the smaller finches and waxbills described on these two pages can be recommended for inclusion in a beginner's aviary. They are peaceful and gregarious and will live happily in a mixed collection.

1 Bengalese/society finch
Domestic; 5in(13cm); white or brown and white, some crested; thrives in most accommodation; feed canary seed, millets.

2 Zebra finch *(Taeniopygia castanotis)* Domestic; 4½in (11.5cm); gray, buff, white, chestnut patches spotted with white, red bill; needs winter shelter; feed canary seed, millets, plenty of greenfood.

3 Gouldian finch *(Poephila gouldiae)* N. Australia; 5in (13cm); green, purple, yellow, lilac, red, black in solid patches; feed millets, canary seed, greenfood; vitamin and mineral supplements advisable.

4 Black-headed mannikin/nun *(Lonchura malacca atricapilla)* India; 4½in(11.5cm); black head, neck, throat, remainder dark chestnut; feed canary seed, millets, spray millet, greenfood.

5 Spicebird *(Lonchura punctulata)* India, Sri Lanka; 4½in(11.5cm); brown, underparts white and brown; feed canary seed, millets, greenfood.

6 Red avadavat *(Amandava amandava)* India, Sri Lanka; 4in (10cm); males in color are red, brown, black, and white, males in eclipse and females are brown and white; feed yellow and panicum millets, spray millet, greenfood.

7 Orange-cheeked waxbill *(Estrilda melpoda)* W. Africa; 4in(10cm); gray, brown, black, red rump and bill, orange cheeks; feed millets, spray millet, canary seed, greenfood.

8 Cordon bleu *(Uraeginthus bengalus)* Tropical Africa; 4½in (11.5cm); fawn with sky-blue underparts, red cheeks; feed mixed millets, millet spray, canary seed, greenfood, insects.

Care is straightforward. Their principal diet is seed, with supplements of greenfood and a supply of grit and cuttlefish bone. Breeding birds should be given some insects to maintain good condition. All these birds adapt well to life in an outdoor aviary and become hardy once acclimatized. They enjoy bathing and should be provided with a dish of clean water every day.

Hardbills (2)

The hardbill species included on these two pages can all be kept in an outdoor aviary, but care is needed when choosing birds for a mixed selection. Weavers, whydahs, and larger finches and finch-like birds are typically more aggressive, boisterous, and restless than are smaller finches, which they are likely to bully.

In most respects care is similar to that for other hardbills

1 Fischer's whydah *(Vidua fischeri)* E. Africa; 5in(12.5cm); breeding males black, buff, and white with 7in(17.5cm) tail; others sparrowlike; seed diet with mealworms, maggots.
2 Paradise whydah *(Steganura paradisea)* Africa; 4in(10cm); breeding males black, chestnut,

white with 8in(20cm) tail; others brown; feed as Fischer's.
3 Napoleon weaver *(Euplectes afra)* W. Africa; 5in(13cm); breeding males black, yellow; others brown; feed as Fischer's.
4 Cut-throat finch *(Amadina fasciata)* Africa; 5in(12.5cm); beige with dark scale-like

(see p. 344), but some species need a higher insectivorous content in their diet. Breeding, too, may be more complicated. Weavers are interesting to breed as they build elaborate nests, but unfortunately they do not breed freely in captivity. Male whydahs have attractive breeding plumage, but they too are difficult to breed, being both polygamous and parasitic (see p.340).

markings; male has red throat patch; feed seeds, greenfood.

5 Rainbow bunting (*Passerina leclancheri*) Mexico; 5½ in (13.5cm); males bright yellow, blue, green; females pale yellow, olive green; seed and greenfood diet with 2-3 mealworms daily.

6 Java sparrow (*Padda oryzivora*) Indonesia; 5½ in(13.5cm); gray, black markings, white cheeks; seed diet with greenfood.

7 Green cardinal (*Gubernatrix cristata*) Brazil, Argentina; 7½ in(19cm); males olive-green and yellow with black crest; females duller; seed diet with greenfood and mealworms.

Softbills

Included on these two pages are representatives of a large group of birds commonly known as softbills. They have characteristically slender, pointed bills totally unsuited to the hardbills' basic diet of seeds but ideal for the softbills' own basic diet of insects and fruit. Softbills are popular with aviculturists since many become very tame. The shama is noted for its fine song, and the hill mynah

1 Pekin robin *(Leiothrix lutea)* S. China, Himalayas; 6in(15cm); olive-green, yellow; feed coarse insect mixture, fruit, plus seeds, greenfood, live food.

2 Shama *(Copsychus malabaricus)* India; 11in(28cm) including tail; black, chestnut, white in tail; house pairs alone; feed fine insect mixture, plus live food, cheese, raw ground beef.

3 Emerald-spotted tanager *(Tangara guttata)* N. South America; 5in(13cm); green, white, black spots; winter indoors; fruit diet, insects.

4 Red-vented bulbul *(Pycnonotus cafer)* India, Sri Lanka; 8in(20cm);

for its mimicking ability allowing it to "talk."
Softbills are best kept in a planted aviary since trees and plants serve to attract insects as valuable live food. Grit is not needed for softbills. A daily bath should be provided. The perches and food dishes of fruit-eaters require frequent cleaning. Many softbills must have a secluded aviary if they are to breed.

brown, black, white, red vent; coarse insect mixture, fruit, 6 mealworms daily.

5 White-crested jay-thrush (*Garrulax leucolophus*) India; 12in(30cm); brown, white, gray, black; noisy; feed coarse insect mixture, fruit, live food.

6 Purple glossy starling (*Lamprotornis purpureus*) W. and C. Africa; 9in(23cm); dark blue with purple/green sheen; fruit plus insect mixture.

7 Hill mynah (*Gracula religiosa*) S. Asia; 13in(33cm); black, yellow wattles; good mimics if obtained young; feed coarse insect mixture, fruit, live food.

©DIAGRAM

Nectar-eaters

Some birds feed on nectar, sweet fruit juices, and small insects. They include the hummingbirds, members of the order Apodiformes. The use of artificial nectar mixtures, together with a plentiful supply of live insects, has made it possible to keep these birds in captivity with some success. Strict cleanliness is essential. Nectar-eaters are only recommended for experienced aviculturists.

1 Yellow-winged sugarbird
(Cyanerpes cyaneus) C. and S. America; 4½in(11.5cm); males in breeding plumage iridescent blue and black, legs red; others green; fruit diet with cake soaked in honey, insects.

2 Golden-fronted fruitsucker
(Chloropsis aurifrons) India, Burma; 8in(20cm); green, throat patch blue, black edged with yellow, head yellow; aggressive; winter indoors; fruit diet with nectar mixture, live food daily.

3 Van Hasselt's sunbird
(Cinnyris sperata) S.E. Asia; 4in(10cm); males black, maroon with blue, green, purple metallic patches; females olive; keep in planted conservatory; feed nectar mixtures, live food.

4 Violet-eared hummingbird
(Colibri coruscans) S. America; iridescent green with purplish blue patches; needs skilled care; planted conservatory, or garden aviary in summer; feed nectar mixture and fruit flies.

Toucans

Toucans and toucanets with their distinctive large bills are members of the order Piciformes. The toco toucan is an attractive, easily tamed large bird. It should not be kept in an aviary with smaller birds. The toucanet, however, can be safely housed with larger softbill species. Both toucans and toucanets destroy aviary vegetation, and both are unfortunately very difficult to breed in captivity.

1 Toco toucan (*Ramphastos toco*) South America; 20in(50cm); plumage black and white, with yellow around breast and red under tail; bill orange with black; keep in a large aviary; protect from bad weather; feed fruit with insect mixture, raw meat, occasional dead mice.

2 Spot-billed toucanet (*Selenidera maculirostris*) South America; 10in(25cm); male black and dark green with orange and red, bare blue patch by bill; female (illustrated) brown in place of black; winter indoors; feed fruit with insect mixture and some raw meat.

©DIAGRAM

351

Budgerigars

Budgerigars are among the most popular of all pets. These hardy, colorful, and friendly birds thrive either in an outdoor aviary or indoors in a simple wire cage (p. 330). The budgerigar *(Melopsittacus undulatus)* is a type of parakeet, a member of the parrot family. Native to Australia, budgerigars breed freely in captivity and are now regarded as domesticated. Type and size do not vary

1 Normal budgerigar
7in(17.5cm); light green, yellow face, dark markings on head, back, wings; blue cere (hard skin above beak) in males, buff in females; feed canary seed, mixed millets, greenfood, grit, canary soft food, cuttlefish bone; lifespan 6-15 years.

Other color varieties have been developed from mutations. Loss of yellow gives blue and white versions of the normal green budgerigar. Greens and blues come in shades from dark to light. Whites lack yellow and most of the blue.
2 Albino is pure white with red

as in the canary, but there is a considerable range of colors produced by selective breeding from mutations. Pet budgerigars should be acquired when young if they are to be properly tamed. Many learn to talk. They are lively and playful, but although toys are a useful distraction cages must never be cluttered. Budgerigars should be bathed with a bird spray (p. 338).

eyes and no tinge of blue. In the green series, lutinos are pure yellow with red eyes.

3 Rainbow is a bright, many-colored variety produced by combining yellow-faced blues with opalines and clearwings (those with normal body shades and wings with no markings).

4 Opaline shows a difference in markings, with the head markings being lighter and a loss of markings on the back.

5 Danish recessive pied has broken coloring on the wings, back, and neck. The upper chest is clear; body color appears in a patch on the stomach.

Parakeets

Parakeets are long-tailed, typically bright colored members of the parrot family. With the exception of the budgerigar, parakeets do not become particularly tame. They are, however, generally quite easy to manage and make ideal aviary subjects. Lengthy flights allow exercise and show their brilliant colors to best advantage. Grass parakeets — including Bourke's parakeet, the turquoisine

1 Bourke's parakeet *(Neophema bourkii)* C. Australia; 9in(23cm); gray-brown, blue, pink; can be housed with finches and softbills; feed canary seed, millets, spray millet, hulled oats, sunflower seeds, greenfood.
2 Turquoisine grass parakeet *(Neophema pulchella)* S.E.

Australia; 7½in(19cm); blue, green, yellow, red; best in a spacious flight; feed as Bourke's.
3 Elegant grass parakeet *(Neophema elegans)* S. and W. Australia; 9in(23cm); olive-green with blue and yellow; hardy, quiet; feed as Bourke's.

grass parakeet, and the elegant grass parakeet — do not destroy vegetation and can be kept with small finches and softbills. Rosella parakeets destroy vegetation. Plum-headed parakeets should only be housed with birds of similar size. Most of these species will breed quite easily in captivity. Like other seedeaters, all of them require grit and cuttlefish bone.

4 Golden-mantled rosella
(Platycercus eximus cecilae) S. Australia; 15in(38cm); red head and breast, white throat, rest black, yellow, and blue; needs a lengthy flight; feed as Bourke's.
5 Red-rumped parakeet
(Psephotus haematonotus) S. Australia; 11in(28cm); green and yellow, red rump; keep alone; lengthy flight; feed as Bourke's.
6 Plum-headed parakeet
(Psittacula cyanocephala) India, Sri Lanka; 14in(36cm); green, black throat and collar, male has plum-colored head, red shoulder patches, female has blue-gray head; feed as Bourke's.

Parrot-like birds

The bee bee, or tovi, and the peach-faced lovebirds are attractive small parrot-like birds that are fairly easy to care for and become very tame. They are best housed in pairs in a small outdoor aviary but can also be kept as indoor pets. Other parrot-like birds include the nectar-eating lorikeets and lories. Dietary and hygiene requirements make these birds more difficult to care for.

1 Bee bee parrot *(Brotogerys jugularis)* S. America; 6½in (16.5cm); basically green, some with yellow, orange or white; feed seeds and fruit.
2 Peach-faced lovebird *(Agopornis roseicollis)* E. Africa; 6in(15cm); green, yellow, blue, with pink head; seeds, greenfood.

3 Swainson's lorikeet *(Trichoglossus haematodus)* Australia; 12in(30cm); blue, red, green, yellow; nectar mixture, fruit, seeds, live food, greenfood.
4 Purple-capped lory *(Domicella domicella)* Assam; 12in(30cm); red, green wings, purple cap; nectar, soft fruit, some seed.

Cockatiels and cockatoos

Cockatiels and cockatoos have characteristic head crests. In overall appearance, however, the cockatiel with its long, pointed tail has more in common with the parakeets, while the cockatoo is more like a parrot. Except when breeding, cockatiels can be kept in a mixed aviary. Cockatoos make interesting pets but chew wood and vegetation, and shriek loudly. Some live 80 years.

1 Cockatiel *(Nymphicus hollandicus)* Australia; 13in (33cm); gray, white, yellow crest, orange cheeks; gentle; provide lengthy flight; seed diet with greenfood and apple.

2 Lesser sulphur-crested cockatoo *(Kakatoe sulphurea)* Celebes; 14in(36cm); white, with yellow crest, pale yellow cheeks; feed seed diet, fruit, carrots, greenfood.

©DIAGRAM

Parrots

Large parrots are famous for their bright colors and amusing ability to imitate human speech. African grays are the best "talkers" and can accurately mimic tones of voice. Amazon, and to a lesser extent, Senegal parrots also pick up many words and phrases but their intonation is less effective. Parrots are typically sociable, and many become attached to their owners to the point of devotion.

1 African gray *(Psittacus erithacus)* Africa; 14in(36cm); silvery gray with red tail; needs exercise; aviaries must have strong mesh; feed canary seed, sunflower seeds, nuts, buckwheat, fruit, and greenfood.
2 Yellow-fronted Amazon *(Amazona ochrocephala)* S. America; 14½in(37cm); green,

yellow; care as African gray.
3 Senegal parrot *(Poicephalus senegalus)* W. Africa; 10in(25cm); green, yellow, head gray; seed diet, greenfood, fruit.
4 Blue and yellow macaw *(Ara ararauna)* C. and S. America; 37in(95cm); blue with yellow breast; needs large aviary; seeds, fruit, greenfood.

They also have strong likes and dislikes — quite often preferring humans of the opposite sex to themselves. Only tame parrots will talk. These are usually kept in indoor cages. The problem of finding a large enough cage can to some extent be remedied by clipping one wing and allowing as much freedom as possible. Parrots' beaks are very strong and they need soft, unpainted wood to chew.

©DIAGRAM

Fowl

Keeping fowl

Chickens, turkeys, Guinea fowl, quail, pheasants, and peafowl are all Galliformes, or fowl-like birds. All have thick-set bodies, small heads, and strong feet adapted for scratching the soil in search of food. They are essentially terrestrial and can run well. They eat mostly seed, grain, and greenfood, and must have grit for digestion. Males are typically aggressive, and some have spurs for fighting. Fowl do not make particularly responsive or intelligent pets, but some have proved very useful to man while others are kept primarily for their attractive appearance. Some species of fowl have been domesticated for thousands of years. Chickens, in particular, have been selectively bred for domestic requirements, resulting in numerous distinct types and breeds. Turkeys are rather more troublesome for the backyard keeper. Ornamental fowl include Guinea fowl, different types of quail and pheasant, and the splendid peacock. Housing requirements range from simple sheds and enclosures for chickens to aviaries for ornamental quail.

Red jungle fowl *(Gallus gallus)*
Illustrated right, this fine red, gold, and black bird is the ancestor of our modern chickens. It is still found wild in the forests of Asia.
Representations in art
a Painting of a cock from an Egyptian tomb (c.1350BC).
b Aztec depiction of a demon in the form of a turkey.
c Two pheasants — detail of a Persian manuscript produced for Prince Salim in 1604.

a

b

c

Galliforme families Commonly kept types of fowl belong to three different families.

1 Pheasants (Phasianidae) In addition to the pheasants, this family also includes quail, peafowl, and the genus *Gallus*. The latter includes the red jungle fowl, ancestor of our modern domestic chickens. There are now over 70 chicken varieties, differing in their appearance and domestic uses.

2 Turkeys (Meleagridae) There are two wild species. The domestic turkey was developed from the common wild turkey *(Meleagris gallopavo)*, native to North and Central America. The turkey was first introduced into Europe in 1541.

3 Guinea fowl (Numididae) The seven African species in this group are sometimes treated as a subfamily of the Phasianidae.

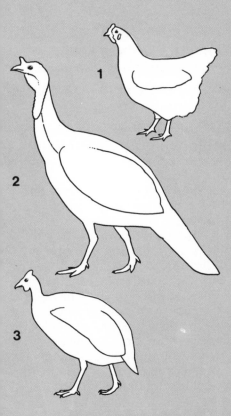

Parts of a hen (Cocks are similar but with spurs on their legs, and longer tail feathers).
1 Wattles.
2 Hackles.
3 Breast.
4 Hock.
5 Shank.
6 Fluff.
7 Saddle feathers.
8 Sickles.
9 Ear.
10 Comb.
11 Beak.

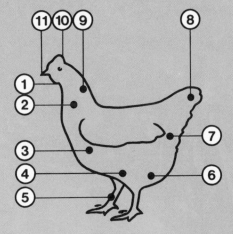

Obtaining Fowl can be obtained through poultry breeders, pet stores, and advertisements in trade papers. Choose only healthy individuals, and resist the temptation to buy day-old chicks. Chicks can be reared with success, but require a lot of initial care and attention. Young chicks are difficult to sex, and novices will make mistakes. Legal restrictions apply in many areas about the keeping of fowl in backyards. It is the owner's responsibility always to ensure that his birds do not trespass, make unacceptable noise, or attract vermin.

Housing fowl

All housing for fowl should provide cover from bad weather, nesting space, and room for exercise and scratching. Shelters must be well ventilated to prevent the spread of respiratory diseases. Fresh air is necessary; drafts are harmful. The roof of the shelter should be insulated to retain heat. Good, secure fencing is a necessary feature. Ground-dwelling birds are particularly

Poultry sheds For the backyard keeper, a simple wood poultry house is adequate provided there is ample space for an open run. Each bird needs 2sq.ft (0.18sq.m) floor space and 8in(20cm) roosting room. No more than 100 birds should be kept per acre (0.4 hectares).
1 Secure fence 6ft(1.8m) high, made of corrugated metal and wire mesh, extending 2ft(60cm) below ground to keep out rats.
2 Lean-to roof.

3 Shed floor raised off ground.
4 Pophole with sliding door and ladder.
5 Attendant's door.
6 Mesh front for ventilation.
7 Protective overhang.
8 Internal fittings — dry floor covered with straw or shavings, perches, a droppings board fixed above the floor underneath the perches, nest boxes on a side wall, a grit box, drinking vessel, and a feeding trough. A dust box for bathing is essential.

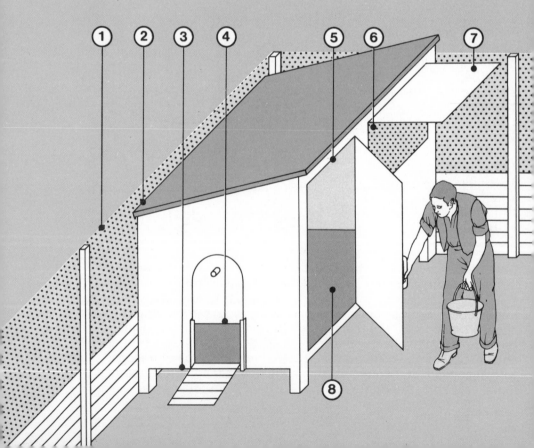

vulnerable to predators like dogs and foxes. Vermin bring in disease and spoil food.
The size, design, and type of housing will vary according to how many birds are kept and the special needs of the different species. Most fowl have similar requirements although details of management differ. Consider any restrictions that apply to housing fowl in urban areas.

Alternative types of housing

Movable units are practical if there is enough land for the unit to be moved daily without returning it to the same place for 2 weeks. The shelter of the ark **(a)** is attached to a mesh-covered run with an open floor to allow grazing, and a closed area for food and water.

Bantams are housed like chickens but require less room.

Turkeys also need similar accommodation, but require at least 5sq.ft(0.5sq.m) floor space, and 2ft(60cm) perching space. All shelters must be raised 3ft(90cm) off the ground. A sun-porch **(b)** gives shelter to birds allowed free range. To prevent disease, never use equipment once used for chickens.

Guinea fowl find their own shelter in bushes, but may use a night shelter if given one. A high fence is essential, and wing-clipping prevents escapes.

Pheasants can have garden liberty. If confined, each bird needs 100sq.ft(9.3sq.m). A rough shelter, shrub cover, and a dust bath are needed.

Peafowl need plenty of room to display. Protect from predators and supply a shelter. Two birds need a house 15 x 15 x 6ft (4.5 x 4.5 x 1.8m), with perches 3ft(90cm) off the ground.

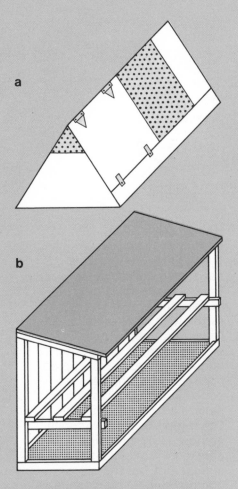

Cleaning Strict cleanliness is an essential part of raising healthy birds. All shelters and their fittings must be washed regularly. If possible, chickens should not always be kept on the same piece of land — their droppings are messy and soon make the land go stale.

©DIAGRAM

Feeding fowl

Fowl need a basic diet of seed, grain, and greenstuff, with grit and fresh water always available. Some of the food, particularly the grain ration, can be fed on the ground to enable the birds to scratch for it. This helps to prevent boredom and the disruption that tends to follow. Seed is often fed in hoppers, but care must be taken to keep rats and other vermin away from the supply.

a

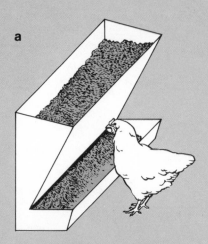

b

Types of food All fowl must have fresh water available at all times. Grit can be freely distributed on the ground, or mixed with grain or seed.
Chickens Feed whole wheat grain, fish meal, greenfood, surplus beans, bread, apples, house scraps, and oats, barley, or cracked maize. Commercial pellets are also available.
Other fowl Bantams and peafowl can be fed like chickens. Turkeys also have a similar diet, but there are commercial pellets specially designed for them. Guinea fowl eat grain and insects, which form the basis of their natural diet. Quail need grain, seed, insects, greenfood, and bread soaked in water and then squeezed dry. Pheasants eat wheat, greenfood, and hen or turkey pellets.

Methods of feeding
a Seed hopper is used to feed a mixture of dry grain. It can be left open all day and even installed inside houses or arks. This method of feeding prevents hens from scrambling for their food. Hoppers must be rat-proof.
b Common type of water vessel that allows several hens to drink at once.
c Free range — oats, barley, and maize are best scattered on poor grass to allow scratching.

Diseases

The control of diseases affecting domestic fowl depends on the maintenance of adequate, hygienic living conditions. At the first sign of trouble, contact a veterinarian to prevent a rapid spread of disease. Litter is often a source of infection. Overcrowding, humidity, and improper diet may result in respiratory ailments or stimulate boredom vices such as feather plucking.

Signs of illness
1 Purple-colored head parts.
2 Eye losing color.
3 Discharge from eye.
4 Nasal discharge.
5 Gaping mouth in chicks.
6 Cough or difficult breathing.
7 Pale head color.
8 Feather loss.
9 Diarrhea (often yellow).
10 Lameness, strange gait.
11 Nervous fits.
12 Lack of appetite, decline in egg production, listlessness.

Turkey diseases Turkeys suffer from a number of diseases that occur in chickens, but the most serious is blackhead, a parasitic infection attacking the liver and intestines, and causing diarrhea and listlessness. Turkeys catch this disease from chickens — never mix the two species.

Ailments
a) Fowl pest (Newcastle disease) is a serious viral disease that is highly infectious and often fatal. There are a number of symptoms — diarrhea, cough, misshapen eggs. Vaccination is the best means of prevention.
b) Bacillary white diarrhea is most common in chicks.
c) Chronic respiratory disease results in nasal discharge and is often due to overcrowding.
d) Avian leucosis complex of diseases can affect the liver, nerves, or eyes.
e) Avian pox causes skin lesions.
f) Fowl cholera is common in backyard flocks; may be fatal.
g) Ringworm causes lesions.
h) Chicken parasites range from lice to internal worms causing coccidiosis, blackhead, or gapes.

Eggs and breeding

Most people keep chickens for their eggs. It is not necessary to keep a cockerel unless the flock is to be increased. Fowl breed easily, and given the right conditions, need little assistance to rear their young. Since cockerels are noisy and aggressive, some people wishing to raise chickens prefer to buy fertilized eggs and hatch them under a broody hen or in an incubator.

Nest boxes Provide one nest box for every four hens. Designs vary. A typical one measures 12x14x12in (30 x 35 x 30cm). The nest box illustrated right is made of wood, with a wire mesh floor through which the eggs fall onto a sloping, straw-covered, removable tray.

A simple nest box with wood sides and a wood floor is quite effective; provide straw, wood shavings, or sawdust bedding. Remove eggs three times daily.

Egg-laying A top-class hen can lay 250-300 eggs a year, but hens kept in a small backyard flock are likely to average far fewer. There are two laying seasons, separated by a summer molt period, during which time laying stops. A good layer usually takes 6-8 weeks to molt. A long molt will be followed by reduced winter egg production.

To produce eggs with a good shell, hens should be fed oyster shell as well as grit during laying seasons. If a hen never lays eggs or suddenly stops laying during a laying season, it may be ill or receiving inadequate care. Consult a veterinarian.

Winter laying Most hens lay fewer eggs in the winter, but artificial lighting in the hen house for 14 hours daily will considerably increase production.

Egg-binding Sometimes a hen is unable to pass an egg. Signs are straining and a protruding vent. Often the condition occurs in cold weather. The problem is usually solved by holding the hen over steaming water, or placing it in a warm box lined with straw bedding.

Broodiness Occasionally a hen becomes broody, indicating a desire to incubate eggs. Signs are refusal to come off the nest, refusal to lay, loss of breast feathers, and aggressive pecking when approached. Broody hens can be useful to hatch fertile eggs, even of other species, provided the eggs are similar in size.

If chicks are not wanted, broodiness can be cured by placing the hen in a coop with a slatted floor for 3 days, giving food and water as usual.

Candling To determine whether an egg is fresh or stale, hold the egg up to a bright light in a darkened room. The egg should be held at a level below the eye. In fresh eggs, the air space will be small. A large air space indicates staleness. Blood spots can also be seen.

a

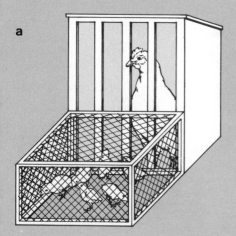

b

Natural rearing If hens run with a cockerel, their eggs will be fertile. Incubation takes 21 days, during which time the hen should be allowed off the nest for 15 minutes daily. After hatching, feed and water the hen on the nest, then transfer the hen and chicks to a coop with a run (**a**). The hen will start laying again after 5 weeks. Or buy day-old chicks and raise them with a broody. (First let her sit on china eggs for a week.)

Artificial incubation Fertile eggs can be hatched in a poultry incubator. Take care to follow the manufacturer's instructions. After hatching, transfer the chicks to an electric or infra-red brooder (**b**) set at 95°F (35°C). Reduce the heat gradually over a 6-8 week period until the chicks can live in normal conditions. If the brooder is too hot, the chicks will be on the outer edge of the brooder, if too cold, they will huddle in the center.

Feeding chicks Chicks should be started on chick crumbs or pellets, fed every 4 hours. After 6 weeks, they can be fed a normal adult diet. Water vessels should be shallow to prevent drowning — if ordinary vessels are used, place stones in the bottom.

©DIAGRAM

369

Chicken breeds

Chickens are easily the most useful of all domestic fowl to keep. In return for looking after them, the backyard poultry keeper can be sure of a dependable supply of eggs. Chickens are fairly nervous animals, are not particularly intelligent or responsive, and require secure protection against dogs and foxes.

Chickens were probably domesticated over 5,000 years

Chicken *(Gallus gallus)*
Domestic; 4-10lb (1.8-4.5kg); small, neat head; brightly-colored comb; wattles on either side of beak; erect carriage; deep body; short wings; dense plumage; strong, medium-length legs; lifespan 8-10 years. Color and size vary according to breed.

1 Light Sussex Hen and cock illustrated. British dual purpose breed. Basically white with black on neck and tail.
2 Leghorn Light breed from Italy. Common in white, black, and brown. Prolific layer of white eggs. Often crossed with Rhode Island red.

ago in Asia, and since then many different breeds have been developed to cater for domestic needs. Some breeds were developed for their qualities as table birds, others primarily for their value as egg-producers. There is a basic division into heavy and light breeds. Heavy breeds include the Rhode Island red and the Wyandotte. Examples of light breeds include the Leghorn and Ancona.

3 Ancona Another light breed from the Mediterranean. Black with white markings. Developed for egg production.
4 Rhode Island red Excellent heavy breed developed in the USA. Noted for its rich chestnut color. A good breed for novice poultry keepers.

5 Plymouth Rock Another dual purpose breed from the USA. Several color varieties.
6 Wyandotte Heavy breed from the USA. Short, deep bird most popular in black and white.
7 Orpington Heavy English breed. Profuse plumage. Most popular in black, white, blue.

© DIAGRAM

Bantams

The bantam — or "poor man's peacock" — is a miniature chicken usually bred for ornamental purposes. Some bantams are reduced versions of farmyard chickens; others are breeds in their own right. They are usually only one-quarter the size of ordinary chickens, and so need less space and food. Bantams generally lay about 100 eggs per year, and usually make good brooders.

Bantam breeds For showing purposes breeds are divided into four groups — heavy, light, ornamental, and game.
1 Sebright Ornamental breed. White or cream with every feather edged in black.
2 Old English game Hen is brown; cock is like a small red jungle fowl (see p.362).
3 Black Pekin/Cochin An ornamental breed with profuse plumage and foot feather.
4 White Japanese Ornamental breed with small, deep, low body and long tail feathers.
5 Frizzle Ornamental breed with soft, curling feathers.

Turkeys

Turkeys are the most difficult of the domestic fowl to keep and are therefore not recommended to novice poultry keepers. They have a natural lifespan of only two years and are exceptionally prone to disease. Turkeys are nervous and unintelligent. They are terrified by loud noises. Poults often have to be taught to eat, and often suffocate each other by crowding into corners.

Domestic turkey *(Meleagris gallopavo)* Wild turkeys are native to North and Central America. A number of domestic breeds have been developed, varying in size and color. In general, domestic turkeys are larger and heavier than their wild ancestors.

1 American bronze Similar in color to wild turkey — bronze, with black and white flight and tail feathers. Males may weigh 40lb(18kg); females 22lb(14.5kg).
2 British white Another popular breed. All-white plumage. Not as heavy as the bronze, but possibly easier to care for.

©DIAGRAM

Guinea fowl

Wild Guinea fowl are found in the open woodlands and grasslands of northern Africa. Domestic breeds are descendants of these birds; common varieties are the pearl, lavender, and African white. Guinea fowl are easy to keep. They roost in trees and find cover under bushes and shrubs, rarely flying. Neighbors may object to their call, which is a loud, repeated cackling.

Guinea fowl *(Numida meleagris)* Africa, domestic; 17-30in (43-76cm) depending on breed; usually black or dark plumage with white polka dots all over (**1**); bare head and neck; bony crest; wattles at base of bill; make repeated cackling call; lifespan 4-5 years.

Domestic breeds do not vary in appearance from the wild variety except in the color of the background plumage which may be pale gray, purplish gray (lavender), or white (**2**). All breeds have characteristic white dots over the plumage, and speckled and barred wings.

Quail

Ornamental quail are the smallest of the Galliformes. Like other members of this order they are principally ground dwellers, and for this reason they are often kept in mixed aviaries to provide interest at ground level. Pairs are devoted to one another. They require clumps of grass or other low vegetation in which to hide their nests. Quail are hardy and live five or six years.

1 Californian quail *(Lophortyx californicus)* Western USA; 10in (25cm); mainly gray with black and white markings on face and throat; males have black crest, females brown crest.
2 Chinese painted quail *(Excalfactoria chinensis)* S. Asia; 5in (13cm); brown mottled with black and lighter markings, black and white throat, gray flanks, underparts chestnut.
3 Rain quail *(Coturnix coromandelica)* India; 6in (15cm); males brown with black markings on throat, neck, and breast, sides of head black and white, females brown.

375

Pheasants

Pheasants are among the most attractive and simplest of all aviary birds to keep. They are hardy, quiet, and have brilliant plumage with long tails. Males are pugnacious, however, and all pheasants should only be kept with the larger aviary birds. A shelter is useful for protection. Pheasants can be kept at liberty if there is enough ground cover. They live 10-15 years.

1 Golden pheasant
(Chrysolophus pictus) China; males 45in(114cm), gold, black, red, green, dark blue; females 26in(66cm), brown, black.
2 Silver pheasant *(Lophura nycthemerus)* Asia; 27in(69cm); males white and black; females brown with white.

3 Lady Amherst pheasant
(Chrysolophus amherstiae) Asia; males 60in(152cm), blue, white, green, red, yellow; females 26in(66cm), brown, black.
4 Brown-eared pheasant
(Crossoptilon mantchuricum) China; 40in(102cm); both sexes brown, white, and black.

Peafowl

Peafowl, or peacocks as they are commonly called, have been kept in captivity for centuries and revered for their brilliant plumage and enormous fan-shaped tails. They must be given plenty of space in which to display, and need secure protection against predators. A major disadvantage for owners is their voice, which varies between a cat-like yowling and an ear-splitting scream.

Common/blue peafowl (*Pavo cristatus*) India, Sri Lanka; males 45in(114cm) plus 45in(114cm) train; females 38in(99cm); males iridescent neck and breast, green back, black rump, black and white face, head crest, upper tail coverts form metallic bronze-green train with purplish, black-centered, coppery "eyes" shown only in display; females brown, green, white, live 15-20 years.

Other varieties Both the white and black peafowl appear to be varieties of the common peafowl. The green Java peafowl (*Pavo spicifer*) is a different species.

©DIAGRAM

377

Pigeons and doves

Keeping pigeons and doves (1)

Pigeons and doves belong to the order Columbiformes, and strictly speaking there is no zoological distinction to warrant classifying any of the 500 species in this order as either a pigeon or a dove. The names have been used interchangeably over the centuries. The most important bird in this group with respect to domestication is the rock dove *(Columba livia),* which Darwin proved to be the ancestor of all domestic breeds of pigeon.

The pigeon has been domesticated for 5,000 years. It has played a symbolic or sacrificial part in many religions. The Romans were the first to use pigeons to carry messages in wartime, and up to the First World War, pigeons were still performing this service on a large scale. The sport of pigeon racing, however, is much newer; it was invented by the Belgians at the beginning of the nineteenth century. Over 200 breeds of pigeon are now officially recognized. Apart from the sporting breeds, there are a great many others bred purely for their appearance and interest.

Columbiformes There is no basic scientific difference between doves (**a**) and pigeons (**b**). It is usual for the smaller and lighter species to be called doves. The characteristics of the group as a whole include a small head in relation to the body, dense plumage, and soft, fleshy feet. Most species lay two eggs per clutch. Pigeons and doves do not drink like other birds — they plunge the whole bill into the water and suck.

Handling Pigeons should never be held by the wings. The feet should be placed side by side between the first and second fingers with the wings folded naturally and the thumb covering the primary flight feathers. The other hand can be placed on the breast for balance.

Feeding The basic diet of pigeons is grain. Commercial mixtures of peas, beans, and corn are widely used. Millet, wheat, and rice can be given in small amounts. Feed from a hopper. Fresh water, grit, and mineral salt should be available at all times.

Doves eat dari, wheat, white millet, and bread soaked in water and squeezed dry. The diamond dove eats only white and brown millet. Fresh water and fine grit must be available at all times.
All take occasional greenfood, especially when breeding.

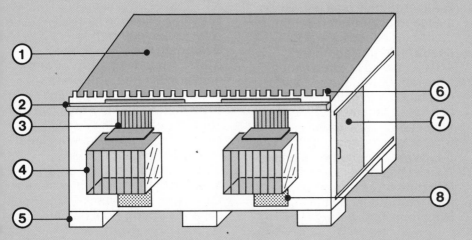

Housing Doves and the more delicate show pigeons should be housed in an aviary. Other pigeons can be kept in a loft. Guard against overcrowding and protect from vermin.
Basic loft for 15 pairs, 12×6× 7ft(3.7×1.8×2.1m), wooden with two interior compartments divided by a partition. Clean superficially every day, and thoroughly every few weeks.
1 Sloping roof.
2 Gutter.

3 Wire trap with landing board.
4 Bay fitted with glass sides and sliding dowel front.
5 Floor raised on concrete piers.
6 Fence to prevent roof-landing.
7 Door.
8 Ventilation holes (also at ceiling height at back), covered with vermin-proof mesh.
Interior fittings
a Box perches for racing birds.
b Inverted V perches for show birds.
c Nest box and bowl.

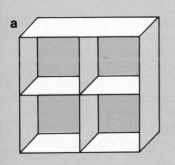

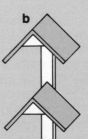

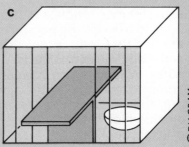

©DIAGRAM

381

Keeping pigeons and doves (2)

Disease Many pigeon diseases can be prevented by good loft hygiene, balanced diet, and isolation of ailing birds. Vaccination is available for some diseases. At the first sign of trouble, notify the vet, and isolate the affected bird.

Common ailments

1 Canker (see p.339).
2 Aspergillosis (see p.339).
3 Pigeon pox either resembles canker, or causes warts on the head and legs. Vaccinate.
4 Paratyphoid is often caught from rat-contaminated food. It may be fatal in young birds, and can cause lameness. Vaccination is available.
5 Coccidiosis (see p.339).
6 Lice are common on pigeons.
7 One-eyed cold is a respiratory infection often brought on by poor ventilation. It causes cold symptoms and watery eyes.

Breeding Pigeons naturally form strong pair-bonds. Segregate the sexes in the winter. Provide nest boxes and nest bowls filled with wood shavings in the early spring. After mating, the hen lays two eggs. Incubation is 17 days. For the first 5 days, parents feed young on "pigeons' milk" (regurgitated food). Parents need extra food and water at this time. After a few weeks, separate young from parents.

Pigeon racing Owners wishing to race their birds should join a club. Training racing pigeons is designed to reinforce the birds' natural homing instinct. At 10 weeks birds are accustomed to a traveling basket and then taken for release only a short distance from home. This distance is progressively increased. Birds are also trained to enter their lofts as soon as they return home. Race lengths range from 60mi (95km) for young birds to 600mi (950km) for older birds. It is usual for race officials to take birds to the starting point. There they are fitted with a race ring and their time of release is noted. When the bird arrives home its owner takes the race ring and feeds it into a sealed clock, which is then sent for official checking.

Traps Racing lofts are fitted with traps that allow pigeons to return to the loft, but prevent them from leaving again. The wire trap shown above is a popular design: wires set at 1in (2.5cm) intervals are attached to a rail inside the loft so that they hang down over the entrance.

Doves

Those species of the order Columbiformes generally known as doves tend to be smaller than pigeons and lighter in build. Doves make excellent aviary birds and can even be allowed periods of liberty. They should never be kept indoors in cages. Several species have been domesticated for centuries, but unlike the pigeon, there is not a wide variety of diverse breeds to choose from.

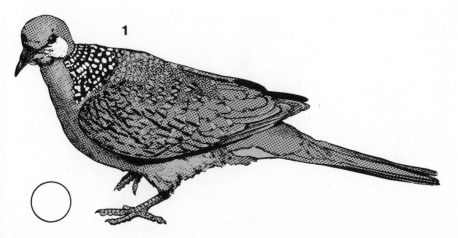

1 Spotted/Chinese dove *(Streptopelia chinensis)* Asia; 12in (30cm); pink, gray, brown, and blue, with white spots on back and wing coverts.

2 Diamond dove *(Geopelia cuneata)* Australia, domestic; 7½in (19cm), one of the world's smallest dove species; blue-gray with tiny white spots on wings; ideal for a mixed aviary collection but aggressive among selves, keep one pair.

3 Barred ground dove *(Geopelia striata striata)* Malaysia; 8in (20cm); brown with pinkish fawn underparts, black bars on flanks and breast.

©DIAGRAM

383

Pigeon breeds

There are two main types of pigeon — those bred for racing, and those bred for their appearance, "fancy" pigeons. Racing pigeons are selected for their ability to fly long distances, and bear a close resemblance to wild and feral pigeons. Fancy pigeons often show exaggerated features, such as profuse foot feather, or enlarged crops which they display in courtship.

1 Racing pigeon *(Columba livia domesticus)* 8-14in(20-36cm); sleek bird in shades of blue; lifespan 5-15 years.
Fancy pigeons are different breeds of the same species. Most fancy breeds of pigeon come in many different colors, and also often vary in shape.

These subdivisions of breeds are known as varieties. Many breeds have been in existence for centuries. Fancy pigeons do not usually fly well.
2 Exhibition homer, a show version of a pigeon developed for strong flight and "homing" ability. Noted for long face.

3 Tumbler, a show variety of a somersaulting pigeon, often short-faced with a small beak.
4 Carrier, an unusually tall, slim fancy pigeon variety with large, swollen-looking wattles.
5 Brunner pouter, one of the types known for extreme crop inflation during display.

6 Silver fantail has a wide spreading tail and carries its head thrown back in display.
7 Fairy swallow has profuse feathering on the legs and feet.
8 Modena is an Italian breed with a stocky, rounded shape resembling that of a domestic chicken. Lifts tail above body.

©DIAGRAM

Keeping waterfowl (1)

Ducks, geese, and swans belong to the family Anatidae which is one of the oldest living groups of animals, known to be in existence over 80 million years ago. It is now very difficult to give an exact classification as the various kinds have become so interrelated. There are two main groups: the subfamily Anserinae, which is composed of swans and geese, and the subfamily Anatinae, which contains all of the ducks. All waterfowl are essentially aquatic birds, with webbed feet and an oily waterproof plumage.

Most domestic ducks descend from the wild mallard, while the ancestors of farmyard geese are the greylag or swan geese. Swans have no true domestic equivalent, but the European mute swan often chooses to live near humans and can be said to be partially domesticated. Waterfowl are attractive, highly adaptable, hardy, and independent, and live out healthy, long lives in a collection kept on an ordinary pond or lake. Many of the domestic breeds make tame and affectionate pets.

1

2

3

Types of waterfowl
1 Ducks (Anatinae) are grouped in 10 tribes, and are found worldwide. They are small waterfowl, with short necks and legs. Most species show a marked difference in plumage between males and females. All have a colored patch called a speculum on their wings.
2 Geese (Anserinae) are large, heavy birds, with longer necks than ducks, but short legs. Sexes have similar plumage. Geese are sociable and often very noisy. Domestic breeds make very tame and generally longlived pets.
3 Swans (Anserinae) are the largest waterfowl, with long necks, and in northern varieties, entirely white plumage. They require a lot of space, and free access to water, where they spend most of their time.

Obtaining Domestic ducks and geese can be bought from breeders, either as newly-hatched birds, or as adults. Keep more than one bird — they are gregarious, and need company. Before starting a waterfowl collection, visit a good collection in a park or nature reserve to get an idea of the varieties available. Most male ducks are more brightly colored than females, but do not keep males only. Waterfowl are happiest when kept in family groups. Check on any local regulations that might restrict the keeping of waterfowl.

a

b

Handling Domestic ducks and geese become tame, especially if hand-reared. Other waterfowl may be more nervous, and should be disturbed as little as possible. Many of the larger birds can be aggressive if frightened, and may inflict injury. At certain times, birds may need to be caught — for wing-clipping, administering medicine, or transporting. Ducks should be held with the palm of one hand under the chest, and the legs caught between the fingers of your other hand (**a**).
Larger birds should be carried with the head pointing away from your body, using both hands to support and restrain the bird (**b**). The help of an assistant is usually necessary. All captive waterfowl must be restrained from flying.

Restraining There are several ways of restraining flight in captive waterfowl. Wing-clipping (see p.338) must be repeated after each molt, but does not involve a permanent change in the bird.
Pinioning is the amputation of the forearm of one wing (**c**). The operation should be carried out by a vet as soon as possible after hatching. The bird will never be able to fly. Restrict pinioning to special circumstances.

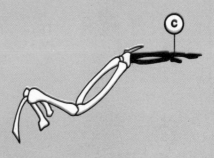

©DIAGRAM

Keeping waterfowl (2)

Keeping waterfowl Waterfowl can be kept in small collections in an ordinary backyard. All need a strong enclosure to keep out predators, a pond or stretch of water, and some type of ground cover, bushes, and vegetation. The amount of water and space needed varies with each family.
Ducks need at least a small stretch of permanent water. A pool of 8sq.yd (7sq.m) is enough for two pairs of ducks.
Geese only need enough water to bathe and submerse in — a tin bath sunk in the ground is adequate. They must also have a large area for grazing, with short, fine grass. If overcrowded, geese will turn lawns into muddy tracks.
Swans need much more space and are best kept on natural ponds or lakes, where they will be almost self-supporting.

Domestic ducks and geese must have access to water deep enough to submerge heads and bills. In the day, they can be kept free range, or in pens. At night they should be shut in dry, vermin-proof houses. A lot of space is required for geese to graze. Strong fences are needed.
Typical waterfowl enclosure
1 Fence at least 6ft(1.8m) high with overhang, extending under the ground to deter vermin.
2 Secure gate for access.
3 Shrubs, small trees, and other ground cover to provide nesting sites and shade.
4 Pond — either natural or concrete with sloping sides. Depth and size depend on the number and species kept.
5 Waterside vegetation.
6 Shelter for less hardy species.
7 Grass lawn for geese and swans.

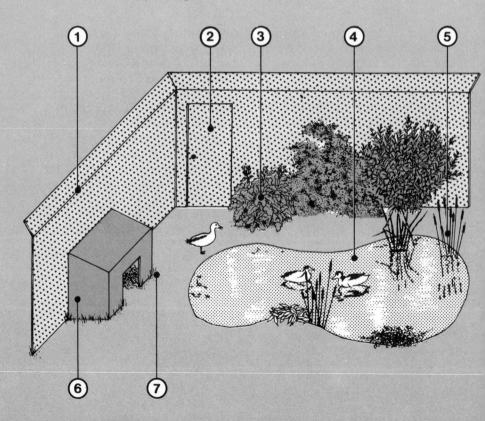

Feeding Waterfowl are very easy to feed. If kept on natural water, feed pellets and corn (wheat) in equal portions. Add a small percentage of biscuit meal if the birds are kept on water that does not have a supply of live food and plants. Supplements in the form of frog spawn, maggots, worms, aquatic weed, lettuce, nuts, seeds, berries, household scraps, and apples can be given. Sand and grit should be available. Geese need access to fresh, short grass. Swans mainly eat water plants, grass, and other greenfood.

Disease Waterfowl are hardy, but call a vet as soon as disease is spotted.
1 Sunstroke affects young.
2 White-eye causes watery eyes and crusts on the plumage.
3 Aspergillosis (see p.339).
4 Pneumonia. Supply warmth.
5 Sprawls — vitamin deficiency. Young birds are unable to stand.
6 Duck virus hepatitis. Vaccinate.
7 Coccidiosis (see p.339).
8 Cramp. Cure by placing bird in hay-lined box for 24 hours.

Breeding Many of the common species breed freely in captivity. Birds should be fed extra protein rations to bring them into condition. A choice of nest sites is important, with boxes if required. Many waterfowl hatch their own eggs easily but tend not to rear the chicks well. A bantam brooder or incubator can be used as alternatives (see p.369). Domestic ducks and geese can be supplied with nest boxes and are often good layers.

Nest boxes should be supplied for breeding waterfowl to simulate the conditions found in the wild. A variety should be made available, placed in secluded, covered areas.
Examples of next boxes
a Box nest covered with plants suitable for dabbling ducks.
b Raised house with ladder suitable for all types of duck.
c Wigwams constructed from twigs or straw suitable for ducks and geese.

a

b

c
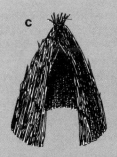

©DIAGRAM

Domestic ducks

Domestic ducks are pleasant, useful birds, and can make good pets. Most domestic breeds are descendants of the mallard, a dabbling duck. The muscovy is another popular domestic breed, especially in European countries.
As large as smaller breeds of geese, the muscovy belongs to the group of ducks known as perching ducks. It is native to Central and South America.

Domestic duck (*Anas* species) Length 20-28in(51-71cm); weight 3-10lb(1.4-4.5kg); broad bill; medium-length neck; long, boat-shaped body; pointed wings; short tail; broad, webbed feet; dense plumage; males and females different colors in some breeds; lifespan up to 10 years.

Examples of domestic breeds
1 **Aylesbury** White; orange feet.
2 **Rouen** Resembles mallard.
3 **Muscovy duck** (*Cairina moschata*) A large duck with black, brown, white plumage, and bare red skin on head.
4 **Indian runner** Long and thin; plumage white, brown, or gray.

Domestic geese

Domestic geese are hardy, affectionate, and intelligent. They are alert and scare intruders, but neighbors may object to their noisy cackling. Geese mate for life, and pairs are usually devoted to one another. Always keep geese in pairs or family groups — they are very sociable and do not thrive alone. Domestic breeds are descendants of the greylag or swan goose.

Domestic goose (*Anser anser*) 30-35in(76-89cm) and 10-34lb (4.5-15kg) according to breed and sex; long neck; deep body; sturdy legs; large, webbed feet; plumage usually shades of gray or white; sexes have similar plumage but males are heavier; lifespan 25 years.

Examples of domestic breeds
1 Toulouse Popular domestic breed; plumage gray and white.
2 Embden Largest domestic goose; white with orange feet. (The Toulouse and Embden are descended from the greylag; also popular is the Chinese, a descendant of the swan goose.)

©DIAGRAM

Ornamental ducks

Many species of wild duck thrive in outdoor collections, are easy to care for, and very hardy. All ducks belong to the subfamily Anatinae, but the classification of the various groups within this subfamily is made difficult by the interrelation of the different species.
Generally, the best ducks for wildfowl collections are those broadly classed as surface feeders, or dabbling

1 Mallard *(Anas platyrhynchos)* N. Hemisphere; 23in(58cm); male gray and brown with green head, white collar, black and white tail; female brown; each with purple speculum; dabbler.

2 Cape teal *(Anas capensis)* S. Hemisphere; 14in(36cm); both sexes gray with brown spots, flat, pink bill, green speculum; dabbling duck.

3 Chiloe wigeon *(Anas sibilatrix)* S. Hemisphere; 19in(47cm); sexes alike, white and chestnut with black head; dabbler; needs grazing.

4 Northern pintail *(Anas acuta)* N. Hemisphere; 22in(56cm); male has long tail, gray body, brown head, white stripe on head; female brown; dabbler.

5 Red-crested pochard *(Netta rufina)* Mediterranean; 22in (56cm); male brown, black, white, head red with crest; female brown and gray; diver.

6 Tufted duck *(Aythya fuligula)* N. Europe; 17in(43cm); male dark and white with crest; female dark brown; diver.

7 Carolina wood duck *(Aix sponsa)* N. America; 17in(43cm); male blue-black, brown, white throat, crested; female duller; perching duck.

8 Common shelduck *(Tadorna tadorna)* C. Asia; 24in(61cm); male black, chestnut, white; female duller; dabbler; belligerent; keep in isolated pairs.

9 Barrow's goldeneye *(Bucephala islandica)* N. Hemisphere; 18in(46cm); male blue, black, white; female duller; diver; feed fish and livefood; keep on natural water; difficult.

10 Smew *(Mergus albellus)* N. Hemisphere; 17in(43cm); male white with black; female dull; keep as Barrow's goldeneye.

ducks. Diving ducks also adapt well, as do certain perching ducks, but ocean-going ducks, like the smew and goldeneyes are more difficult to keep. They require fresh fish and livefood and must always be kept on natural water, where they can find small aquatic animals to eat. All collections should contain males and females, although the females are often duller in coloring.

Ornamental geese

There are three groups of true geese: gray, black, and snow. Examples of each group are included here: the pink-footed goose (gray), Canada and red-breasted geese (black), and Emperor goose (snow). In all true geese there is no plumage difference between the sexes. Geese are the easiest of all waterfowl to care for, breed well in captivity, and can become very tame.

1 Pink-footed goose *(Anser brachyrhynchus)* N. Hemisphere; 24in (61cm); gray, dark head and neck, black bill, pink legs.
2 Canada goose *(Branta canadensis)* Canada; 38in (97cm); gray-brown with black head and neck, white chin patch; large, noisy; several types.

3 Red-breasted goose *(Branta ruficollis)* N. Hemisphere; 21in (53cm); black and white with red breast and red patch on head, small black bill.
4 Emperor goose *(Anser canagicus)* Alaska; 28in (71cm); blue-gray with white and black, pink bill, orange legs.

Swans

There are eight true swans, but no domestic varieties, although the mute swan, common on rivers and park lakes, is considered to be semi-domesticated. Swans need a substantial expanse of natural water, as they are too heavy to be comfortable for long on land. Mating is usually for life, and swans can be relied upon to breed and rear their young without assistance.

1

2   3

1 Mute swan *(Cygnus olor)* Europe; 60in (150cm); white plumage, orange bill with black base, black knob; sexes similar as in all swans; not entirely mute — may hiss when angry.

2 Black-necked swan *(Cygnus melanocoryphus)* S. America; 40in (102cm); white with black head and neck, white eye stripe, blue bill, red knob, pink legs; adults carry cygnets on backs.

3 Black swan *(Cygnus atratus)* Australia; 40in (102cm); black with white flight feathers, curled wing coverts; red bill with white band; black legs; savage with other waterfowl.

©DIAGRAM

Keeping birds of prey (1)

Birds of prey belong to the order Falconiformes, which contains five families. They are diurnal, large, strong, and fierce birds, built for a predatory life. Birds of prey are associated with man almost entirely through the sport of falconry, which dates back over 4,000 years, and achieved great popularity in medieval Europe, although it originated in China. Today, falconry is necessarily limited due to the decline of these birds in the wild, and their inability to breed successfully in captivity. Many species are protected and it is an offense to take them from their natural habitat. No bird of prey should ever be kept as a "pet." In many countries a license is required, supplied only upon proof of the handler's intentions. Birds may be taken from the wild only for falconry or for scientific research. A falconer must train his bird to fly free from his arm and to return with its prey. Only persons prepared to dedicate a great deal of time and effort to the care and training of their birds should even contemplate taking up this activity.

Peregrine falcon *(Falco peregrinus)* Historically the most highly praised falconers' bird, females were flown by princes, whereas males, called tiercels, could be flown by lower ranks. Today, peregrines are endangered and must never be taken from the wild.

Types and uses Although most types of bird of prey have been used for hunting at some time, it is the hawks and falcons that have been used most often. In this context, the terms hawk and falcon are used generally and not strictly scientifically. Falcons, or long-wings, have dark eyes and long, pointed wings. They hunt by waiting in the air for a quarry and then diving down to grasp it. Hawks, by contrast, have yellow eyes and short, rounded wings, hence the name short-wing. They fly directly at their quarry from the hawker's fist. Different species are used over different types of terrain, according to the conditions in which they would hunt in the wild. They should never be flown in unsuitable areas or at the wrong type of prey.

Falcons and hawks The birds drawn above may sometimes be available. Females are shown as they are most often used. Males tend to be smaller, and mainly gray on the upperparts, where females are brown.

1 Merlin *(Falco columbarius)* 13in(33cm); for open country.

2 Kestrel *(Falco tinnunculus)* 13½in(34cm); open woods, farms.

3 American kestrel *(Falco sparverius)* 8½in(21cm); open woods, farms.

4 Sparrowhawk *(Accipiter nisus)* 15in(38cm); woods, farms.

5 Goshawk *(Accipiter gentilis)* 24in(61cm); wooded areas.

© DIAGRAM

401

Keeping birds of prey (2)

Obtaining Birds were formerly taken from the nest just as they had learned to fly. In most countries, this practice is now illegal, or severely restricted. Imported birds are also now more difficult to obtain. Before birds of prey are acquired, legal restrictions must be checked and licenses obtained.

Housing At night, birds of prey are housed in a dark, dry shed or "mews." They should have a screen perch (**a**), a long pole 4ft (1.2m) from the ground fitted with a curtain so the bird can get back on its perch when it flies off. Outdoors, hawks will use a bow perch (**b**), which has a padded top and wire laced across the circular framework, to enable the bird to regain its perch, without hanging upside down and suffocating. Falcons use a wooden block perch (**c**).

Equipment

1 A hood is used on falcons to reduce nervousness. Worn before the bird is released, the hood must cover the eyes. It is fastened by leather braces.

2 A bell is attached to each leg by a bewit or leather strap. Each bell has a different tone. This makes the sound carry better over distances, and helps in the location of a lost bird.

3 Leather jesses attach to each leg and are fastened to a swivel. The swivel ends are undone to release the bird. Flight jesses are made without a slit in the end to prevent the bird getting caught in a tree when flying.

4 A strong metal swivel joins jesses and leash.

5 A leather leash is attached to the swivel.

6 A special knot ties the leash to a ring on the perch.

Feeding Food should be taken from the trainer's hand. Feeding is usually once daily, but in an attempt to reproduce natural conditions some owners allow their birds to gorge one day a week and then not eat at all the next day. Birds of prey should be fed raw meat, preferably birds, mice, rabbits, or chicken heads. "Tirings" such as chicken wings are given to prevent boredom. Every few days roughage in the form of fur and feathers is needed. To prevent overfeeding, weights of birds and food require daily checking.

Health Surroundings must be dry and free from drafts, and birds should not be flown in rain or mist. Cleanliness is vital, and baths should always be available during the day. Warmth and light food may help cure some minor ailments.

Training This is a complicated and demanding process requiring expert instruction. The first step is to tame the bird, often by depriving it of sleep for 2 days. The bird is then accustomed to hand feeding and handling before it can be taken outside. The next step is to fly the bird at increasing distances from a leash, and then from a long line, using a lure (usually a pigeon wing) for falcons (**b**).

Flying Birds show readiness to fly by "rousing" or ruffling their feathers. They should be flown only when "sharp set" and hungry (before a meal). Falcons are taken out hooded and worked with dogs. On spotting the prey, the hood is removed, the jesses released from the swivel, and the bird soars before swooping. Hawks are taken out unhooded and fly straight at their prey.

Holding A right-handed falconer takes the bird in his gloved left fist (**a**), with the two jesses in the palm of his hand, coming out between his third and fourth fingers so that the swivel rests on his knuckles. The leash is caught up in two loops by his little finger.

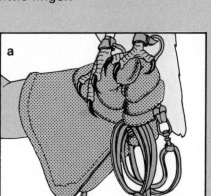

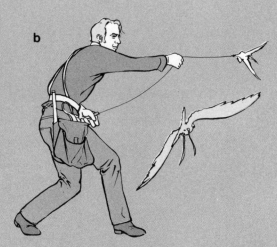

Losing The longer a bird stays free, the less likely it is to return. Lost birds should therefore be traced as quickly as possible, using leg bells as a guide. A falcon in a tree may be attracted by a lure, but a long wait may be needed if it has eaten its prey.

7

Conservation

With his superior intelligence, man has been able to devise ingenious ways of exploiting his environment. This century, we are beginning to count the cost to the natural world. Many species are endangered, while others have been lost for ever, their loss threatening whole systems of life due to the many complex interrelationships existing in nature.

Trade in wild animals, for their products, or as pets, has done irrevocable damage to certain species. Legislation to control the taking, importing, and exporting of animals now exists in many countries. Vigilance on the part of every animal lover is vital if illegal dealing is ever to be stamped out.

The observation and study of local wildlife can provide hours of enjoyment. It is also possible to be of practical help in the preservation of local species.

Right Animals saved from the Flood. Illustration of Noah's Ark from "Biblia Sacra Germanica" c.1478 (Mansell Collection).

NOE

Controlling the pet trade

The threat to wild animals from the pet trade comes in two forms. Overcollecting has led to the extinction of some species in the wild, and the hazards of transport from the country of origin inflicts appalling cruelty on animals in transit, many of which will not survive the journey. Legal restrictions are often difficult to enforce, especially in the countries where the animals are caught.

Dangers for imported animals
Wild animals (1) are caught by hunters — many more than are needed because of high death rates. Birds are netted (2), others are trapped. Many die from shock or starvation on the way to the dealer (3). Cages (4) are overcrowded, diet is poor, and disease rife in pet markets. Animals are crated for export. After delays, survivors are sent by sea or air (5). Noise, heat, cold, shock, starvation, lack of air, and overcrowding cause deaths. On arrival (6), many must be destroyed because of disease. Others are held in quarantine (7), where many die from disease or the after-effects of their journey. Pet shops (8) receive those that are left, which may then be exposed to new diseases. Most die within a year of capture, from delayed shock, though failure to acclimatize, or because of the ignorance of their owners (9).

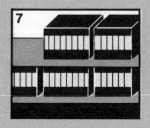

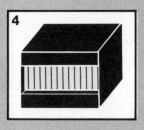

High profits for dealers and people involved in the trade routes mean that the fines incurred in prosecutions are not always effective in stopping the trade. The best way to safeguard these animals is to stop the demand for them. Efforts should be made to stop the irresponsible importation of wild animals. No animal from an endangered species should ever be taken as a pet.

Endangered species

Restrictions now prevent the taking of certain endangered species from the wild. Permits are required to keep others. Never buy or obtain any animal known to be from an endangered species.

Species unsuited to captivity

The importing or taking of some wild animals is controlled or banned because they do not thrive in captivity. Disruption of natural behavior patterns means they do not breed and many soon die.

Transport controls

Regulations exist to protect animals in transit, but cases of cruelty are common. There is still no effective means of enforcing international agreements concerning the carriage of live animals.

Health controls

Many countries now have complete bans on certain animals because of disease. Periods of quarantine are common for species that carry diseases, which, like rabies, can be transmitted to humans.

Other controls

Non-native animals may escape and become agricultural pests. Others are dangerously aggressive. Local laws may ban the keeping of some species, or require owners to obtain permits as a means of control.

Species in danger

Nearly 900 species of animal and 30,000 types of plant are today in serious danger of extinction. Man is largely responsible, due to his unique ability among animals to disrupt natural balances. When a species becomes extinct, it is lost forever, and cannot be recreated. The loss of one species puts others at risk because of the interdependence of different forms of life.

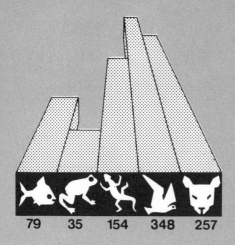

79 35 154 348 257

Endangered species occur in all groups of living things. The diagram shows the numbers of fish, amphibians, reptiles, birds, and mammals known at present to be seriously threatened with extinction. Approximate total numbers of species in each group are: fish 15,000 (79 endangered), amphibians 3,500 (35 endangered), reptiles 5,000 (154 endangered), birds 9,000 (350 endangered), mammals 5,000 (257 endangered).

The size of the problem For every species shown right, there are 35 others in danger. These examples have been selected to indicate the range of groups involved, and also to illustrate some of the more familiar endangered species.
1 Atlantic sturgeon.
2 Gila trout.
3 Pine barrens tree frog.
4 Japanese giant salamander.
5 Komodo dragon.
6 Two-striped garter snake.
7 Tuatara — the sole survivor of a reptilian order. The other species in the order died out 100 million years ago.
8 American alligator — 25 other crocodilians are in danger.
9 Green turtle.
10 Cape Barren goose.
11 Spanish Imperial eagle — the rarest bird in Europe. Many birds of prey are endangered.
12 Whooping crane.
13 Grass parakeet — 29 types of parrot are in danger.
14 Seychelles owl.
15 Ivory-billed woodpecker — the rarest bird in the world.
16 Ponapé great whiteye is a passerine. 141 others from this order are endangered.
17 Galapagos penguin.
18 White-throated wallaby.
19 Orangutan — 41 primate species are endangered.
20 Maned wolf.
21 Giant panda — symbol of the World Wildlife Fund.
22 Tiger — other endangered big cats include the leopard, cheetah, jaguar, and ocelot.
23 Javan rhino.
24 Persian fallow deer — 30 deer species are endangered.
25 Blue whale. Most whale populations are severely depleted through hunting.

Conservation in the garden

Increased urban development has deprived many species of their natural habitat. The clearance of wooded areas, and the filling in of ponds often means a loss of nesting and breeding places. Anyone with a garden can help local species by growing plants to serve as food, and by providing shelter and nest boxes. Animals attracted in these ways can then be observed at close quarters.

Attracting animals

1 Areas planted with hedges or dense undergrowth provide shelter and nesting areas for birds and small animals.

2 Bird table for feeding.

3 Food hung on tree branches for birds.

4 Nest boxes fixed to trees or walls supply valuable nesting space. Do not provide too many, or fighting over territory will result. Bat boxes high up in trees give roosting places for bats.

5 An area of wild plants is ideal for breeding insects, especially butterflies. Highly cultivated plants are generally less attractive to insects.

6 Plants on the pond's edge give protection for salamanders.

7 Ponds are good breeding places for frogs and newts.

8 Water plants attract insects and support small water animals.

9 Bird bath. Make sure the water does not freeze in cold weather.

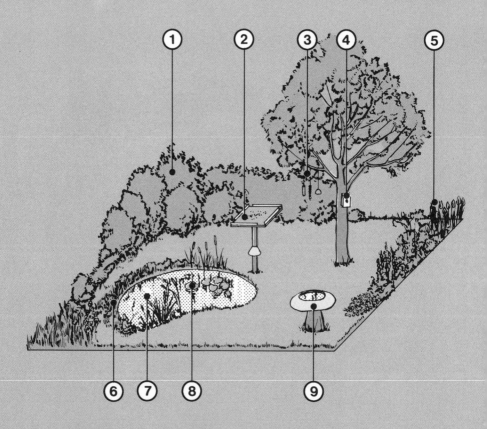

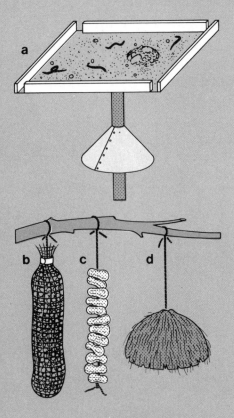

Feeding birds Providing food for birds is an ideal way to help preserve local species, especially during a hard winter. It is important to continue to put food out once the birds start to come regularly to the garden, otherwise those dependent on the supply may starve during a spell of bad weather. Food can be scattered on the ground or placed on a bird table (**a**), at least 2ft(60cm) square, with holes for drainage and a baffle to stop cats from climbing up. Feed table scraps, seeds, dried fruit, meat, and fat. Chickadees (tits), and other acrobatic birds, like nuts or seeds suspended from a branch in a mesh bag (**b**), or peanuts in their shells on a string (**c**). Half a coconut can also be hung on a branch to enable the birds to pick out the filling (**d**).

Attracting butterflies Many species of butterfly are now nearing extinction. These insects can be encouraged to breed by planting a selection of wild flowers and plants as food for adults and caterpillars. Examples include the milkweed (**a**), the food of the monarch butterfly caterpillar *(Danaus plexippus),* and the nettle (**b**), which is the food plant for the red admiral *(Vanessa atalanta)* and various other species.

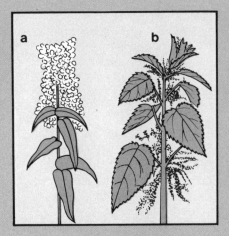

Ponds can play an important part in the conservation of frogs, newts, and other water animals. They are easy to construct (see p.182). Site the pond away from trees to prevent it becoming clogged with leaves. It should be at least 18in(45cm) deep so that it does not freeze over in cold weather. Stock the pond with water plants collected locally, to attract insects and birds. Water insects, mollusks, and small crustaceans can be added, as well as small fish. In time, frogs and newts may breed there.

©DIAGRAM

Nest boxes for birds and bats

A selection of boxes for birds and bats can help compensate for the loss of natural nesting and roosting sites caused by the destruction of woodlands and the extension of urban and cultivated areas. Each bird pair needs its own territory so do not put too many nest boxes in a small garden. To allow the birds time to become used to them, always put up nest boxes well before spring.

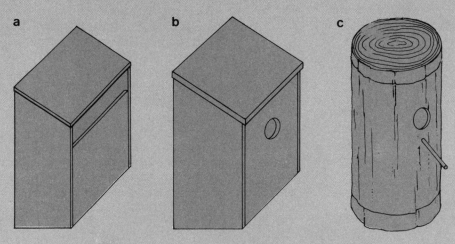

a   b   c

Nest boxes for birds can be made or bought in various sizes. The size of the entrance hole determines which birds use a box. All boxes should be placed on a south-facing wall or tree, out of the wind. They must also be out of the reach of cats and squirrels. There are many types of design, but all should have drainage holes in the bottom, and a hinged top for cleaning out at the end of the season. Never disturb nesting birds.
a Box 10x6x4in (25x15x10cm) with an open front suitable for small bush and tree nesters.
b Box 11x5x5in (28x13x13cm) with a round entrance hole 1in (2.5cm) in diameter for small hole nesters like chickadees (tits) or 2in(5cm) in diameter for wrens, sparrows, or starlings.
c Nest box for hole nesters made from a hollowed log.

Bat boxes Bats are nocturnal animals that roost upside down during the day. The destruction of suitable roosting places has led to a decline in many bat species. The provision of bat boxes should help check this decline. A suitable bat box is illustrated below (**d**). It is an 8in (20cm) hollow cube of rough-sawn timber, with a ¾in(2cm) slit at the bottom for entry. Bat boxes should be placed at least 6ft(2m) up a tree.

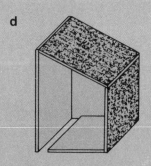

d

Helping wild animals

Always take great care when trying to help an injured wild animal or bird. Animals in pain often react aggressively, and may be dangerous. Many cases are beyond home remedies, and it is better to get a veterinarian to help, or to let nature take its course. Remember that a young animal on its own is not always an orphan, and is most probably not in need of assistance.

Orphaned animals and birds

Most of the young creatures that people assume to be lost are not orphans at all. Parents may be close by, gathering food, or distracting predators. Always leave a young creature where it is unless absolutely sure the parents are dead. Care of orphaned young is extremely difficult. Always seek advice. Do not attempt to make a pet of an orphaned animal. Return it to the wild once it has grown.

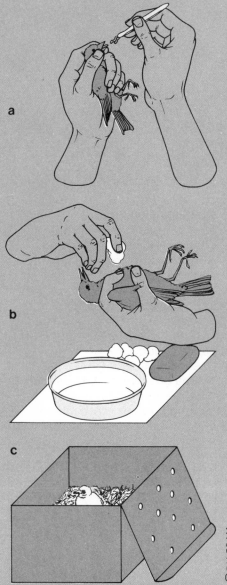

a

Care of wild birds

Feeding a young bird is done by simulating the action of the parents, which thrust their beaks into the throats of their young. Prise the beak open, and push the food down with blunt tweezers (**a**).

Simple injuries Birds are often victims of cuts and scratches, commonly caused by cats. Clean the affected areas with soap and water, holding the bird firmly with its wings closed (**b**). Damage caused by oil pollution is rarely treatable because affected birds have normally ingested too much oil in efforts to clean their own plumage. A stunned bird should be put into a cardboard box (**c**) with some warm bedding. Put the lid on the box and release the bird as soon as it can be heard moving about.

b

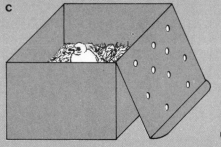

c

© DIAGRAM

413

Observing wildlife

Wildlife observation is an ideal way to understand and appreciate the systems of nature, and can lead to many practical ways of conserving local species. Many people can watch and record wildlife in their gardens or in local woods and fields. Urban areas, too, are often rich in wildlife. To see rare species it may be necessary to go farther afield or to some form of wildlife sanctuary.

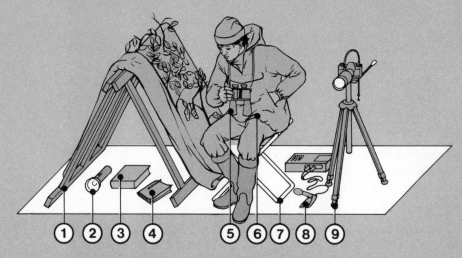

Observing wildlife The commonest form of wildlife observation is birdwatching. Birds are active during the day, and although timid, can be discovered by listening for their songs. They have a poor sense of smell, so observers can go unnoticed if they are quiet and patient. Mammals are best observed at night from a hide placed downwind. All observers must be careful not to disturb nesting birds or scare animals.

Equipment
1 Hide — a dark blanket placed over a clothes horse, covered with twigs and branches.
2 Flashlight with red filter for night observation.
3 Reference book or field guide.
4 Notebook for observations.
5 A good pair of binoculars.
6 Dull or dark clothing for camouflage.
7 Collapsible stool.
8 Tape recorder.
9 Camera with telephoto lens.

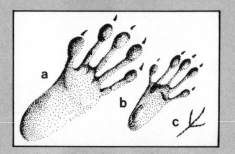

Animal signs Animals leave various signs that can be found by wildlife observers. These include footprints (spoors), like those of the raccoon (**a**), squirrel (**b**), and sparrow (**c**). Other signs are discarded food husks or shells, fur, feathers, droppings, smells, and noises.

Wildlife locations

The world's first national park was Yellowstone Park, founded in the United States in 1872. Today, the United Nations lists some 1200 areas as national parks or equivalent reserves. There are also many smaller areas with similar objectives. Together these form an essential part of conservation programs, and make excellent places for the observation and study of wildlife.

National parks

A national park is an area set aside to conserve nature. It must be mainly wilderness. The public are allowed access, but must not settle there. Game reserves in Africa are now called national parks.

Nature reserves

A nature reserve is usually smaller, and may exist to protect a single species. Very similar are bird sanctuaries and sites of special scientific interest, all of them linked with natural history societies.

Wildlife parks

Wildlife parks are privately run concerns where the public may go to see exotic creatures in a semi-natural setting. Unfortunately many do not meet adequate standards of care, or provide suitable environments.

Zoos

The old type of zoo was little more than an animal prison, but zoos today aim to provide "open" enclosures where species can live naturally. Many breed in captivity — a major conservation achievement.

Local parks

Local parks and botanical gardens often offer the chance to see a variety of birds, especially waterfowl, and free-roaming animals like deer. They provide nesting sites for many types of bird.

© DIAGRAM

Zoonoses

Over 100 diseases can be transmitted from animals to humans. These diseases are known as zoonoses; most are now rare in Western countries, but some, due to the rise in the pet population, are on the increase. Fear of disease should not usually prevent anyone from keeping a pet, but it is every pet owner's responsibility to ensure that his animals are kept in clean and healthy conditions,

Disease	Symptoms and signs
Rabies	Marked change in behavior; fits; aggression; salivating; death.
Cat-scratch fever	Swelling; tender lymph nodes near wound; ulceration.
Leptospirosis/Fort Bragg fever	Vomiting; diarrhea; fever. In untreated animals, convulsions follow, leading to death.
Salmonellosis	Vomiting; diarrhea; fever; septicemia; chronic infections.
Brucellosis/undulant fever	Symptoms in man resemble chronic influenza.
Ornithosis (psittacosis)	Respiratory disease resembling pneumonia.
Lymphocytic choriomeningitis	Headaches; coughing; fever; general discomfort.
Ringworm	Circular patches of red spots on skin; itching; hair loss on head.
External parasites	Fleas, lice, ticks cause itchy bites; may carry other diseases.
Toxoplasmosis	In children, resembles common cold; may cause fetal brain damage in pregnant women.
Other infestations	Tapeworms, hookworms, roundworms, and *toxocara canis* or *cati* cause various conditions from diarrhea to blindness.

and that they are given any vaccinations recommended by a veterinarian. Modern vaccines for animals have largely controlled diseases like rabies, but to prevent renewed outbreaks it is essential that animals are vaccinated even when risks are low. The chart below gives a selection of common zoonotic disorders; many of these are troublesome rather than serious.

Source	Action
Bite or close contact with rabid animal, eg fox, squirrel, dog.	Vaccination; immediate reporting; isolation of suspected cases.
Scratch or bite usually from cat; more common in children.	Not serious; doctor should examine infected area.
Contact with contaminated urine of dogs, farm animals, rats, or wild animals.	Vaccinate dogs if endemic; seek prompt medical or veterinary advice if disease is suspected.
Many species are carriers, but turtles are often infected.	Isolate new turtles; wash hands after handling; test regularly.
Contact with infected animal, eg cattle, or urine of breeding dogs.	Isolate infected animal; seek medical and veterinary advice.
Contact with diseased birds; recovered birds may be carriers.	Treat cases with antibiotics for 45 days; isolate new birds.
Contact with feces of infected rodents, especially hamsters.	Prevent by keeping rodent pets isolated from wild species.
Contact with affected dogs or cats; sometimes other species.	Children susceptible; use prescribed ointments and drugs.
Contact with animals, bedding, or other infested areas.	Clean living conditions; treat animals regularly; not serious.
Contact with infected cat's feces; pregnant women should not change cats' litter trays.	Prevent by hygienic living conditions for cats; wash hands after handling cat litter.
Handling feces of infected animals; from contaminated soil; usual carriers are dogs and cats.	Prevent by regular deworming of pets; strict hygiene; do not allow dogs to foul public parks or other urban areas.

©DIAGRAM

Zoological classification

The modern science of classifying forms of life, known as taxonomy, developed from the work of Swedish naturalist Karl von Linné (1707-78). Linnaeus, as he is usually called, grouped all known animals and plants according to their physical similarities, and gave each of them a descriptive Latinized name. Even today, when Latin is less commonly known, it is extremely useful to have a system in which

Kingdom	The most basic division of life is into two kingdoms: plant and animal. Animals are living things able to move freely.
Phylum	The animal kingdom contains 26 phyla. Animals with backbones are Vertebrata (vertebrates), a sub-phylum of one of these.
Class	The sub-phylum Vertebrata is divided into five classes — Mammalia, Aves (birds), Reptilia, Amphibia, and Pisces (fish).
Order	Classes are further divided into orders. Carnivora (carnivores) is one of 19 mammalian orders. Flesh-tearing teeth are a characteristic.
Family	The next division, into families, is the first at which similarities of appearance are seen. The dog family — Canidae — is an example.
Genus	Members of a genus resemble each other more closely, eg the wolf (*Canis lupus*) and the domestic dog *(Canis familiaris)*.
Species	The species is the only natural grouping. It comprises all animals that interbreed with fertile results, eg domestic dog.

animals and plants have precise, internationally recognized names. Following the work of Charles Darwin (1809-82), the developed system also shows evolutionary relationships. Each species has two or sometimes three names: first the name of the genus to which it belongs, followed by one or two names specific to the species or sub-species. Constant updating occurs with new findings.

Below The diagram illustrates the classification of several mammalian pets within the order Carnivora (carnivores). Three families are represented: the domestic dog (*Canis familiaris*) belongs to the Canidae, the domestic cat (*Felis domestica*) to the Felidae, and the ferret (*Mustela putorius*) and skunk (*Mephitis mephitis*) to the Mustelidae. The ferret and the skunk belong to different genera within the same family.

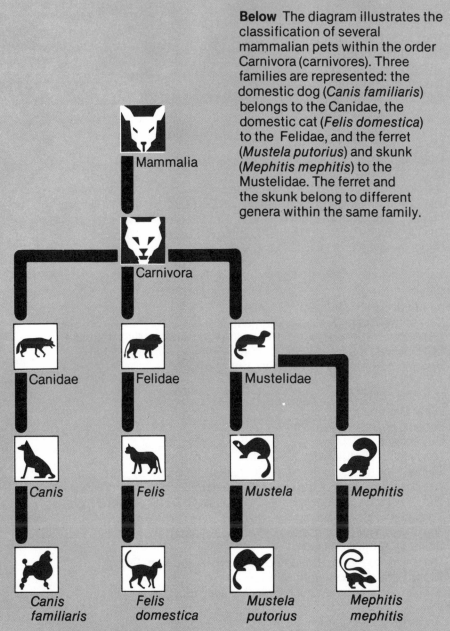

Mammalia

Carnivora

Canidae

Felidae

Mustelidae

Canis

Felis

Mustela

Mephitis

Canis familiaris

Felis domestica

Mustela putorius

Mephitis mephitis

Further reading

General
A Practical Guide to Impractical Pets, E. Dolensek and B. Burn (Viking)
Animals in Art, J. Rawson (British Museum Publications)
ASPCA Guide to Pet Care, D. Henley (Taplinger)
Great Pets! S. Stein (Workman Publishing Company)
Larousse Encyclopaedia of Animal Life (Hamlyn)
Pet and Fancy series (Cassell)
Pet Animals and Society, ed. R. Anderson (Balliere Tindall)
Phil Drabble's Book of Pets, P. Drabble (Fontana)
The Family Naturalist, M. Chinery (Macdonald and Jane)
The Life of Mammals, L. Matthews (Weidenfeld and Nicholson)
The Life of Vertebrates, J. Young (Oxford University Press)
The Living World of Animals (Reader's Digest)
The Natural World (Mitchell Beazley)
The Wonderful World of Pets (Orbis)
Traveling With Your Pet (ASPCA)
Your Pet's Health from A-Z, D. McKeown DVM and E. Strimple DVM (Dell)

Dogs
Dog Training, Sports Illustrated (Lippincott)
Dogs, W. Boorer (Bantam)
Judging Dogs, R. Smythe (John Gifford)
The Common Sense Book of Puppy and Dog Care, H. Miller (Bantam)
The Dog: Structure and Movement, R. Smythe (Foulsham)
The Observer's Book of Dogs, S. Lampson (Frederick Warne)
Understanding Your Dog, Dr. M. Fox (Bantam)

Cats
All About Cats, C. Burger (W. H. Allen)
Cats of the World, M. Warner (Bantam)
The Common Sense Book of Kitten and Cat Care, H. Miller (Bantam)
The Observer's Book of Cats, G. Pond (Frederick Warne)
Understanding Your Cat, Dr. M. W. Fox (Bantam)

Other Mammals
Rabbits, H. Dyson (Cassell)
Exhibition and Pet Cavies, I. Turner (Spur Publications)
Fancy Mice, R. Hutchings (Cassell)
Guinea Pigs and Chinchillas, K. Denham (Bartholomew)
The Complete Book of the Horse, E. Edwards and C. Geddes (Ward Lock)
The Observer's Book of Horses and Ponies, R. Summerhays (Frederick Warne)
The Pony-Lover's Handbook, T. Webber (Pelham)
Goats, H. Jeffrey (Cassell)
The Backyard Pig and Sheep Book, A. Williams (Prism Press)
Exotic Pets, C. Roots (John Gifford)
Wild Animals Around Your Home, P. Villiard (Scribners)

Fish

Aquarium Fishes, J. Prescott (Bantam)
Aquarium Fishes in Colour, J. Madsen (Blandford)
Freshwater and Marine Aquarium Fishes (Simon and Schuster)
The Home Aquarium Book, W. Simister (David and Charles)
Tropical Fish, C. Harrison (Bartholomew)
Tropical Freshwater Aquaria, G. Cust and P. Bird (Bantam)
Tropical Marine Home Aquariums, G. Cox (Bantam)

Invertebrates

A Field Guide in Colour to Insects, Dr. J. Zahradnik (Octopus)
Beetles in Colour, L. Lyneborg (Blandford)
Butterfly Culture, J. Stone and H. Midwinter (Blandford)
Discovering Beekeeping, D. More (Shire Publications)
The World of Spiders, W. Bristowe (Collins)

Reptiles and Amphibians

A Field Guide to Reptiles and Amphibians of Eastern and Central North
    America, R. Conant (Houghton Mifflin)
A Field Guide to Western Reptiles and Amphibians, R. Stebbins (Houghton
    Mifflin)
Encyclopedia of Reptiles and Amphibians, J.Breen (TFH Publications)
Keeping Reptiles and Amphibians, A.Leutscher (David and Charles)
Reptiles and Amphibians, Z. Vogel (Studio Vista)
Reptiles of the World, C. Gans (Bantam)
Snakes of the World, J. Stidworthy (Bantam)

Birds

Aviary Birds in Colour, D. Avon, T. Tilford, F. Woolham (Blandford)
Beginner's Guide to Birdkeeping, R. Low (Pelham)
Cage and Aviary Birds, D. Risdon (Faber)
Seedeating Birds as Pets, C. Rogers (Bartholomew)
The Dictionary of Birds in Colour (Michael Joseph)
Guide to Pigeons of the World, A. McNeillie (Elsevier)
Practical Poultry Management, J. Rice and H. Botsford (John Wiley)
The Practical Guide to Ornamental Waterfowl, J. and P. Parker (Arco)
Wildfowl in Captivity, R. Martin (John Gifford)
Falconry for You, H. ap Evans (John Gifford)

Conservation

Airborne Birds, T.Inskipp (RSPB)
All Heaven in a Rage, T. Inskipp and G. Thomas (RSPB)
Endangered Species Act 1976 (HMSO)
International Trade in Endangered Species 1977 (US Fish and Wildlife
    Service)
Wildlife Crisis, HRH The Prince Philip and J. Fisher (Hamish Hamilton)

Index